GCSE

ECONOMICS

Barry Harrison and Robert Nutter

 LONGMAN

LONGMAN GCSE STUDY GUIDES

SERIES EDITORS:
Geoff Black and Stuart Wall

TITLES AVAILABLE:
Biology
Business Studies
Chemistry
Economics
English
English Literature
French
Geography
German
Information Technology
Mathematics
Mathematics: Higher Level
Music
Physical Education
Physics
Psychology
Religious Studies
Science
Sociology
Spanish
Technology
World History

Pearson Education Limited
Edinburgh Gate, Harlow,
Essex CM20 2JE, England
and Associated Companies throughout the World.

© Longman Group Limited 1988
This edition © Addison Wesley Longman Ltd 1997

First published 1988
Second edition 1995
Updated edition 1997
Third impression 1999

ISBN 0 582 31539 5

British Library Cataloguing-in-Publication Data

A catalogue record for this book is available from the
British Library

Set by 27QQ in 10/12pt Century Old Style
Printed in Singapore (COS)

CONTENTS

ACKNOWLEDGEMENTS

The authors are grateful to the following examination groups for permission to reproduce their questions. The answers provided are the responsibility of the authors.

> Edexcel Foundation (London) (ULEAC)
> Midland Examining Group (MEG)
> Northern Examinations and Assessment Board (NEAB)
> Northern Ireland Council for Curriculum Examinations and Assessment (NICCEA)
> Southern Examining Group (SEG)
> Welsh Joint Education Committee (WJEC)

We are also indebted to the Controller of Her Majesty's Stationery Office and *GCSE Regulations and Criteria*, SCAA, March 1995 for permission to reproduce extracts from the National Criteria.

We are grateful to the following for permission to reproduce copyright material:

Acquisitions Monthly for Figure 12.1; Anforme Ltd for Figure 16.2; Crown copyright is reproduced with the permission of the controller of HMSO for Tables 5.4, 6.1, 10.1, 14.5, 14.6, 15.1, 17.1 and 17.2; Figures 6.3, 6.4, 6.6, 12.2, 12.3, 13.4, 15.1 and 15.3; and the extract 'Public Money 1991–92' on p. 184; *Financial Times*, 30/11/95 for Figure 16.1; *Social Justice: Strategies for National Renewal*, Commission on Social Justice/IPPR for Figure 17.2; Solo Syndication Limited for the Figure in examination question 3, p. 167.

Though every effort has been made to trace the owners of the copyright material, in a few cases this has proved impossible and we take this opportunity to apologise to any copyright holders whose rights may have been unwittingly infringed.

CHAPTER 1

THE EXAMINATIONS & ASSESSED COURSEWORK

GETTING STARTED

All members of a society are involved in making *economic* decisions. We must all decide how much of our *limited time* to use in following different activities. Shall I use my Saturdays to earn income from a weekend job, follow a sport or hobby, catch up on homework set during the week and so on? Shall I spend my *limited income* on a new compact disc this week, going to a special concert or play, or on a new book? In other words we are all involved in *allocating* scarce resources amongst alternative uses. This is the same problem faced by the *firm* when deciding how to use its limited amount of labour, land and capital equipment. It is also the problem faced by *governments* in deciding how much of their limited budget to spend on health, education, pensions, and so on.

In this book we shall look at how the *individual person*, and the *single firm* operate. This has traditionally been called *micro* economics. We shall also look at the activities of *all* the persons and firms in the economy; this is often called *macro* economics.

All this will be in the context of your GCSE course in economics. In this chapter we look at the aims of GCSE Economics, the topic areas in your course and the ways you will be assessed.

GENERAL AIMS

CHOICE OF TOPIC

PREPARATION

PRESENTING INFORMATION

OBJECTIVE DISCUSSION

CONCLUSION

THE AIMS OF GCSE IN ECONOMICS

1 > GENERAL AIMS

Subject-specific criteria have been established by the School Curriculum and Assessment Authority (SCAA) for all subjects to be examined at GCSE. An *Economics* GCSE course must enable you to develop knowledge and understanding of the working of economic systems and of the interdependence and dynamics in economic behaviour. Candidates should be able to:

i) demonstrate knowledge and critical understanding of the specified subject content;
ii) apply the specified terms, concepts, theories and methods effectively to address problems and issues;
iii) select, organize, interpret and use information from various sources;
iv) evaluate evidence, make reasoned judgements and present conclusions accurately and appropriately.

The above skills are classed as 'assessment ojectives' by the examination groups.

An economics syllabus requires candidates to demonstrate specified knowledge and understanding of:

i) the basic economic problems and decisions which give rise to economics as a discipline;
ii) the economic behaviour of individuals, groups, organizations and governments within local, national and international communities.

In relation to the above, candidates should demonstrate specified knowledge and critical understanding of:

i) the concepts, theories and methods needed to analyse issues from an economics perspective (*covering, for example, price elasticity of demand in relation to tax policy; price and consumer behaviour*);
ii) economic terms, classifications and indicators (*covering, for example, money, inflation, exchange rates, fixed and variable costs, income per head, General Index of Retail Prices*);
iii) the institutional and organizational framework within which economic behaviour takes place (*covering, for example, the Bank of England and the operation of monetary policy, government and the promotion of training*);
iv) the criteria against which economic behaviour might be assessed (*covering, for example, productivity as a measure of efficiency; profit as a measure of success*).

These criteria are very important because they set out the **aims** of all GCSE courses in economics. Since the aims are known we also know the **skills** that it is necessary to demonstrate in order to succeed. For all GCSE examinations these skills will be tested in two ways: by formal examination and by coursework assessment.

IMPORTANCE OF THE TOPIC AREAS

The importance of each of the topic areas for the different exam groups is set out in Table 1.1.

Clearly the topic areas are similar across all the exam groups. However, you should be aware that different groups place **different emphasis** on the topics given in the grid reference. For example, population and national income may only be briefly covered by one exam group, whereas another group may require detailed coverage. It is therefore very important to check the topics covered in the chapters of this book against your own particular syllabus. You may be able to obtain a copy of the syllabus from your teacher. If not, then you can write to the exam groups. The addresses and telephone numbers are given at the end of this chapter.

Chapter and Topic		University of London Examination and Assessment Council (ULE AC)	Midland Examining Group (MEG)	Northern Examinations and Assessment Board (NEAB)	Northern Ireland Council for Curriculum, Examinations and Assessment. (NICCEA)	Southern Examining Group (SEG)	Welsh Joint Education Committee (WJEC)	IGCSE
3	The economic problem	X	X	X	X	X	X	X
4	Types of economic system	X	X	X	X	X	X	X
5	The resources and production	X	X	X	X	X	X	X
6	Population				X			X
7	Demand supply, and price	X	X	X	X	X	X	X
8	Applications of price theory	X	X	X	X	X	X	X
9	Revenue, cost and profit	X	X	X	X	X	X	X
10	Wages and trade unions	X	X	X	X	X	X	X
11	Business organization and finance	X	X	X	X	X	X	X
12	Growth, location and market structure	X	X	X	X	X	X	X
13	National Income and the circular flow			X	X			
14	International trade and payments	X	X	X	X	X	X	X
15	Money and financial institution	X	X	X	X	X	X	X
16	Public revenue, expenditure and policy	X	X	X	X	X	X	X
17	The distribution of income and wealth	X	X	X	X	X	X	X

Table 1.1 Syllabus coverage chart

THE EXAMINATIONS

The next section describes in detail the various examination papers set by each group. You can see the proportion of the total marks gained from that paper (the 'weighting'), the time available and the types of question set. Many of these papers will have their first examinations in 1996.

From the 1996 papers onwards, GCSE Economics will be examined by a written paper with two tiers of assessment plus optional coursework. Each tier of assessment in the written paper will be targeted to a certain range of GCSE grades as shown in the example below:

Tier of entry	Grades targeted
Foundation	C–G
Higher	A*–D

As you can see there is a grade overlap for each tier. A candidate can be entered for one tier only.

The above written examination paper will usually carry 80 per cent of the marks and the coursework 20 per cent. There are some exceptions to this (see detailed breakdown of papers below). Both the written examination and the coursework include an assessment of spelling, punctuation and grammar. Coursework is not a compulsory part of the examination as from 1996.

THE EXAMINATION PAPERS

ULEAC

i) ECONOMICS

Candidates will be assessed by means of a terminal examination, consisting of a written paper, weighted at 80 per cent of the total marks, selected from Papers 1, 2 and 3 and coursework weighted at 20 per cent of the total marks. The terminal examination will be by means of an externally marked written paper, and the coursework will require candidates to submit *two* assignments which will be set and marked by centres and moderated by the Council.

The scheme of assessment is designed to ensure that candidates across the ability range are provided with the opportunity to show what they know, understand and can do. To allow awards to be made across grades G to A* the terminal examination will offer three tiers of assessment and require a choice to be made from three differentiated papers targeted at different grades; the papers will differentiate by outcome:

		Grades targeted
	Paper 1: Foundation – 2 hours	C–G
or	Paper 2: Higher – 2½ hours	A*–D

Paper 1: Foundation (2 hours)

This paper will be marked out of 80 and will be divided into two sections:

Section A will consist of a range of compulsory short answer stimulus and data response style questions and will carry a maximum of 40 marks.

Section B will consist of four structured questions; candidates will be required to answer *two* of these questions. Section B will carry a maximum of 40 marks.

Paper 2: Higher (2½ hours)

This paper will be marked out of 100 and will be divided into two sections:

Section A will consist of a range of compulsory short answer stimulus and data response style questions and will carry a maximum of 40 marks.

Section B will consist of five structured questions; candidates will be required to answer *three* of these questions. Section B will carry a maximum of 60 marks.

ii) BUSINESS STUDIES AND ECONOMICS

Candidates will be assessed by means of a terminal examination consisting of two written papers (two Foundation or two Higher) weighted at 75% of the total marks and coursework known as a Portfolio weighted at 25% of the total marks.

The terminal examination will be by means of two externally set and marked written papers. The Portfolio will require candidates to submit *two investigations*, from the range of completed work. These two will be set and marked by centres and moderated by the Council.

The scheme of assessment is designed to ensure that candidates across the ability range are provided with the opportunity to show what they know, understand and can do. To allow awards to be made across Grades G to A* the terminal examination will offer two tiers of assessment and require a choice to be made from two differentiated papers targeted at different grades.

		Grades available
Paper 1:	Foundation tier 1¼ hours	Grades G to C
Paper 3:	Higher tier 1¼ hours	Grades D to A*
Paper 2:	Foundation tier 1¼ hours	Grades G to C
Paper 4:	Higher tier 1¼ hours	Grades D to A*

Coursework, in the form of the Portfolio, will be differentiated by outcome; the assessment of each investigation will be related to marking criteria designed to reward positive achievement.

Papers 1 & 3: Foundation and Higher (1 1/4 hours). Problem solving

Each paper will be weighted at 35% of the total subject mark. It will consist of case material which candidates will be advised to spend fifteen minutes reading. The core of this material will be identical for both tiers. This paper is based on an issue and poses a problem to which candidates will provide a solution, drawing on the stimulus material provided and their knowledge of Business Studies and Economics. Each paper will be divided into two sections:

Section A will consist of stimulus material followed by an average of 6 compulsory questions. These will range from short answer questions to those requiring a longer response.

Section B will consist of a structured problem solving question based on the initial stimulus material.

Papers 2 & 4: Foundation and Higher (1 1/4 hours). Perspectives

Each paper will be weighted at 40% of the total subject mark. The stimulus material will consist of evidence of differing perspectives on issues and events. Candidates will be expected to use the information and their knowledge of Business Studies and Economics to evaluate the evidence and come to reasoned conclusions. This will encourage them to develop a critical awareness of economic systems and the business environment in order to make informed evaluative judgements.

There will be three questions and candidates will be required to answer two.

MEG

There are two tiers available and candidates will enter for one tier and take two papers. The grades which can be awarded for each tier are shown below.

Foundation tier	C–G
Higher tier	A*–D

Paper 1 will consist of short questions and longer structured questions based on data. All questions will be compulsory and this paper will carry 60 per cent of the marks.

Paper 2 will contain a series of questions related to a common case study. All questions will be compulsory and this paper will carry 40 per cent of the marks. There is no course work in this examination.

NEAB

NEAB candidates may choose to do *either* Option A *or* Option B

Option A	**Option B**
Paper 1: 82½%	Paper 1: 82½%
Coursework: 17½%	Paper 2: 17½%

Paper 1 will contain between five and eight questions which will consist of short answer and structured questions based on given data and other stimulus material. There will be some opportunities for extended writing.

Paper 2 (option B only) will be in the style of a case study with a variety of data, and will consist of structured questions.

Each of the written papers will be set and marked by the NEAB. Each candidate must take the written paper(s) at one of the two tier of assessment as follows:

Tier	Targeted grades	Time	
		Paper 1 *(Options A and B)*	*Paper 2* *(Option B only)*
Foundation	C–G	2 hours	1 hour
Higher	A*–D	2½ hours	1 hour

Candidates must be entered for only one of these tiers. Within each tier differentiation will be achieved by outcome. Paper 2 will only be taken by those candidates not completing a coursework assignment. Coursework titles are provided by the examination board.

No award will be made outside the targeted grades, this candidates failing to reach grade G on the Foundation tier, or grade D on the Higher tier will be ungraded.

NICCEA

The scheme of assessment consists of the assessment of coursework (20%) and a terminal examination (80%).

There are two tiers of entry for the examination:

Tier S	Target grades C–G
Tier T	Target gardes A*–E

With each tier candidates are required to sit two written papers, which are externally assessed, and to submit coursework for assessment by the teacher.

Candidates must be entered for one tier only at the appropriate time of entry. In judging what is the more suitable tier of entry for a candidate, centres should consider the candidate's record of performance throughout the course. Each tier will include two examination papers. These are described below:

Paper 1 (20%)

Paper 1 (One hour and fifteen minutes duration) will be a case study exercise. Case study material for both tiers of entry will be supplied by the Council and will be based on an economic issue, problem or event. The material may be in a variety of forms, e.g. written, graphical, statistical, pictorial.

The case study material will be distributed to schools for issue to candidates approximately eight school weeks before the date of Paper 1. Centres will be notified of the authorized date for issuing the material to candidates.

Paper 2 (60%)

Paper 2 (two hours and fifteen minutes duration) will examine content drawn from across the syllabus, and will examine both groups of assessment objectives.

The Tier S paper will consist of two sections. Section A will contain approximately five short answer type questions. Section B will contain two compulsory stimulus response questions.

The Tier T paper will consist of two sections. Section A will contain two compulsory stimulus response questions. Section B will consist of a choice of structured essay type questions. Candidates will be expected to answer two questions from a choice of five.

Coursework (20%)

The school-based component will consist of one coursework assignment set by the Council. The assignment should not exceed 2,000 words.

SEG

Candidates must take *one* written paper. This component is externally set and marked by SEG. The written paper carries a weighting of 80 per cent of the candidate's total GCSE mark.

Two tiered papers are available, each giving access to a different range of levels. Candidates should be entered for the tier which is most suited to their abilities.

	Papers and weighting	
Paper 1	(2 hours) Foundation (C–G) Higher (A*–D)	80%
Paper 2	Coursework	20%
GCSE Total		100%

Written examination

Paper 1: written paper, 2 hours (80 per cent of total GCSE mark)
   The paper will consist of two sections:

Section one will contain about four compulsory questions based upon the same stimulus material which will be included within the paper. This material may consist of charts, tables, graphs or written extracts, or a combination thereof, and will deal with important economic issues such as unemployment, inflation or government policy.

Section two will consist of about five questions, each with separate stimulus material. Candidates will be required to answer two questions. Each question will be divided into four sections which will test the range of skills and knowledge of the candidates in the same way as Section one.

Coursework

Paper 2: coursework (20 per cent of total GCSE mark)
   Candidates will be required to submit two pieces of work covering all of the assessment objectives.

WJEC

For the terminal examination, there will be two tiers of assessment targeted as shown in the grid below. Levels may be awarded at one level below and one level above the targeted range.

Tier of entry	Grades targeted
Higher	A*–D
Foundation	C–G

A tier must allow for awards up to two grades below the targeted range (one grade below if there is overlap between the targeted grades of the tiers or where grade G is the lowest targeted grade). A tier may allow for exceptional awards one grade above the targeted range, except in the case of grade A*, which can only be awarded on a tier which targets that grade. A candidate may be entered for *one* tier only.

Examination papers

The written examination papers will be of 2½ hours duration and will account for 80 per cent of the total subject mark. In all questions the WJEC examiners and moderators will be asked to ensure that the range of language in the questions, and where appropriate, the data used, is accessible to the ability range of the candidature. The questions will be of varying types, e.g. short answer, data response, structured essay and unstructured essay.
   A summary of the structure of examination papers is set out below:

	WEIGHTING OF QUESTION TYPE ON PAPER (%)			
Tier of assessment	Short answer	Data response	Structured essay	Unstructured essay
Higher	–	40	40	20
Foundation	40	40	20	–

Table 1.2

Coursework

Coursework will be a written assignment of approximately 2000–3000 words and will account for 20 per cent of the total subject mark.

IGCSE

Candidates who have followed the core curriculum and take the relevant papers are eligible for the award of grades C to G only. Candidates who have followed the extended curriculum are eligible for the award of grades A to E only.

Candidates will be required to take three papers:

Core curriculum Grades available: C–G	*Extended curriculum* Grades available: A–E
Paper 1 (45 minutes) 40 multiple choice items (all questions to be answered). **Paper 2** (1 hour 30 minutes) Structured questions (all questions to be answered).	**Paper 3** (1 hour) 40 multiple choice items (all questions to be answered). **Paper 4** (2 hours) Structured questions. Candidates must answer Section A and three questions in Section B.
There will be some common questions between Papers 1 and 3 and between Papers 2 and 4.	
Paper 5 Coursework (School-based assessment)‡ *or* **Paper 6** (1 hour 30 minutes) A variety of questions which test enquiry skills. Novel data will be presented for interpretation and analysis of a real economic situation.	

‡ Candidates choose two topics from a list provided by the exam group. No piece of coursework should exceed 1000 words in length.

Paper	Weighting
1	25%
2	50%
3	25%
4	50%
5 or 6	25%

COURSEWORK

Coursework is an element in assessment at GCSE, although it is no longer a compulsory part of the examination. In economics, coursework will take the form of a project or projects and the weight of coursework is usually 20 per cent of the total mark. As can be seen from the information on the examination papers, in some cases the weight of coursework is less than 20 per cent. However, it is especially important to realize that in cases where no coursework is submitted, no final grade will be awarded by any examining group.

The basic skills that will be assessed through coursework can be summarized in the assessment objectives listed on p. 2. To be awarded high marks for coursework it is necessary to demonstrate these abilities and skills, and they should be uppermost in your mind when preparing coursework. These are some other points to bear in mind:

2 ⟩ CHOICE OF TOPIC

Some exam groups, such as the NEAB and NICCEA, can specify the titles of coursework assignments. Others leave students a free hand. In the latter case your teacher might provide advice and there is nothing wrong in asking for this. But remember, your teacher is not allowed to write the project for you! If you wish to select a topic for yourself, you should still discuss it with your teacher and make sure that it will enable you to demonstrate the necessary skills and abilities.

3 ⟩ PREPARATION

This is the important background work to a thorough and well-organized project. There is no substitute for planning and preparation! The sort of areas you should think about include:

    i)   title of the project;
    ii) brief summary of the aims of the project;
    iii) investigation – the data you are going to collect and how they will be obtained. How the data are to be organized, analysed and presented.

4 ⟩ PRESENTING INFORMATION

This is one of the most important aspects of all projects. Data must be presented in a logical way and be used to support, illustrate and further the theme of the project. This is the hallmark of a good project! There are several ways of presenting data. Bar charts, pie charts, tables and graphs can all be used with great effect. Remember that the subject-specific criteria state that students will be expected to use simple techniques of presenting information.

Make sure you have an **introduction**, where you outline briefly the aim of your project and how you are going to meet that aim. Then have a series of paragraphs, perhaps one for each main point. If you present a table or graph, make sure you discuss it in your project. Make sure your project has a beginning, a middle and an end.

5 ⟩ OBJECTIVE DISCUSSION

Take care to avoid pure statements of opinion that cannot be supported by reference to the facts. Economists refer to such statements as **normative statements**. They are quite different from **positive statements**, which can be checked against the facts. For example, there is no way we can test the validity of the statement 'unemployment is too high'. We might feel that this is correct but we have no way of measuring what we mean by 'too high'. However, we can say that 'unemployment has increased during the last twelve months'. This statement *can* be checked against the facts and shown to be either correct or incorrect. It is therefore an objective, or positive, statement.

6 ⟩ CONCLUSION

It is best to finish your coursework with some kind of **conclusion**. This should summarize the results of your investigation. You might say whether your results support or contradict any view with which you may have started your project.

Never leave coursework until the last minute. The preparation and presentation of coursework is a time-consuming process. It is unlikely to gain high marks if it has been rushed. When starting coursework set yourself a realistic deadline and try to stick to it. Allow time for things to go wrong. They often do! Investigating an issue often takes more time than you expect. Remember this!

At the end of each chapter we suggest some useful **sources of information** and data for that topic area. A good investigation will depend largely on the use of relevant, up-to-date data. We also suggest some issues within each chapter, each of which you might consider as the possible basis for your project.

Try to plan your coursework so that you have enough time for each stage.

EXAMINATION TECHNIQUES

SHORT ANSWER QUESTIONS

DATA RESPONSE QUESTIONS

STRUCTURED ESSAY QUESTIONS

MULTIPLE CHOICE QUESTIONS

CASE STUDIES

GETTING STARTED

Despite the importance of coursework, examinations still usually count for 80 per cent of the overall mark on most GCSE courses. Many students fail to do justice to their ability in examinations because of a lack of *technique*. We are all different, and what works for me may not work for you. Nevertheless there are well-tried ways of *preparing* for examinations and actually *sitting* examinations that may help improve your performance. Some of these are considered in this chapter.

One vital thing you must be familiar with is the *type* of question you are likely to face in the exam. We consider the various types in this chapter. Actual questions are provided at the end of each of the following topic-based chapters to give you practice. There are outline answers and fuller *tutor's* answers. There are also, from time to time, *student's* answers with examiner comments to help you see what is expected of you.

TYPES OF QUESTION

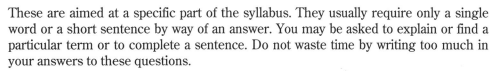

The *type* of question will clearly influence the method or technique you adopt in preparing an answer. There are basically four types of question used in the GCSE examination. Not all of them are used by each exam group and you should check Table 1.1 for information on the types of question you will be asked to cope with in your examination.

These are aimed at a specific part of the syllabus. They usually require only a single word or a short sentence by way of an answer. You may be asked to explain or find a particular term or to complete a sentence. Do not waste time by writing too much in your answers to these questions.

These present information in various forms such as charts, graphs, newspaper articles, tables and so on. Questions are then set on the data. Extract as much information as you can from the data and wherever possible *use* the data to answer questions that are set. Data response questions often test whether you can recognize economic principles, in real-world data or in imaginary data. Use your knowledge of economics to help you understand the data. Watch out for *trends* in data that show how a particular variable, such as unemployment, has changed over time.

These ask a series of questions, sometimes relating to a single theme or topic, sometimes covering several topics. The marks to be awarded for each section are usually given and you should pay attention to these. They tell you how much time to spend on each part of the question. Remember to answer the longer parts of the question as you would write any other essay – in other words, introduction, main points, conclusion. Avoid brief notes or lists of relevant points. It is possible that unstructured essays may be set for Higher tier papers.

These are useful for examination purposes in that they enable a wide range of the syllabus to be tested in a relatively short period of time. To score well on this paper you will have to be thoroughly prepared, but you will also need to concentrate. It is not always easy to decide which is the correct answer. If you cannot decide which is the correct answer, miss out the question but remember to return to it later. If you still cannot decide which is the correct answer, eliminate as many of the options you think are incorrect as you can, and make an educated guess at which of the remaining options is correct. You do not *lose* marks for an incorrect answer.

CASE STUDIES

Some exam groups make use of case studies in their assessment of candidates either as part of the written examination paper or in place of coursework. A case study involves presenting candidates with a quantity of information such as extracts from newspaper articles, tables and graphs. The information is on a specific subject area, e.g. tourism. Candidates are required to answer questions which test their economic understanding of various areas of the syllabus from issues raised by the information given. Usually all the questions in the case study are compulsory.

EXAM PREPARATION

Passing exams is really about preparing properly for them. In particular, do not leave revision until the last few weeks before the examination. You will simply put yourself under too much pressure and because of this you will find it very much more difficult to concentrate, to understand and to remember what you are trying to revise. Be organized in your efforts and allow yourself plenty of time. Make a revision time table and try to stick to it. In drawing up your time table allow yourself more time than you think you are going to need. Revision usually takes longer than at first thought!

Try to answer examination questions in the time you would have in the examination. You might attempt the questions given in this book and then check your answers against the ones given in outline or in full at the end of the chapter. The 'outline answers' which are given are a brief outline of the points the examiner is looking for. There is also a 'tutor's answer' at the end of each chapter. This gives a more detailed answer to the question, of the type that would give you high marks in the exam. Finally, there is a 'student's answer' to a question at the end of some chapters. You will find comments from the examiner throughout the answer to help you see how you can gain marks. There are also 'review sheets' at the end of every other chapter. These give you a chance to check whether you really have understood the content of the previous two chapters, and provide still more questions for practice before the exam.

IN THE EXAMINATION

Before you attempt any questions in an examination, read the **instructions** on the front of the question paper very carefully. Make sure you understand what the instructions mean in terms of the sections you can choose questions from, the number of questions that have to be attempted and so on. You should also pay particular attention to the time the examination will finish and divide your time between questions accordingly. An unfinished exam paper is a common cause of low marks. Where you are required to choose a certain number of questions from a particular section, you should read all the questions in that section before attempting any of them. Tick the questions you think you can answer and then go back and examine each question carefully. When you have done this you will be in a good position to decide *which* questions you think you can answer best. Now you can start to write your first answer. Many teachers and examiners advise students to tackle their favourite question first. This helps you to gain confidence early on in the examination and to put marks 'in the bank'.

Take care to have a **plan** before you attempt a question. If you start to answer a question without a plan you might find that the question is more difficult than you thought at first and, worst of all, you might find you have started a question which you are unable to finish! A plan will also help you to keep a clear structure to your answer and to avoid wandering off the point.

Answer the question, the whole question and nothing but the question

Remember to deal with the specific issues raised in the question. No marks are awarded for including irrelevant material, however interesting you think it might be. Avoid the tendency simply to reproduce your notes on a particular topic. Examiners are used to seeing this and although you will be awarded marks for whatever relevant material you have included, you are unlikely to score highly. This is because your notes will have been **general**, whereas the question is likely to ask you to apply your knowledge to a **particular** situation. If you just write 'all you know' about a topic, a lot of this is likely to be irrelevant to the question actually set.

When answering questions try to avoid the use of **normative statements**, in other words opinions that cannot be supported by reference to the facts. These will gain no marks. Questions on such topics as trade unions, privatization and the distribution of income and wealth often lead to students writing a political answer to what is an economic question. Political answers are unlikely to gain high marks. We all have opinions about what we think would be best for society. Questions on an economics paper will not have asked for a discussion of these political issues. You must answer all questions in terms of the understanding and knowledge you have gained from your study of economics.

CHAPTER

THE ECONOMIC PROBLEM

GETTING STARTED

It might seem odd to choose 'The economic problem' as the title of a chapter, because this seems to suggest that there is only one economic problem. However, most people can list many economic problems. If you asked the person in the street to identify some economic problems they would probably include such things as inflation, unemployment, poverty and so on.

These are most certainly economic problems and economists are very concerned with them. But they are in fact only *part* of a much greater problem, that of matching resources to needs. It is this greater problem which economists refer to as 'The economic problem', and it is to an explanation of this that we now turn.

SCARCITY

CHOICE

OPPORTUNITY COST

PRODUCTION POSSIBILITY CURVES

ECONOMIC GOODS AND FREE GOODS

ESSENTIAL PRINCIPLES

SCARCITY

Scarcity is at the heart of the economic problem. However, by scarcity economists do not necessarily mean that something is rare, in the sense that there isn't much of it. Instead, scarcity is defined as a situation that exists when more of something is desired than is currently available.

In this sense most of the goods and services we can think of are scarce. There is no doubt that for society as a whole there are many unsatisfied desires. This is what the economist means by scarcity.

The question we must ask is, why are goods and services scarce? In fact the answer is simple. Goods and services are scarce because they are made from **resources** which are scarce. We shall see in Chapter 5 that resources include such things as labour and raw materials. At any moment in time there is a limited supply of raw materials as well as of labour. However, there is no limit on the **desires** of society for the output that these resources can produce. This means that some of society's desires will never be satisfied. In other words, some goods and services will always be scarce.

> **Desires are unlimited, but resources are limited**

CHOICE

Because society cannot have all the goods and services it desires at any one time, it is forced to make **choices**. In other words, because of scarcity, society is forced to choose. The choices which all societies must make are discussed in more detail on p. 15. However, it is clear that one important choice is deciding *which* goods and services the available resources are going to produce. If they are used to produce one thing, they are not available to produce something else. Society must therefore choose which goods and services it is going to produce from its scarce resources.

3 OPPORTUNITY COST

We have seen that because resources are limited they cannot produce everything that is desired. This provides us with an important way of looking at cost. If resources are used to produce one thing, then we must do without the *alternative* goods or services that could have been produced with those same resources. The alternative which is forgone is called the **opportunity cost** of what is produced. For example, suppose the Government, on behalf of society, chooses to build a new university, using £80 million of public money. This public money might otherwise have been spent on a new hospital or housing estate. We might therefore say that the opportunity cost of the university that was produced was the new hospital or the new housing estate that was forgone.

Great care must be taken here. In this case the opportunity cost of the university is *not* the hospital *and* the housing estate. Society does not do without both of these. If, in order of preference, society would have chosen a university first, a hospital next and a housing estate last, then the opportunity cost of the university is only the hospital, because it is the hospital that society will do without by using its resources to build the university. In other words, opportunity cost is the **next best alternative which is forgone**.

In practice, most of society's choices about the use of its resources do not mean choosing one thing in preference to another. They involve choosing *more* of one thing and having **less** of something else. For example, if society chooses to produce more **home** computers from its limited resources, then it may have to make do with fewer **business** computers, as skilled operatives and equipment are transferred to the production of home computers.

Opportunity cost is equally important to individuals. They must also choose whether they will buy one good or service in preference to another good or service. For example, when we receive a gift of money we choose which goods and services to spend it on. In choosing what we are going to purchase, we also choose what we are going to do without. Any decision we take must therefore have an opportunity cost. If someone receives £15 as a birthday present they must choose what they are going to buy with it. Possible choices, in order of preference, might be a compact disc, a book or a new shirt. If the compact disc (as first on the list of priorities) is purchased, the opportunity cost of the compact disc is the book, because this is the next best

> **Opportunity cost is the *next best* alternative forgone**

alternative which is forgone.

Sometimes opportunity cost is illustrated by means of a **production possibility curve**. A production possibility curve simply shows the different combinations of output that society can produce at any one time when all of its available resources are used or employed. For example, if we assume that society produces only two goods, **good X** and **good Y**, we can illustrate a typical production possibility curve as in Figure 3.1.

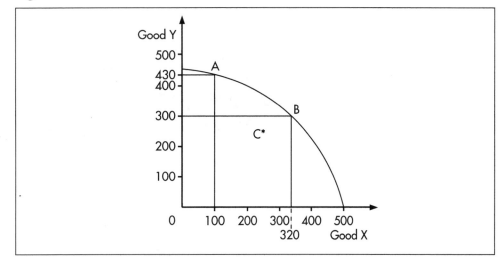

Figure 3.1

Since a production possibility curve shows the maximum amount that can be produced from society's scarce resources, it follows that any point actually resting on the curve, such as A or B, is a point of full employment. Any point *inside* the curve, such as point C, is a point at which not all of society's resources are fully employed. In other words, there are unemployed resources in the economy.

> Movements *along* the curve involve an opportunity cost

outside the curve ?

It is clear from Figure 3.1 that when the economy is at point A it is producing 100 units of good X and 430 units of good Y, whereas when the economy is at point B it is producing 320 units of good X and 300 units of good Y. We can see from this that if the economy is at point A, the only way of increasing the production of X is by using some of the resources currently used in producing Y; in other words there are no spare or unemployed resources available. In this example the opportunity cost of increasing the production of X from 100 units to 320 units is 130 units of good Y. This is because the increased production of X is possible only if the production of Y is reduced by 130 units.

On the other hand, if the economy is at point C, that is, currently producing 250 units of good X and 250 units of good Y, it is possible to increase the production of *both* goods at the same time. It is also possible to increase the production of one good *without* reducing the production of the other. In other words, when the economy is at point C, increased output has no opportunity cost. The reason is that at point C there are unemployed resources which can be drawn into production.

Economists sometimes distinguish between economic goods and free goods. **Economic goods** are those goods which are created from *scarce resources*. Because they are created from scarce resources there is a limit on the amount of economic goods that society can produce at any given time. However, not all goods are created from scarce resources. An example of such a good is sand in the desert. This is freely available in the desert and increased consumption by one person does not deprive another person of the ability to consume. Because of this only economic goods have an opportunity cost.

A review sheet to check your understanding of the materials in this chapter can be found at the end of Chapter 4.

IDEAS FOR COURSEWORK

It is unlikely that you will ever write a project solely on the material covered in this introductory section. However, in any project you do undertake do not neglect to consider opportunity cost if it is at all relevant. Opportunity cost is one of the most important concepts in the study of economics. It is relevant to many decisions taken by individuals, firms and governments and therefore it will easily fit into a great many projects. Let us take a single example to illustrate this point.

Suppose you are looking at how a local farmer uses his land. If he has a field near a major road does he consider using the grazing land for car boot sales or possibly for caravans? What is the best use for his land in terms of revenue? What will be the next best alternative that will be sacrificed as a result of implementing his decision?

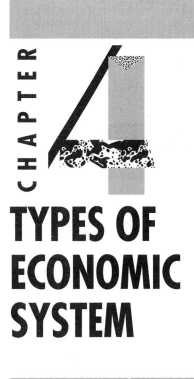

CHAPTER 4

TYPES OF ECONOMIC SYSTEM

GETTING STARTED

We have seen in Chapter 3 that the basic economic problem facing all societies is that of scarcity. This is because **wants** are unlimited, but the **means** to satisfy those wants are limited. Individuals and societies must therefore make choices. In the case of a society, this means deciding on *how* to allocate the scarce economic resources of land, labour, capital and enterprise.

In fact this problem of how to allocate scarce resources really involves all societies in making three fundamental choices: what, how and for whom to produce.

a) **What to produce**   Since society cannot produce *all* of the goods and services it desires, it must decide which goods and services it is going to produce. Because of opportunity cost, more of one thing means less of something else.

b) **How to produce**   There are various ways of producing any given output. Economists usually identify two extreme ways: **capital intensive** production and **labour intensive** production. In the former, production uses mainly large amounts of capital and comparatively little of the other resources. In the latter, labour is used mainly in comparison with other resources. By using different *combinations* of resources, society is able to produce its output in different ways. Which way is a choice all societies must make.

c) **For whom to produce**   Society must decide how its output is to be distributed among consumers. Will there be equal shares for all, or will some people have more output than others and if so, how much more?

Although the problem is the same for all societies, there are different approaches to allocating scarce resources. Here we consider only two very simplified approaches: the **free market economy** and the **centrally planned economy (command economy)**. These are extreme types of economic system that do not actually exist in the real world. Nevertheless, most real-world economies can be thought of as being *more like* one system than the other, though inevitably containing elements of both.

THE FREE MARKET ECONOMY

ADVANTAGES OF A FREE MARKET ECONOMY

DISADVANTAGES OF A FREE MARKET ECONOMY

CENTRALLY PLANNED/ COMMAND ECONOMIES

ADVANTAGES OF CENTRALLY PLANNED/ COMMAND ECONOMIES

DISADVANTAGES OF CENTRALLY PLANNED/ COMMAND ECONOMIES

THE MIXED ECONOMY

ESSENTIAL PRINCIPLES

The main feature of this type of economy is that the Government plays no part in how resources are allocated. Instead, what is produced is decided by consumers and producers, although of course these do not communicate directly with each other. To see how this is so we must consider the main features of a **free market economy**. These are summarized below.

PRODUCTION IS UNDERTAKEN FOR PROFIT

In free market economies, production is undertaken for profit. We say that producers are guided by the **profit motive**. This simply means that producers produce those goods and services which offer the highest profit (revenue minus cost).

FREEDOM OF CHOICE

An important feature of free market economies is that there is **freedom of choice**. This means that consumers are free to choose the goods and services they buy. Workers are free to choose which occupations they will enter. Producers are free to choose which goods and services they will supply and so on.

ABSENCE OF GOVERNMENT INVOLVEMENT

The Government does not make any attempt to influence what is produced, how it is produced or for whom it is produced in a free market economy. It is important to note that this also means that there are no state benefits of any kind, such as pensions, supplementary benefit, free school meals and so on.

PRIVATE PROPERTY

In free market economies there are no legal barriers to prevent people from owning private property. This means that individuals are free to own the means of production, such as land and capital (factory buildings, machinery, etc.). Such individuals are able to undertake production themselves, or they can hire out their private property to others who wish to undertake production.

THE PRICE MECHANISM

> ❝❞ Of all the features make sure that you understand this ❞❞

This is the most important feature of free market economies since it is the mechanism through which resources are allocated to different uses. When consumers buy particular goods and services they are in effect casting a vote for the continued production of those goods or services. When particular goods or services become *more* popular, then *more* votes are cast for these than was previously the case. The result is that the price of these goods and services rises. The higher price encourages producers to increase their output. As a result, resources move into the production of those goods and services which have become more popular with consumers.

The mechanism also works in reverse. Where goods and services become less popular, their price will fall. This reduces profits available from production. Because of this producers will supply less, and fewer resources will now be used to produce these goods and services.

CONSUMER CONTROL

One of the main advantages of free market economies is that **consumers** have the power to influence what is produced. By purchasing more of some goods and services and less of others, they influence what producers supply.

EFFICIENCY

Because production is undertaken for profit, producers are encouraged to be as **efficient** as possible. Firms which are more efficient than others have lower costs of production and can therefore earn higher profit. The profit motive also encourages firms to change their output *quickly* when there is a change in what consumers buy. Firms which do this will earn higher profits than firms which change production slowly.

AUTOMATIC OPERATION

The price mechanism operates *automatically* and does not need people to supervise its operation. Consumers influence what is produced. This means that it is not necessary to employ people just to *decide* what is produced, how it is produced and so on. They are therefore available to produce other goods and services which add to the amount available for society to consume. Put another way, the price mechanism helps to reduce the need for taking decisions through a large administrative bureaucracy.

3 ›DISADVANTAGES OF A FREE MARKET ECONOMY

While market economies have many advantages, they are also considered to have many disadvantages. These can be summarized as follows.

UNEQUAL DISTRIBUTION OF INCOME AND WEALTH

Market economies are associated with great inequality in the distribution of income and wealth. The few who own resources such as land and capital might be very rich compared with the majority of people who would own only one resource: their own labour. Some idea of the kind of inequality that might exist can be seen if we look at how the majority of people lived in eighteenth- and nineteenth-century Britain. A few people lived in very fine houses, but the majority of people were very poor indeed.

BOOMS AND SLUMPS

Over time, all economies experience periods of **boom** and periods of **slump**. During a boom, output and employment rise and most people have jobs. However, during a slump the opposite happens, and output and employment fall. Since there is no government involvement in free market economies, those people who become unemployed are likely to experience great hardship, since there will be no social security system.

EXTERNAL COSTS

Because production is undertaken for private profit in free market economies, producers pay little attention to any undesirable effects of production on the community, such as pollution. Pollution damages the environment and causes health problems, but these costs are imposed on the community through production of the good, rather than on the producer. In others words, they are **external costs** – costs imposed by private firms on an unwilling community. For example, the burning of fossil fuels such as coal in UK power stations causes **acid rain** to fall on parts of Scandinavia.

> The idea of *external* costs will appear in many areas of economics

The producer is concerned mainly with **private costs** such as wages and raw materials, trying to make these as low as possible for the level of output produced. The producer is unlikely to take steps to reduce pollution since this would increase private costs and therefore reduce profit. Because of this, external costs of production may be higher in a free market economy than under other economic systems. **Social costs** are equal to private costs plus external costs.

PUBLIC GOODS AND MERIT GOODS

In free market economies only those goods which are profitable will be produced. However, some goods which are considered necessary in modern economies can never be profitable. One example is street-lighting. No person would ever pay individually for this because if it is provided for one person it is *automatically available* to every other street user without charge. Goods like this, for which a charge cannot be made, are known as **public goods**. Since they can never be profitable they would not be provided in a free market economy.

A different problem arises with **merit goods**. These are goods which benefit the consumer, but which also benefit non-consumers. Examples include healthcare and education. A healthy, well-educated workforce will be more efficient and so will produce more output per head, benefiting employers and indeed the nation as a whole. In market economies, merit goods would be provided only for those people who were willing and able to pay for them. Because merit goods would not be provided for everyone, society as a whole would be worse off.

MONOPOLIES

Because there is no government involvement in free market economies, there will be no legal restrictions to stop firms from growing into a **monopoly**, in other words becoming the only supplier of a product. Firms which are monopolies might be able to charge higher prices for their products, and consumers will have to pay these prices.

In this other extreme type of economy there is no private ownership of property. The state owns all of the land and capital and the Government decides what to produce. To do this the Government makes a **plan** in which it sets target levels of output for all firms in the economy. Because the Government decides what to produce and how to produce it, there is no consideration given to profit.

It is possible for the Government to plan the distribution of output by a system of **physical rationing**. This simply means that everyone receives a fixed amount of output. However, it is unlikely that people would accept this forever and even in a full **centrally planned economy** it is more likely that consumers would have freedom to decide which goods and services to purchase.

5 > ADVANTAGES OF CENTRALLY PLANNED ECONOMIES

Centrally planned economies are thought to have several advantages over other types of economy.

PROVISION OF PUBLIC AND MERIT GOODS

In centrally planned economies production is *not* undertaken for profit. The Government decides what is to be produced. This means that public goods and merit goods can be produced in the quantities the Government thinks best for the population.

MORE EQUAL DISTRIBUTION OF INCOME AND WEALTH

In centrally planned economies there is no private ownership of property. This means that no one can obtain income from hiring out land or capital. Apart from those on state benefit, the only other income received will be from employment. Because of differences in wages there will almost certainly be some inequality. However, it will not be as great as in a free market economy.

REDUCED EXTERNAL COST

We have seen that production is not undertaken for profit in a centrally planned economy. If it chooses, the Government can therefore ensure that external costs of production, such as pollution of the environment, are taken into account in planning decisions. This might mean that external costs will be lower than in a free market economy. However, recent evidence suggests that the former Soviet Union did little to preserve the environment, despite being a centrally planned economy.

GREATER ECONOMIC STABILITY

Because the Government plans output in a centrally planned economy it can avoid the booms and slumps that typically occur in a free market economy. In particular this means that employment is more stable in a centrally planned economy.

CONSUMER PROTECTION FROM MONOPOLY

In centrally planned economies governments have the power to fix prices. This means that where production is controlled by a monopoly, consumers will not be charged higher prices in order for the monopoly to obtain higher profits.

PLANNERS MAKE DECISIONS

It is often suggested that a major disadvantage of planned economies is that consumers have far less influence over what is produced. Decisions about what is produced are taken by **planners** and are basically nothing more than guesswork. Once a plan has been implemented, that is, put into operation, it is difficult to change even if the range of goods and services demanded by consumers changes. This lack of flexibility is considered a serious disadvantage of centrally planned economies.

OPPORTUNITY COST OF PLANNERS

Planning involves collecting and coordinating a great deal of information. This in turn involves the labour of thousands of people who could otherwise be employed producing goods and services for consumption. In other words the **opportunity cost** of planning is high, in terms of sacrificing the many goods and services which could otherwise be produced.

INEFFICIENCY IN PRODUCTION

The profit motive plays no part in the allocation of resources in centrally planned economies. Firms are given production targets and instructions about how many workers to employ and so on. There is therefore no incentive to reduce costs by improving efficiency. Indeed, in many centrally planned economies there is a great deal of inefficiency. Because of this it is argued that resources could be used more efficiently in other types of economic system.

The shortages of consumer goods and the failure to raise living standards to anywhere approaching those in the market and mixed economies of Europe and North America has led to the almost total collapse of the centrally planned economy throughout the world (see below).

In the real world there are no completely free market economies and there are no completely centrally planned economies. All economies are a mixture of both. This does not, of course, mean that there are no differences between economies. There are major differences. Some economies are more like centrally planned economies than market economies. Others, such as the economy of the USA, are more like market economies than centrally planned economies. In all economies what is produced is partly determined by the Government and partly by consumers.

> Actual economies will lie *between* the two extremes

Figure 4.1

In recent years a number of former centrally planned economies such as China and the former Soviet Union have relaxed state controls. Market forces have been allowed to operate in these economies and private enterprise has been encouraged. Many former centrally planned economies of Eastern Europe such as Hungary and the Czech and Slovak Republics have implemented policies of **deregulation, liberalization**, and **privatization** in an effort to provide the prosperity that failed to materialize under planning. While these countries have been successful, to date Russia has found the change from planning to market forces much more difficult, suffering in particular from rampant inflation and rising unemployment. Such has been the rejection of the centrally planned/command system in recent years that only Cuba and North Korea still run their economies in this way.

In a mixed economy, the Government has a variety of ways in which it influences what is produced. It can simply pay firms to produce a particular good or service. For example, in the UK the Government pays firms to resurface the motorways. However, the Government can also influence what is produced by taxing some goods to discourage consumption and therefore production. Other goods can be subsidized to encourage consumption and therefore production.

The Government can also seek to influence consumers by advertising, as in health warnings on the danger of AIDS. The Government can also insist that producers provide information to the public, for example the health warnings on cigarette packets.

TYPICAL EXAM QUESTIONS

1　i)　What is meant by a mixed economy?

　　ii)　Why are there so many economies of this type?

2　In recent years the Government has privatized gas, electricity and water. This has made the UK less of a mixed economy and more like a market economy.

　　i)　What are the main differences between a market economy and a command economy?　　　　　　　　　　　　　　　　　　　　[8]

　　ii)　Using examples explain the view that the UK is still a mixed economy.　　[8]

　　iii)　Why are so many countries mixed economies rather than market or command economies?　　　　　　　　　　　　　　　　　　　[8]

　　　　　　　　　　　　　　　　　　　　　　　　　　　　　WJEC, 1994

3　i)　What is meant by a market economy?

　　ii)　What are the advantages and disadvantages of this system?

OUTLINE ANSWER TO Q. 1

i)　It is best to begin your answer to this question with a clear definition of a mixed economy. Quite simply a mixed economy is one that contains features of *both* free market economies and centrally planned economies. It is necessary therefore to go on to describe the essential features of both free market and centrally planned economies in turn.

　　A market economy is one where the factors of production are privately owned and where people are free to set up their own businesses and produce goods and services for profit. All goods and services have prices which are determined by supply and demand, and only those goods and services which yield profits will be produced. The Government does not interfere in the economic system.

　　A centrally planned economy is one where the factors of production are owned by the state. What is produced and how it is produced are decisions which are taken by central planning committees. These will also decide the prices at which goods and services are sold and therefore the incomes earned by the people producing them.

　　In the typical mixed economy, most firms are privately owned and will continue in business only if they make a profit. However, some industries will be owned by the state. In addition, the Government will also control the way private firms run their businesses. In the UK we have the Factory Acts, the Monopolies and Mergers Acts and a great deal of legislation designed to protect the consumer. All of these are designed to regulate the behaviour of firms.

ii)　The second part of the question really asks why society has never found the pure market economy or the centrally planned economy totally acceptable. The disadvantages of these systems have already been covered (see pp. 19–21). A mixed economy attempts to obtain the best features of both market and centrally planned economies.

TUTOR'S ANSWER TO Q. 2

i) A market economy answers the economic questions of what, how and for whom to produce by the operation of the market mechanism. The forces of demand through consumers and supply through producers determine prices and the allocation of resources. The role of profit is important in that it provides an important role in rewarding risk and providing signals to the market mechanism. Resources are drawn towards the production of goods in demand where profits are highest. The private sector is most important in this system. Singapore and to a lesser extent the USA are good examples of market economies.

A command economy attempts to solve the economic problem through state ownership and control of the nation's resources. The Government uses planning authorities to direct resources to produce planned production targets. The importance of directives and plans mean that command economies are producer-led rather than demand-led as in market economies. Few examples of command economies exist nowadays, with only Cuba and North Korea remaining faithful to planning.

ii) The UK is still a mixed economy because it has sizable public and private sectors. Although a large number of nationalized industries have been privatized in recent years such as British Gas, British Airways and British Telecom there is still a significant degree of public ownership. The Royal Mail and large parts of the health and education services are in the public sector. Public expenditure still accounts for over 45 per cent of total expenditure in the economy. The private sector's importance has increased in recent years. Examples of important private sector firms which are owned by individuals include Marks and Spencer, Guiness and Esso.

iii) Some goods and services cannot be provided by the private sector, such as defence. Others are too important to the economy or society to be provided by private firms only interested in profit, for example health and education. Goods provided by a single state firm often gain economies of scale which would not be available to a number of smaller private firms. Private sector monopolies may exploit consumers with high prices or poor quality products. Market economies often produce an unequal distribution of income and wealth.

The above points illustrate the failure of the market system and the need for state intervention in an economy. A command economy, however, is often unable to equate demand and supply with regular shortages and surpluses. With no profit motive, command economies are often unable to respond to consumer demand with the result that resources are misallocated. The need for markets and a private sector became clear to the former Soviet Union and China in the late 1980s. The restructuring of these former command economies included the need to have a profit motive for firms and individuals.

STUDENT'S ANSWER TO Q. 3 WITH EXAMINER COMMENTS

Question

i) What is meant by a market economy?

ii) What are the main advantages and disadvantages of this system?

> **If you mention 'four types' name them**

(i) A market economy is one of four major types of economy which deal with economic problems. A market economy will allow freeplay to what are known as market forces, which means there is no intervention by political organizations in the form of price controlling or taxation. Most people in the non-communist world will earn and spend money in societies which are fundamentally market economies. In this type of economy the questions of how what and for whom to produce are decided by the entrepreneur who undertakes decisions and risks involved in production. What to produce is decided mainly by the price mechanism which lets the producer know consumer demands and hence resources can be allocated to produce goods to satisfy consumer demand. Lastly the question for whom to produce can be answered by letting the forces of demand and supply create a market price at which people will be able to purchase it if they can afford it.

> **An excellent introduction, bringing out the role of the price mechanism**

The market economy contains six essential features which separate it from any of the other types of economy. In a market economy individuals have the right to own, control and dispose of private property, i.e. land buildings, etc. The entrepreneurs also have freedom of choice of what they produce and to sell it in markets of their own choice. The entrepreneur is driven by self-interest as the success of the business will be in terms of profit. In the market economy there is a lot of competition as there are many producers of the same commodity. The price mechanism is also a feature of the market economy. When we buy a good or service we are in fact voting for the continuation of the production of the commodity. Goods that the public demands will be produced even if resources have to be diverted from the production of other goods. Lastly, the Government, as we have said before, have a limited vote in a market economy.

> **A very good point**

(ii) This type of economy has many advantages over other economies. Firstly, the goods that consumers want are produced as the price mechanism shows what commodities are in demand, and so the entrepreneur can act on this information. Self-interest is one of the advantages of a market economy as the entrepreneur is driven by the fact that he will get the rewards if the business is profitable. Competition is also an advantage of the market system as prices are forced down when companies producing the same good battle to sell their own

> **Again, some very good points made in this paragraph**

product. This will mean uncompetitive companies will not be able to compete in these markets. Resources are also used efficiently in the market economy as they are allocated through the price mechanism. This will mean resources will not be used on goods the public doesn't want.

The disadvantages of this system are like the advantages, very numerous. The market economy is very susceptible to booms and slumps in the cycle of economic activity. This type of system gives rise to producers forcing their dominance on the market in the form of monopolies. This will mean in some cases lack of competition and exploitation of the consumer by charging prices well above cost. In comparison to command economies, market economies suffer more in terms of unemployment. This is due to competition and technical innovation leaving capital and labour reduction in some industries that are declining. The market economy also leaves no room for the provision of merit goods which need to be available to everyone, eg education and health. This type of economy doesn't take into account social costs when producing goods. The amount of pollution discharged from factories is less important in a market economy as trying to rectify this would add to costs.

One thing that must be noted is the fact that a pure market economy has never existed. Every country's economy will have some form of government influence.

Not very clear!

These are good points

An excellent essay. A good structure, with introduction, paragraphs for the major points and a brief conclusion. Some very good points made in the essay. A high standard of economic knowledge and English expression.

IDEAS FOR COURSEWORK

The following areas might be followed up as the basis of a coursework assignment:

- How has British Rail been privatized?
- What have been the effects of the privatization of British Telecom?
- What are the cases for and against the privatization of the Royal Mail?

SOURCES OF INFORMATION

The following sources provide tables and data relevant to these topic areas:

- *Economic Trends*, Central Statistical Office
- *Employment Gazette*, Department of Employment
- *Monthly Digest of Statistics*, Central Statistical Office
- *Social Trends*, Central Statistical Office

They may be found in the **reference** section of a town central library, or perhaps in your school or college library. Also make use of quality newspapers such as *The Times* or *Daily Telegraph*.

REVIEW SHEET

1 What are the missing words in the following sentence? Any good which is created from _____ _____ is an economic good.

2 Give an example to show how opportunity cost is relevant to each of the following:
   i)   the Government
   ii) a firm
   iii) an individual.

3 Assume that a country produces only two goods, X and Y, and that when resources are fully employed it can produce any of the following combinations of X and Y:

X	Y
100	0
93	20
82	40
64	60
35	80
0	95

   i)   Sketch the production possibility curve for this country.

   ii) What is the opportunity cost of increasing the production of X from 64 units to 82 units?
   _____
   _____

   iii) Show this on your production possibility curve.

4 Why do economic goods have an opportunity cost while free goods do not?
   _____
   _____
   _____
   _____

5 Do all countries face the same basic economic problem
   _____
   _____
   _____
   _____

6 If a consumer wishes to buy a Mars bar and a bag of crisps both costing 25p, what is the opportunity cost of purchasing the crisps?
   _____
   _____
   _____

7   Why are free school lunches for teachers not a free good?

_____
_____
_____
_____

8   If a country is producing at a level of output within its production possibility frontier, what economic problem is it likely to be suffering from?

_____
_____
_____
_____

9   In a free enterprise economy the basic function of the _____ _____ is to allocate resources.

10 In a free enterprise economy why would a change in the distribution of income lead to a change in the allocation of resources?

_____
_____
_____
_____

11 What determines the allocation of resources in a centrally planned economy?

_____
_____
_____
_____

12 What determines the allocation of resources in a mixed economy?

_____
_____
_____
_____

13 A visitor to a particular country noticed long queues for basic commodities such as bread, and long waiting-lists for many consumer durables such as fridges and television sets. Local residents explained that there were shortages of these commodities and that these shortages had existed for many years.

What kind of economy is being described and why do shortages often continue?

_____
_____
_____
_____

14 Listed below are some features of economic systems. Match the feature listed with the following economic systems:

- pure market economy
- mixed economy
- fully planned economy

i)   Resources are allocated entirely by the free choices of consumers.

_____

ii) All industries are allocated a target rate of output.

_____

iii) Producers have total freedom to decide what to produce.

_____

iv) Some resources are allocated by the Government.

_____

v)   There is no private property.

_____

15 In free market economies the consumer is said to be **sovereign**. Why is this?

_____

_____

_____

_____

16 Which one of the following is most likely to be in the public sector in a mixed economy:
i) car production
ii) postal services
iii) financial services?

17 Name some external costs created by an individual driving a car.

_____

_____

18 Why are increased external costs often seen as the opportunity cost of increased output in an economy?

_____

_____

_____

_____

19 Why may it be undesirable for merit goods to be supplied by the private sector in a modern economy?

_____

_____

_____

_____

20 Give some examples of goods using capital intensive methods of production.

_____

_____

THE RESOURCES & PRODUCTION

GETTING STARTED

The resources of an economy are the **factors of production**, or inputs, which are used to produce an output. They are usually classified as **land**, **labour** and **capital**. However, sometimes a fourth factor of production called the **entrepreneur** is identified. This refers to the role of individuals or groups in bringing together the various factors of production to meet a demand identified in the economy. The word 'enterprise' is sometimes used for this role. Each factor of production is considered separately in the following section. Here it is sufficient to note that *all* output produced in a modern economy depends upon the contribution of *all* of these factors of production. Some output might contain more of one input relative to another. We use the term **capital intensive** when capital equipment is the most important factor input, and **labour intensive** when labour plays the dominant role. However, all units of output contain at least some of each of these inputs.

One term that is frequently used in connection with the factors of production is **mobility**. In fact there are two types of mobility, **geographical** and **occupational**. Geographical mobility refers to the ease with which a factor of production can change its geographical location, that is, physically move itself from one place to another.

Occupational mobility, on the other hand, refers to the ease with which a factor of production can change from one occupation to another.

Production is the process of creating **goods** or performing **services** for which people are prepared to pay. The purpose of all production is the satisfaction of desires. We can say that production includes all those activities that take place before the consumption of any good or service by the final consumer. Production therefore includes activities such as the extraction of raw materials, the processing of raw materials into finished or partly finished goods, and the sale of these goods to the consumer. As an example, take the case of North Sea oil. It is extracted from the North Sea, refined into petrol (fuel oil) and other products. These are then sold through wholesalers and retailers to customers, e.g. petrol through garages.

ESSENTIAL PRINCIPLES

1 ▷ LAND

Early economists defined **land** as 'all the free gifts of nature', and this is still a useful definition. In fact land is defined to include all natural resources such as forests, seas and lakes, mineral and ore deposits, fields and all land which is built upon, etc.

Clearly, a great deal of land is very mobile in terms of the use that can be made of it, but highly immobile geographically. The mountains of Scotland cannot be moved to the South-East of England!

A special characteristic of land is that in its *natural* state it has no cost of production. It is quite literally provided freely by nature.

2 ▷ LABOUR

The input of **labour** refers to the input of human effort, both physical and mental. It is therefore the **services** of labour which are bought and sold. The supply of labour to the economy depends on many factors such as the size of the population, the age and sex structure of the population (see Chapter 6), the length of the working week and so on.

GEOGRAPHICAL MOBILITY

❝❝ Remember the two types of mobility: geographical and occupational **❞❞**

In any town, or even within a particular neighbourhood, there are countless examples of **geographical** mobility of labour. Different accents identify people from different parts of the country and sometimes even from different countries. However, this does not necessarily mean that labour is always geographically mobile.

Barriers

In particular we can identify several **barriers** to the geographical mobility of labour. These include the following.
- **Ignorance:** Workers might be unaware of the opportunities that exist in different parts of the country.
- **Cost of movement:** The cost of moving from one part of the country to another can deter movement. This is especially true in the case of a person who has to move the family to another part of the country. There is the cost of transporting household items, and perhaps the costs involved in buying and selling a house. This can be a particular problem when a person moves from one part of the country where house prices are relatively low, such as North Wales, to another part of the country where they are relatively high, such as the South-East of England.
- **Availability of housing:** The problems and costs involved in buying and selling a house will tend to discourage people from moving. Mobility of labour will also be reduced if there is a shortage of rented accommodation in the areas to which people wish to move.
- **Social ties:** When people live in a community they establish social and family ties which they might be reluctant to give up. Unwillingness to leave friends and family reduces the geographical mobility of labour.

OCCUPATIONAL MOBILITY

This refers to the willingness and ability of a worker to change from one occupation to another. For example, a school teacher who becomes a salesperson would provide an example of **occupational** mobility.

Barriers

The main barriers which limit occupational mobility are detailed below.
- **Natural ability:** Some occupations require a particular ability that not everyone possesses. For example, not everyone has the intelligence and dexterity to become a brain surgeon or the balance and strength to become a professional footballer.
- **Training:** Some occupations require considerable training. People will be deterred from entering these occupations if they receive relatively low wages during training. They will also avoid these occupations if the wage on qualifying is not high enough to 'compensate' them for the years spent training.

WHY IS MOBILITY IMPORTANT?

Mobility of labour is considered important for several reasons:

- **Higher and more flexible output:** The demands of the population for goods and services are constantly changing. Where the labour force is mobile it is able to help firms change the types of goods and services produced with comparative ease.
- **Lower inflation:** A mobile labour force, by being able to respond quickly to changes in consumer demands, is able to influence inflation. For example, when consumers suddenly demand more of a particular product its price will tend to rise. However, the more mobile the workforce the more quickly output can be increased in response to an increase in demand. This will help to reduce the upward pressure on prices.
- **Lower unemployment:** Sometimes there is demand for workers in a particular part of the country or in a particular occupation. Some firms may be short of labour. Only if the labour force is mobile will they be able to recruit workers from areas of high unemployment or from workers with other skills. A greater mobility of labour would therefore help to reduce unemployment.
- **Technological advances:** New technology changes the way in which goods and services can be produced. In particular technological advances tend to reduce the average cost (see pp. 92–3) of producing output. To take full advantage of these advances the labour force must be mobile, in the sense of being willing to learn how to use the new technology and to move to those firms adapting to the modern methods.

3 **CAPITAL**

Capital is defined as any **man-made** aid to production. These man-made aids to production can be classified as either **fixed capital** or **working capital**.

Fixed capital includes such items as factories, machines, dockyards and so on. These items do not change their form when used in the process of producing other goods and services.

Working capital, on the other hand, does change in the course of production. It consists of stocks of raw materials and stocks of semi-finished and finished goods awaiting purchase by consumers. Working capital is sometimes called 'circulating capital'.

> Make sure you know the difference between *fixed* and *working* capital

Whether a good is classified as an item of capital depends on what it is to be used for. For example, a car which is used solely as a taxi is clearly an aid to the 'production' of that service, and therefore an item of capital. On the other hand, a car which is used by a family for social purposes is clearly not an item of capital.

CAPITAL ACCUMULATION

The total amount of capital in existence at any one time is referred to as the **stock** of capital. Additions to this stock are the result of **investment**. To the economist, investment is the creation of additional capital. However, if resources are used to create additional capital the same resources cannot be used to produce other goods or services. There is therefore an **opportunity cost** associated with the creation of capital. The existence of this opportunity cost is summed up in the sentence: **Capital accumulation involves abstention from current consumption.** In other words, society must forgo the output that resources could otherwise produce in order that they can be used for the creation of capital.

4 **THE ENTREPRENEUR**

Modern production would be impossible if the three factors already considered were not coordinated and regulated. This task of coordination and regulation is one function of the **entrepreneur**. However, the bulk of production takes place in **anticipation** of demand. This means there is a **risk** of loss for any person (or group of people) who does not correctly anticipate consumer demand. If the anticipated demand does not materialize, so that output is produced which no one will buy, the result will be a business loss. Bearing this risk of loss is another function of the entrepreneur.

5 **CLASSIFYING PRODUCTION**

In general we can classify production into one of three categories: primary, secondary and tertiary. Figure 5.1 provides an illustration of these activities and Table 5.1 shows their relative importance in the UK in 1991 and 1994. There is a continual shift in employment away from the primary and secondary sectors towards the tertiary sector.

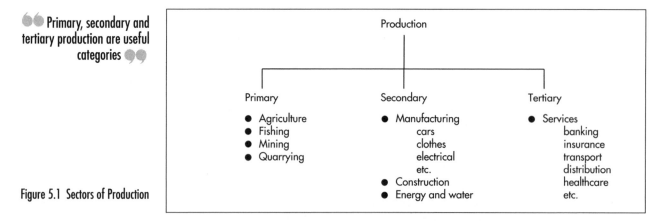

Figure 5.1 Sectors of Production

Table 5.1 Shares of Total Employment (UK)

SECTOR OF ACTIVITY	% OF TOTAL EMPLOYMENT	
	1991	1994
Primary	2.1	1.6
Secondary	29.2	22.4
Tertiary	68.7	76.0
Total	100.0	100.0

A different way of classifying production is to distinguish between **capital goods** and **consumer goods**. We have already seen that capital goods are those goods which are produced as a man-made aid to production. Consumer goods, on the other hand, are those goods desired for their own sake.

Sometimes economists distinguish between **durable** and **non-durable** goods. A durable good is one that can be used many times, such as a washing machine or a television set. A non-durable good, on the other hand, can be consumed only once. Food is the most obvious example of a non-durable good.

PRODUCTIVITY

When discussing production we often hear of the term **productivity**. Productivity refers to the volume of output produced from a given volume of inputs or resources (land, labour and capital). For example, the productivity of labour within a firm can be measured as:

$$\text{labour productivity} = \frac{\text{total output of the firm per period}}{\text{number of workers employed per period}}$$

This means that if a firm produces 1000 bicycles per week and employs 250 people each working a full week, productivity can be expressed as: 1000 bicycles per week ÷ 250 people per week = 4 bicycles per person week.

Productivity is a very important measure of the **efficiency** with which resources are being used. In the example above if we assume that there is no change in the number of workers employed or the hours worked by each person, but that output per week increases to 1250 bicycles, we can say that productivity has increased to 5 bicycles per 'man-week', that is an increase in productivity of 25 per cent.

THE DIVISION OF LABOUR

The division of labour is sometimes called specialization

In modern economies the production of most goods is broken down into a series of highly specialized tasks. Each worker carries out only a small part of the overall production process. This is easily observed in many industries, such as the car industry where cars are put together along an assembly line. Each worker along the assembly line performs only a single task or a small group of tasks. This kind of specialization is referred to as the **division of labour**.

ADVANTAGES OF DIVISION OF LABOUR

● **Increased productivity:** The main advantage of the division of labour is that it makes possible a large increase in the **productivity of labour**. There are several reasons why productivity increases, including the following:

● When workers specialize in a particular task they become more skilful in the performance of this task than would be possible if they performed a variety of tasks. This is summed up by the saying 'practice makes perfect'.

- No time is wasted by workers moving from one machine to another, and all machines can be kept in constant use. This would not be possible if one person was using several machines.
- By breaking down the production process into a number of small tasks which are constantly repeated, it often becomes possible to develop machines that can perform these tasks. In other words, specialization in a particular task often helps producers to see where they can 'mechanize' a task, i.e. substitute machinery (capital) for labour. The main advantage of this is that greater mechanization usually leads to a substantial increase in productivity.

- **Increased range of goods and services:** Another major advantage of division of labour is that greater productivity leads to the production of larger outputs than would otherwise be possible. This has increased the range of goods and services available to the community as a whole. In addition, greater productivity leads to lower costs **per unit of output** (see pp. 92–3). Because each unit costs less to produce, producers can sell them for lower prices than would be possible if each unit was produced individually. This helps to bring many items into the 'price range' of the majority of consumers.

DISADVANTAGES OF DIVISION OF LABOUR

- **Increased boredom:** A major disadvantage of division of labour is that workers perform the same repetitive tasks day after day. Many find this repetition boring. This can lead to poor quality output as many workers lose interest in the job.
- **Lack of variety:** Although division of labour has increased the **range** of goods and services available to consumers, all goods of a particular type are identical. A glance in a car showroom or in clothes shops will confirm this. This lack of individuality is sometimes suggested as a disadvantage of division of labour. However, care must be taken here. It is true that a great deal of output is highly standardized, but it is equally true that in the absence of this standardization, costs of production would be much higher and therefore most people would have to consume less. We might have less choice of *styles* when selecting one particular product, but there is no doubt that we are now able to afford to choose from a substantially greater range of different products than would be the case in the absence of standardization.
- **Worker interdependence:** Because each worker performs only a single task or small group of tasks, industrial action, such as a strike by any group of workers performing the same task, can result in a complete stoppage of production.
- **Greater risk of unemployment:** In modern economies the demands of consumers are constantly changing. New products become available and demand for older products declines. Where workers have been trained in only one skill, it might be difficult for them to find alternative employment if demand for the product they help to produce falls and production is cut back. The main point is that when demand for a product falls, output will be reduced and therefore fewer workers will be required. The way in which changes in demand affect output is discussed more fully in Chapter 7.

LIMITS TO THE DIVISION OF LABOUR

Despite the disadvantages of the division of labour, it is so widespread that society clearly believes the advantages *outweigh* the disadvantages. However, there are limits on the extent to which division of labour is possible. These are considered below.

- **Size of the market:** The main factor that limits the extent of division of labour is the size of the market. Specialization makes possible a substantial increase in output, but it will be profitable to produce this only if there are sufficient consumers willing and able to buy the higher level of output. The larger the market, that is, the greater the number of consumers, the greater the demand and therefore the more likelihood that specialization will take place. The smaller the market, the less scope there will be for specialization.
- **Transport costs:** One factor in particular that might limit the size of the market is the cost of transporting the finished product to the market. Where this is high relative to the value of the finished product, firms might be prevented from taking full advantage of specialization. A good transport network of roads, railways, coastal and

canal boats, airways, etc. will help specialization in an economy by making it cheaper and easier to get the products to the consumer.

● **Nature of the product:** The production of some goods and services cannot be broken down into a small series of tasks. This is true of a great deal of repair work. It is also true in the production of certain goods where a unique item is required, such as a work of art. An element of variety is an important part of many goods and services, such as jewellery or exclusive clothing. Standardization would clearly be less acceptable here. In such cases the market is often served by a large number of small firms, rather than a small number of large firms each producing a standardized product.

8 CHANGES IN PRODUCTIVITY

A change in productivity occurs when there is a change in output per unit of input. It is very rare in modern economies for productivity to fall and so we tend to concentrate on increases in productivity and in particular on increasing the productivity of labour. We have seen that an increase in the productivity of labour occurs when there has been an increase in output per 'man-hour' or per 'man-day'. A different way of saying the same thing is to say that the average output of the labour force increases.

The way in which change in the number of workers employed changes output and productivity is usually explained by the **law of variable proportions**. This is discussed below, but first we must distinguish between the **short run** and the **long run** in production.

THE SHORT RUN AND THE LONG RUN

The ideas of short *and* long *run will appear in other parts of the course*

In economics the short run and the long run are *not* specific time periods such as a month or a year. Instead they relate to the length of time required to change the input of various factors of production. During the **short run** it is possible to change the input of only some factors – the **variable factors**. If at any point in time there is *at least one* factor of production whose input cannot be increased, then the firm is operating in the short run. In other words, the short run is a period of time during which there is at least one **fixed factor** of production. The **long run**, on the other hand, is a period of time during which there are no fixed factors of production, i.e. all factors can be changed.

The short run and the long run are difficult ideas to understand. An example will clarify them. Assume a firm wishes to increase its weekly output. To do this it must obtain more raw materials, more machines and more factory space. It must also hire more labour. Now if the firm has additional factory space, and is able to buy more raw materials and hire additional workers, but is temporarily unable to obtain more machines, it is operating in the short run. All of the inputs are variable except machines. Machines are therefore the fixed factor. In the short run the only way the firm can increase output is if it works the fixed factor (machines) more intensively, perhaps by introducing a shift system.

Although the firm may be temporarily unable to obtain additional machines, as time passes it will be able to obtain them. When this is the case, *all* factors are variable and the company can then operate in the long run.

Although in this example the fixed factor of production was capital, that is machines, it may be any factor of production that is fixed in the short run. It is often the case that in order to expand production firms need to take on more workers, but they are unable to recruit workers with the skills they require. It takes time to train additional workers or to attract them from other occupations or firms. In this case, labour is the fixed factor during the short run.

9 THE LAW OF VARIABLE PROPORTIONS

These laws refer to the short run, *with at least one factor fixed*

The effect on output of changing the input of variable factors can be explained in terms of the **law of variable proportions**. This law can be broken down into two component laws. These are the **law of increasing returns** and the **law of diminishing returns**. We take each in turn.

● **The law of increasing returns:** This states that as more units of a variable factor are added to a fixed factor, output will at first rise **more than proportionately**. When this happens we say that the firm experiences **increasing returns**.

● **The law of diminishing returns:** This law states that as more units of a variable factor are added to a fixed factor, there will come a point when output will rise **less**

than proportionately. When this happens we say that the firm experiences **diminishing returns**.

Putting these two laws together gives us the law of variable proportions. This states that as more units of a variable factor are added to a fixed factor, output will at first rise *more than proportionately*. However, as more units of the variable factor are added, output will, after a certain point, rise *less than proportionately*.

10 > **AVERAGE AND MARGINAL PRODUCT**

When discussing the law of variable proportions or its component laws we often make use of the concepts of **marginal product** and **average product**. These are measured with respect to a specific type of input, usually labour.

The **marginal product** of labour is simply the change in total output when one more worker is employed. The **average product** of labour, on the other hand, is simply total output divided by the total number of workers employed. The relationship between total, average and marginal product is illustrated in

NO. OF WORKERS	TOTAL PRODUCT	AVERAGE PRODUCT	MARGINAL PRODUCT
1	2	2.0	2
2	5	2.5	3
3	10	3.3	5
4	22	5.5	12
5	42	8.4	20
6	62	10.3	20
7	77	11.0	15
8	86	10.75	9

Table 5.2

It can be seen that up to the employment of the fifth worker marginal product is rising. When marginal product is rising total product is rising at a *faster rate* because each additional worker employed makes possible an increase in total product that is greater than that achieved from the preceding worker. This means that total product rises *more than proportionately* and therefore the firm is experiencing *increasing returns*.

With the employment of the sixth worker the situation changes, because marginal product is constant. Employing the sixth worker results in an increase in output that is exactly the same as the increase in output that occurs when the fifth worker is employed. In these circumstances we say that the firm experiences *constant returns* because total output grows by a constant amount, or at a *constant rate*.

After the employment of the seventh worker marginal product begins to fall. This means that the *rate* at which total output rises, as more workers are employed, falls. In these circumstances the firm experiences *diminishing returns*.

The concepts of increasing returns and diminishing returns are illustrated in Figure 5.2, which is based on the data in Table 5.2.

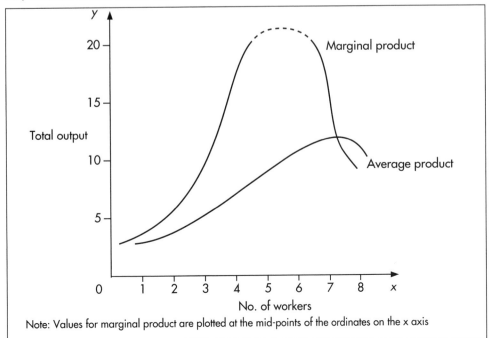

Note: Values for marginal product are plotted at the mid-points of the ordinates on the x axis

Figure 5.2

RETURNS AND THE DIVISION OF LABOUR

The laws of returns discussed and illustrated above are widely known. However, we have not yet explained what *causes* increasing and diminishing returns. In fact, increasing returns are due to the **division of labour**. It was suggested earlier that the major advantage of the division of labour is that it makes possible an increase in productivity. If productivity does rise, this means that output per worker increases. In other words, increasing returns are an illustration of the gains obtained from specialization.

Output per worker (average product) will rise whenever marginal product is greater than average product (see Figure 5.2). You can easily understand this if you think of a game. If your last (marginal) score is greater than your average score, then your average will rise. If the last (marginal) score is the same as your average, your average will be unchanged. As soon as marginal product falls below the existing average product, then average product (productivity) falls. This occurs after the employment of the seventh worker in Table 5.2.

When productivity falls as a result of employing more workers, this is simply an indication of the fact that there is a *limit* to the gains from specialization given that the firm has at least one fixed factor of production. In other words, falling productivity simply indicates that the combination of factors of production used has become less favourable.

RETURNS TO SCALE

> Returns to scale refer to the *long run* when *all* factors can be varied

Earlier we distinguished between the short run and the long run. The short run was defined as a period when there was at least one fixed factor of production. Clearly then, our analysis of increasing and diminishing returns is a short run analysis because we assume that the firm is operating with at least one factor of production which is fixed. This is why we speak of the law of **variable proportions**. By changing the amounts of the variable factors to at least one fixed factor, the *proportion* in which the factors are combined will be variable, i.e. changing.

However, in the long run there are no fixed factors of production. All factors are variable, and firms are therefore able to adjust their input of all factors of production. When firms change the input of all factors of production, we say that there has been a change in the **scale of production**.

When firms change the scale of production this will almost certainly change productivity. When an increase in the input of all factors of production leads to a **more than proportional** increase in output, we say that the firm has experienced **economies of scale**. For example, if the firm increases the scale of production, that is the input of all factors of production, by 10 per cent, and as a result output rises by more than 10 per cent, the firm has experienced economies of scale. On the other hand, when an increase in the input of all factors of production leads to a **less than proportional** increase in total output, we say that the firm experiences **diseconomies of scale**. Thus if the firm increases the scale of production by 10 per cent and output rises by less than 10 per cent, then we say that the firm has experienced diseconomies of scale.

Great care must be taken to distinguish between an increase in productivity that has occurred as a result of an increase in the use of *variable factors only*, and an increase in productivity that has occurred because of an increase in the *scale of production*. Increasing returns and diminishing returns refer to *short run* changes in output, that is, changes in output when the firm has at least one fixed factor. Economies and diseconomies of scale refer to *long run* changes in output, that is changes in output when there are no fixed factors.

For simplicity, economies of scale are sometimes defined as an increase in the scale of production that leads to a *fall* in the average cost of producing each unit. Diseconomies of scale, on the other hand, are defined as an increase in the scale of production that leads to an *increase* in the average cost of producing each unit. More is said about this in Chapter 9 when we also consider why a change in productivity leads to a change in the average cost of producing each unit.

REASONS FOR ECONOMIES OF SCALE

There are several reasons why firms might experience economies of scale as they grow. The main ones are summarised below.

Technical economies

These refer to increases in productivity which result from changes in the **technical** process of production, made possible as a result of an increase in the scale of production. We can identify several technical economies of scale.

- **Increased specialization:** The larger the size of the firm, the greater the opportunities for specialization. We have seen that specialization results in an increase in productivity for a variety of reasons, such as the increased use of specialist machinery.

Technical economies usually refer to the plant, i.e. the production unit

- **Better linkage of processes:** Products often require two or more separate processes in producing the finished item. Suppose a product needs two types of machine, machine A capable of producing a *maximum* output per hour of 20 units, and machine B capable of producing a *maximum* hourly output of 15 units. A firm that possesses only one of each machine has a maximum output per hour of 15 units. This means that one-quarter of the output of machine A cannot be used each hour, i.e. for 15 minutes per hour machine A is not used. The firm therefore has *unused* or *excess* capacity. Now if the firm expands its output to 60 units per hour (assuming it can sell the additional output) there need not be any idle machine time, that is excess capacity. The firm will simply use 3 of machine A (3 x 20 units per hour) with 4 of machine B (4 x 15 units per hour). So it may be possible to use all machines fully only when output grows to a larger size. Here again it is clear that productivity will increase when output is expanded. Question 2 on p. 40 provides you with an opportunity to demonstrate this.

- **Indivisibilities:** It will always be possible for firms to increase productivity by using more efficient capital. For example, if two machines perform exactly the same function, but one machine produces twice as much per hour as the other, productivity can be increased by using the more efficient machine. However, the capital equipment which is most efficient is often large and expensive. In many cases it will be **indivisible**, in the sense that smaller versions are not available. A nuclear power station cannot be scaled down below a certain operating level, and the same applies to an assembly line in a car plant. Only as the firm's output grows will it be able to afford and to *use* these large, more productive items of capital equipment. At relatively low levels of output such indivisible units of capital equipment would be under-utilized and firms would again be operating with excess capacity. Question 2 on p. 40 provides an example of this.

Marketing economies

As well as these technical economies, a firm that grows in size might also benefit from a number of **marketing** economies.

- **Economies of bulk purchases:** Firms which are large can buy in bulk, gaining discounts on raw materials and other items purchased as inputs. This gives large firms a considerable advantage over smaller firms which cannot buy in bulk.

- **Economies of bulk distribution:** Firms which are large can use their own distribution fleets, such as heavy goods vehicles, bulk containers and so on to transport their product to market. This in itself would give them an advantage over smaller firms, but they also gain another advantage. As the size of containers and transport vehicles increases, the **cost per unit transported** falls. It is many times cheaper to transport a barrel of oil from the Gulf using a fully laden supertanker weighing some 2 million tonnes than it is to use a tanker weighing only 150,000 tonnes, for example.

Financial economies

Larger firms can often obtain **finance** more cheaply and easily than smaller firms. Banks and other financial institutions may consider them less risky and be more willing to lend, and at lower rates of interest.

These are some of the major reasons why a firm might experience economies of scale as the size of output rises. However, it is possible that beyond a certain level of output further increases in scale might lead to diseconomies of scale. The suggestion is that large firms become more difficult to manage and run. This might be because of the problems of organizing and coordinating the activities of relatively large firms, with the result that beyond a certain size, such firms become **less efficient** as they grow.

TYPICAL EXAM QUESTIONS

1 Study the graph below which is based on statistics from *H.M. Treasury* and answer the questions which follow.

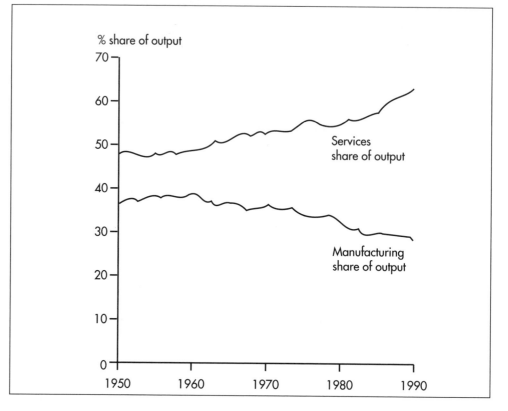

Figure 5.3

i)   Explain the difference between a service industry and a manufacturing industry, giving examples to illustrate your answer. [4]

ii) Describe what has happened to the share of services in total output since 1950. [3]

iii) The change in manufacturing share of output shown in the graph does not necessarily mean that less manufactured goods are being produced. Explain why this is so. [2]

iv) What would be the possible effects on an economy of a growth in the tertiary sector and a decline in the primary and secondary sectors? [12]

NEAB, 1996 specimen

2 This question is based on the following table, which shows how the weekly **output** of a particular firm changes as the **inputs** of labour and capital vary (from 1 to 4 units respectively).

		CAPITAL			
		1	2	3	4
LABOUR	1	50	100	150	200
	2	150	300	500	820
	3	250	450	590	680
	4	100	125	140	150

Table 5.3

i) How does the economist define capital and labour?

ii) What is the total production when a) 4 units of labour and 2 units of capital, and b) 2 units of labour and 4 units of capital are employed?

iii) The firm can produce 150 units of output per week using three different combinations of labour and capital. a) What information do we require before we can say which technique the firm will use? b) Is there any technique the firm will definitely reject?

iv) If the firm produces 150 units of output per week using 1 unit of labour and 3 units of capital, and raises output to 500 units per week by employing an additional worker, what is the change in productivity?

v) a) When the firm is employing one worker and increases output by continually adding an additional unit of capital, what happens to the productivity of capital?

b) When the firm uses one unit of capital and continually increases output by adding an additional unit of labour, what happens to the productivity of labour?

3 Study the table and the passage below and then answer the questions which follow.

	% OF TOTAL UK OUTPUT	
	1980	1990
Agriculture	2.1	1.5
Energy and water	9.7	5.1
Manufacturing	26.8	22.4
Construction	6.1	7.6
Transport & communication	7.3	7.1
Distribution, hotels and catering	12.9	14.6
Financial and business services	7.4	12.7
Public services	16.3	12.9
Miscellaneous services	11.4	16.1
	100.0	100.0

Table 5.4

Source: National Income and Expenditure Blue Book, HMSO

The most notable change has been in the manufacturing sector. In the early 1970s manufacturing accounted for almost one-third of total output in the UK, but by 1980 this was down to about 27 per cent and by 1991 the figure was little more than 20 per cent. Experience has varied from one industry to another. Industries such as chemicals and electronics have prospered for much of the post-1945 period, but others which used to form the backbone of the economy have been in long-term decline – industries such as coal, steel, textiles and mechanical engineering.

There has also been a fall in the public sector's share of output. The change reflects the Government's policy in the 1980s of privatizing and contracting out certain public services.

i) a) Name one financial or business service. [1]

b) Name one public service. [1]

ii) Suggest one reason why a) electronics has prospered and b) coal has declined. [2]

iii) How has the location of industries in the UK altered with the changes in output shown in the table? [4]

iv) a) Calculate the growth in the percentage of total output provided by all service industries between 1980 and 1990. [2]

b) Explain why this growth in service industries took place. (You may wish to consider: income elasticity of demand; deindustrialization; government policy; growth of national income.) [6]

ULEAC, 1994

OUTLINE ANSWER TO Q.2

i) See pp. 32–3.

ii) a) 125 units per week. b) 820 units per week.

iii) a) Cost of labour and capital, so that we can find the **lowest-cost** method of producing 150 units per week. b) Using 4 units of labour with *any* amount of capital, since the fourth person actually *reduces* output.

iv) Changes in productivity are measured as changes in output per head, that is average product. In this case average product increases from 150/1 = 150, to 500/2 = 250. This means that productivity has increased by 100/150 = 66.67 per cent.

v) a) The productivity of capital is constant. In other words there are constant returns to capital, since each extra unit of capital always raises output by 50 units.

b) The productivity of labour increases up to the employment of the third worker but declines with the employment of the fourth worker. In other words the firm experiences increasing returns to labour up to the employment of the third worker, but diminishing returns to labour from then onwards.

TUTOR'S ANSWER TO Q.1

i) Manufacturing industry is the secondary sector of the economy and involves producing a good from raw materials. The manufacture of cars involves the processing of steel, plastics and glass into a finished product. Service industries are the tertiary sector of the economy, producing a service to society rather than a tangible product. Service industries include tourism, banking, health and education.

ii) The share of services as a percentage of total output has risen since 1950 from about 50 per cent to approaching 68 per cent in 1990. This has happened while the percentage share of total output accounted for by manufacturing has fallen from 35 per cent in 1950 to just over 20 per cent in 1990. The rise in services and the fall in manufacturing share has been most pronounced in the period from 1970.

iii) It is possible for the output of manufactured goods to go up but its share of total output to go down. For example, if the total output in an economy is 200 units per year and manufacturing accounts for 100 units, then if total output increases to 400 units per year and manufacturing output rises to 120 units per year, the manufacturing share will have fallen from 50 per cent to 30 per cent. More manufactured goods will have been produced though.

iv) The decline of the primary and secondary sector is a common feature of advanced developed economies in Europe and North America. The expansion of the tertiary sector comes about with the extension of health, education, banking, insurance, tourism and leisure. These services enjoy increased demand as incomes in an economy rise. Exhaustion of finite resources and cheaper sources of supply tend to reduce the importance of the primary and secondary sectors.

The main danger of the trends shown in the data is the increased reliance on visible imports. A country with a shrinking manufacturing sector will possibly see its exports of goods falling and its imports rising. If a country is unable to produce enough manufactured goods it will have to import them. It can, of course, sell services such as tourism, banking and insurance to other countries just as easily as it can sell cars, but that may not be enough to cover the shortfall.

The switch in employment away from manufacturing to services also calls for retraining of workers and possibly new employment patterns. Service sector employment often offers more part-time work and possibly better career opportunities for women.

OUTLINE ANSWER TO Q.3

i)   a) Insurance. (1)
     b) Social services. (1)
ii) Electronics has been a growth industry over the last thirty years. The growth in demand for electrical goods such as dishwashers, freezers, computers etc has helped to make electrical industries profitable. On the other hand there has been a decline in demand for coal for central heating in homes and also in power stations. Alternatives such as gas and oil have been preferred by consumers. (2)
iii) The decline of 'sunset' industries in manufacturing meant that the North and Midlands suffered severe decline in the 1980s. The new high growth sectors such as financial services and distribution are 'footloose' and can locate successfully anywhere in the UK. In recent years the regional imbalance has become much less marked. The 1990s has seen significant inward investment by overseas multinational companies in the North, Wales, and Scotland which traditionally have been areas of high unemployment. (4)
iv) a) In 1980 services accounted for 55.3% of output, by 1990 this had risen to 63.4%, an increase of 8.1%. (2)
     b) The growth in service industries occured at the same time as a rise in incomes in the economy. Many services such as leisure, insurance, and banking are income elastic meaning that as incomes rise the demand for these services rose more than proportionately. At the same time UK manufacturing went through a period of decline, mainly due to foreign competition. This is known as deindustrialisation. During the last fifteen years it has not been government policy to support declining industries such as shipbuilding and thus many jobs have been lost. (6)

IDEAS FOR COURSEWORK

Investigate a particular farm or industry noting the extent to which it uses labour intensive or capital intensive techniques, and also how it makes use of the division of labour.

SOURCES OF INFORMATION

See the list at the end of Chapter 4.

POPULATION

GETTING STARTED

When individuals buy goods and services they are consumers, and the aim of all production is the satisfaction of human wants. However, to produce these goods and services requires the input of labour and this is provided by human beings. So human beings, as consumers, provide the reason for production, and yet at the same time are one of the resources necessary for production. The various aspects of population are therefore an important part of the study of economics.

ESSENTIAL PRINCIPLES

More is said about this and its problems later, on pp. 52–3.

1 ⟩ CHANGES IN POPULATION

Figure 6.1 shows that world population has increased dramatically in recent years. According to the United Nations, it reached 1 billion at the start of the nineteenth century. By 1950 there were over 2.5 billion people on the planet. Since then the total has more than doubled, to 5.6 billion this year. Long-term projections suggest that the number will carrry on growing until after 2200, when the population will stabilize at around 11.6 billion – more than twice as many as there are now.

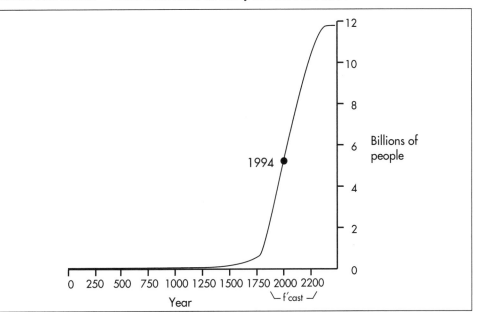

Figure 6.1 World population growth

Despite the rapid growth of world population not all countries have experienced rapid population growth. In particular it is the world's poorer countries which have experienced the greatest growth of population. More is said about this and its problems later, on pp. 52–3. Although the growth of world population is one of the most important questions of our time, we will concentrate initially on the causes of population growth in a single country.

For any particular country there are three factors that affect the rate of population growth: the **birth rate**, the **death rate** and **migration**. Each is considered in turn.

THE BIRTH RATE

The **birth rate** is the number of live births per thousand of population in a given year. Thus in any given year the birth rate is equal to:

$$\text{birth rate} = \frac{\text{number of live births} \times 1000}{\text{total population}}$$

For example, if a country has a population of 50 million and the number of live births in a particular year is 500 000 then the birth rate is:

$$\frac{500\,000 \times 1000}{50\,000\,000} = 10 \text{ per thousand}$$

In the UK in 1992 there were just 13.5 births per thousand of population. This is much lower than the birth rate of almost 19 per thousand in 1964, but a rise from the low point of less than 12 per thousand in 1977.

THE DEATH RATE

The **death rate** is the number of deaths per thousand of total population in a given year. Thus in any given year the death rate is equal to:

$$\text{death rate} = \frac{\text{number of deaths} \times 1000}{\text{total population}}$$

For example, if a country has a population of 50 million and the number of deaths in a particular year is 400 000, then the death rate is:

$$\frac{400\,000 \times 1000}{50\,000\,000} = 8 \text{ per thousand}$$

In the UK in 1992 the death rate was 10.9 per thousand for males, and 11.0 per thousand for females.

NET MIGRATION

When people leave the UK to live in another country this is referred to as **emigration**. When people leave other countries and come to live in the UK this is referred to as **immigration. Net migration** is the difference between the number of emigrants (those who leave a country) and the number of immigrants (those who come into the country). In the UK in 1990 there was a net outflow to all countries of 11 000.

A POPULATION'S NATURAL INCREASE

For any country the difference between the birth rate and the death rate is referred to as the **natural increase** (or **decrease**) in population. Care must be taken when calculating the natural increase because it is unaffected by the changes in net migration.

Using the figures given earlier for the birth rate and death rate, that is 10 per thousand and 8 per thousand respectively, the natural rate of increase can be calculated as 2 per thousand. As a percentage of total population this gives a natural increase or **growth rate** of:

$$\text{natural increase} = \frac{2}{1000} \times 100 = 0.2 \text{ or } = 0.2\%$$

<table>
<tr><td>**2** >   **MALTHUS AND POPULATION**</td></tr>
</table>

❝ Lack of subsistence would, said Malthus, limit the growth of population ❞

One of the earliest writers on population was the Reverend Thomas Malthus. In his *Essay on Population*, which was published in 1798, Malthus suggested a theory of population growth. Malthus' theory was that the growth of population was limited by the means of subsistence. In other words he believed that population growth was limited by the ability of the population to provide food, clothing, shelter and so on for itself.

He was concerned mainly with population growth in the UK and argued that population growth had a tendency to outstrip the growth of the means of subsistence. He expected that the production of food and the other means of subsistence would not keep pace with the growth of population. In these circumstances, an increase in population would reduce the amount of food and shelter available per head. Continued population growth would therefore lead to poorer diets and even starvation for some people. The result of poorer diets and lack of adequate shelter would be an increase in the death rate because of the more rapid spread of disease and ultimately starvation for some people. The spread of disease, famine and death provided what Malthus called **positive checks** on population growth. He believed that the existence of these positive checks would ultimately limit the growth of a country's population.

Clearly Malthus' predictions have not proved to be correct for the UK or for the rest of the developed world. The main reason for this is that the means of subsistence have in fact increased faster than population growth. In particular Malthus believed that *food production* would not keep pace with population growth because as population increased, land which was less and less fertile would be drawn into use and would yield a smaller and smaller increase in the output of food. In other words, Malthus felt that the law of diminishing returns would apply to the use of extra acres of agricultural land.

In fact, in the *developed* countries there has been a widespread and increasing use of fertilizers and pesticides, and the adoption of highly mechanized means of production. Both these trends have raised the output per acre of agricultural land; so much so that the increase in the output of agricultural land has exceeded the needs of the increase in population.

However, the same is not true of many of the world's *developing* countries. Here population growth has sometimes been at such a rate that Malthus' predictions have unfortunately come true. We are all aware of famine in areas such as Ethiopia and Sudan. The relatively high death rates that characterize many developing countries are often due to the effects of poor diet. The lack of food and unbalanced nature of the diet in turn stem from the population growing faster than the means of subsistence.

3 > AN OPTIMUM POPULATION

❝ The population is *optimum* when output per head is at a maximum ❞

A country is said to have an **optimum population** when, with the available amount of resources, **output per head of population** is at its highest level (P_1 in Figure 6.2). In this sense a country is said to be **under populated** if it has insufficient people to make full use of the available resources. Here an increase in population would lead to an increase in output per head. Conversely, a country is said to be **over populated** if its population is so great that an increase in population would lead to a decrease in output per head. In such a case, output per head would increase if population fell.

The idea of a optimum population is based on the laws of increasing and diminishing returns, as Figure 6.2 illustrates.

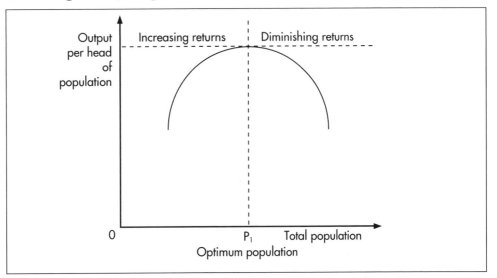

Figure 6.2

For any country, the size of the optimum population (P_1) depends on many factors which are constantly changing. For example, technological advances may increase the productivity of capital, and raise the output of each worker. This will change the size of a country's optimum population, probably raising it, since more than P_1 might now live in the country *before* output per head begins to fall.

However, the size of a country's optimum population will also be affected by changes in the size of its **working population**, its **activity rate** and the **dependency ratio**. Each of these is considered in more detail below.

4 > THE WORKING POPULATION

The **working population** of a country is defined as:

● those in employment
● those serving in the armed forces
● those registered as unemployed (see Table 6.1).

Clearly the main influence on the size of a country's working population is the number of the people of **working age**, that is the number of people above the minimum school-leaving age and below the age of retirement. In Great Britain the size of the working population was about 27.1 million in 1993 with 24.6 million of these in employment.

EMPLOYEES IN EMPLOYMENT		
Males	all	10 507
	part-time	1 107
Females	all	10 337
	part-time	4 792
Total		**20 844**
Self-employed		3 192
HM Forces		250
Work-related govt training		303
Workforce in employment		24 589
Workforce		**27 134**

Table 6.1 Workforce breakdown, June 1994 (GB) (Seasonally adjusted '000s)

Source: Department of Employment

THE ACTIVITY RATE

The working population is less than the number of people of working age, for several reasons. For example, some people remain in full-time education after the minimum school-leaving age, while others take early retirement. For this reason economists are sometimes more interested in the **activity rate** or **participation rate** of the population. This measures the proportion of the population of working age which is in paid employment or is currently seeking such employment. For example, if a country has a working population of 25 million, and of these 15 million are **economically active**, that is, in full-time employment or seeking such employment, then the activity rate for this economy would be:

$$\text{activity rate} = \frac{15\,000\,000}{25\,000\,000} \times 100 = 60.0 \text{ or } = 60\%$$

For Great Britain in 1992 the activity rate for males was 73.0 per cent and for females 52.6 per cent. By 1996 it has been estimated that the male activity rate will have fallen to 71.9 per cent and the female one risen to 53.6 per cent.

THE DEPENDENCY RATIO

For any country, the **dependency ratio** measures the ratio of those in the non-working age groups to those in the working age groups. The term 'dependency' is important since it indicates that the dependent group makes no contribution to current output. Instead it depends on others to produce the goods and services it consumes.

In the UK people in the working age group are defined as those over the age of 15 and under the age of 65. This information is used to calculate the dependent population for the UK. However, let us consider a hypothetical example first. If, for a particular country, the relevant figures are:

Age	Population (millions)
under 16	10
16–64	100
over 65	15

then in this country the dependency ratio would be:

$$\text{dependency ratio} = \frac{25}{100} = 0.25$$

In Great Britain for 1991 the dependency ratio was 0.63 (see data in Table 6.2). This has climbed in recent years because of the ageing of the population.

YEAR	% OF TOTAL POPULATION		
	UNDER 15	16–64	OVER 65
1901	32.5	62.8	4.7
1941	22.7	67.5	10.0
1971	25.5	61.2	13.3
1985	19.3	65.5	15.2
1993	20.5	63.7	15.8
2000*	20.7	63.6	15.7

Table 6.2

AGE STRUCTURE

The **age structure** of the population refers to the numbers of people in each age group of the population. This is important to economists for several reasons. For example, when there is a change in the age structure there will be a change in the demands of consumers for output. A rise in the number of young people with families will tend to increase the demand for the clothing, food and other items bought for babies and young children. Firms like Mothercare will clearly benefit from a change in age structure of this type. There might also be changes in the dependency ratio.

In most countries the average age of the population is rising, and where this is the case we say that countries have an ageing population. The main reason why ageing populations are so common now is that medical advances have vastly increased life expectancy. The economic consequences of an ageing population are considered in more detail on pp. 53–5, while the changes in the average age of the UK population can be estimated from the information given in Table 6.1. We see that 16 per cent of the UK population is now over 65, compared with a projection of 19 per cent for 2021.

SEX STRUCTURE

The **sex structure** of the population refers to the number of males relative to the number of females in the population. Figure 6.3 is called a **population pyramid** and it shows the age and sex structure of the UK in 1991.

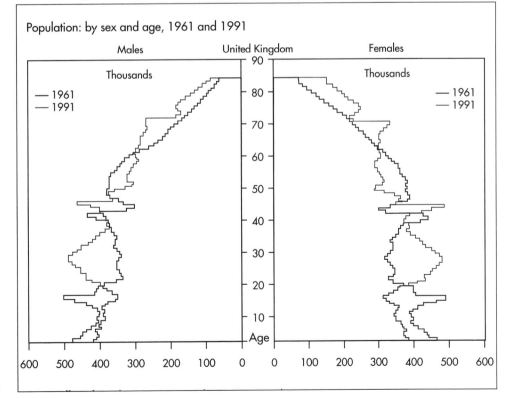

Figure 6.3

Source: Office of Population Censuses and Surveys: General Register
Office (Scotland); General Register Office (Northern Ireland)

The birth rate is roughly the same for males and females, but in almost all age groups the **mortality rate**, that is proportion of deaths, is higher for males than females. The difference is particularly marked in the older age groups, reflecting the higher life expectancy of females.

Again economists are interested in changes in the sex structure of the population, because this will lead to changes in the allocation of resources. For example, when there are more female live births than male live births over a relatively long period of time, then this will lead to changes in demand for different goods and services. The 'average' male in each group buys a different range of goods and services to the average female, e.g. spending more on drink and sports goods, but less on cosmetics. A change in the sex structure will also lead to changes in the mobility of labour, since males tend to move more readily between different parts of the country than do females. We have already seen that males have a higher activity rate than females, so a change in sex structure will also affect activity rates.

REGIONAL DISTRIBUTION

Figure 6.4 shows changes in the **regional distribution** of population in the UK between 1981 and 1991.

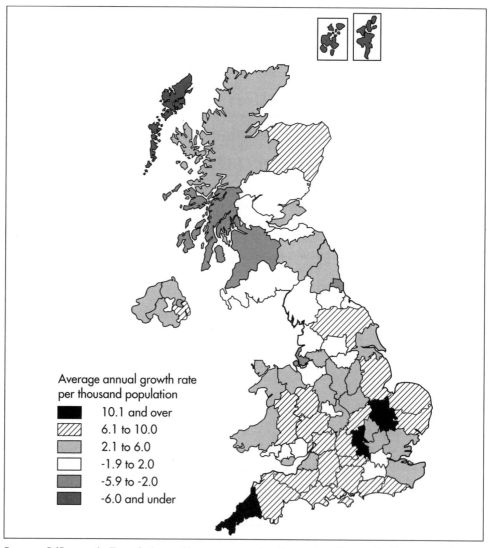

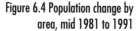
Figure 6.4 Population change by area, mid 1981 to 1991

Source: Office of Population Censuses and Surveys: General Register Office (Scotland); General Register Office (Northern Ireland)

As the map shows, there has been a considerable movement of population *out* of the major cities and conurbations and *into* suburban and rural areas. East Anglia has had the most rapid growth of population since 1981, and the South-East has also seen an increase (except inner London), as indeed have other regions indicated on the map.

OCCUPATIONAL DISTRIBUTION

The **occupational distribution** of the population refers to the proportion of the population employed in different occupations. This is discussed in Chapter 10.

TYPICAL EXAM QUESTIONS

1

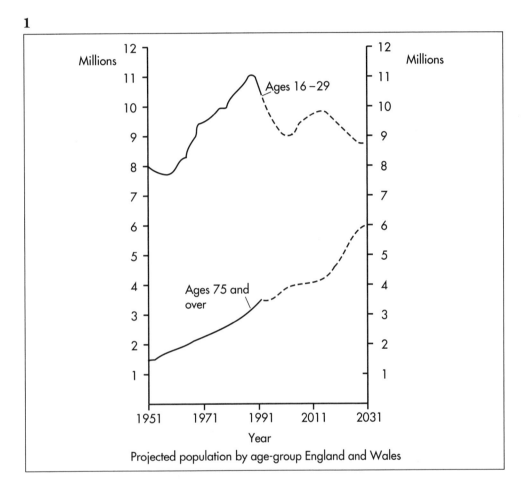

Projected population by age-group England and Wales

i)   a) Using the above information explain what is meant by the term
         'ageing population'   [4]
     b) What factors may explain why England and Wales have an
         'ageing population'?   [4]
ii) Discuss the economic problems faced by a country with an
     ageing population.   [8]
iii) Why does the UK collect information about its population every ten
     years in a census?   [8]

WJEC, 1994

2 The data in Figure 6.5 show a population pyramid for a 'typical' developing country.

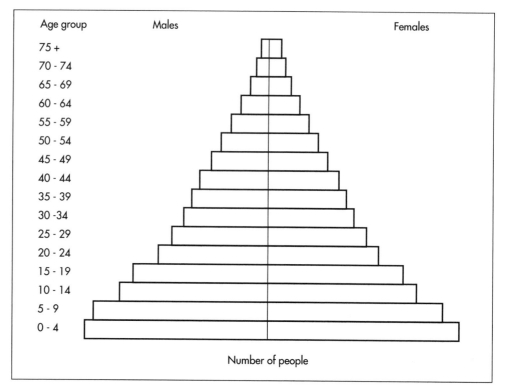

Figure 6.5

i) Comment on the most significant features of this population pyramid.
ii) What problems would you expect an economy with the kind of age structure shown in Figure 6.5 to face?

3 Study the maps and then answer the following questions.

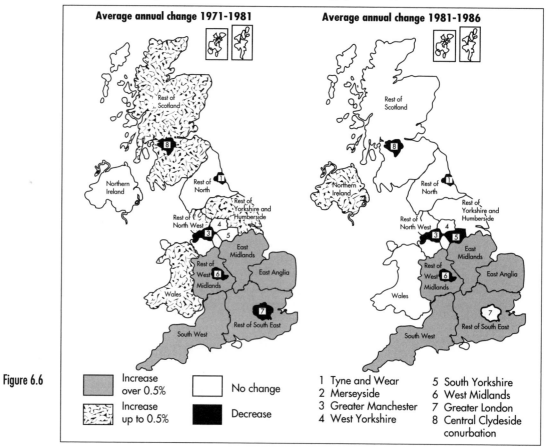

Figure 6.6

Source: Office of Population Censuses and Surveys

i) a) Which three regions had the largest percentage increase in population over the whole period (1971–86) shown by the maps? [1]
   b) Why do you think this occurred? [2]
ii) The 'rest of the North' has shown no change in this period. What reasons might account for this? [3]
iii) What would be the likely effects if the population distribution trends shown by the maps continued? [4]
iv) Why might these trends not continue? [6]

ULEAC, 1991

OUTLINE ANSWER TO Q.2

i) The most significant features of this population pyramid are undoubtedly the high birth rate and high death rate. This implies a relatively low life expectancy in developing countries, and this is confirmed by the fact that in each successive age group the population is smaller than in the preceding age group. Such countries therefore tend to have a large proportion of the population in the younger age groups. Countries with this type of population pyramid also tend to have a low rate of population growth; in other words, the size of the population does not change much from year to year.

ii) One problem that countries with this kind of population structure face is that medical advances in the developed countries can bring about a substantial reduction in the death rate in the developing countries. This can cause a relatively large increase in population in a relatively short period of time. The increasing size of population can cause problems such as starvation, lack of housing, etc.

Another problem facing countries with this kind of population structure is that the large numbers in the younger age groups lead to a relatively large dependency ratio. Having defined this term you should go on to analyse the consequences of a relatively high dependency ratio. In particular it is necessary to stress that a relatively high dependency ratio in developing countries will mean a relatively low income per head. The consequence can therefore be discussed in terms of poverty, starvation, homelessness and so on.

TUTOR'S ANSWER TO Q.1

i) a) A country is said to have an ageing population when the average age of its population is rising. An increased proportion of the population is over, say, 75. From the data it can be seen that there is an increasing number of people over 75 with a decreasing number aged between 16 and 29.
   b) The falling number of 16–29-year-olds is explained by a low birth rate since the late 1960s in the UK. The rise in the number of elderly people is due to a falling death rate.

ii) With an ageing population there will be higher government spending on pensions, healthcare and social services. With the population ageing it is likely that the working population will become a smaller proportion of the total population. This means that those in work may have to pay much higher taxes to pay for the care of the elderly. The wider economy will also need to adapt to changes in patterns of demand for both housing and consumer goods. For example, with an ageing population the demand for smaller houses will increase.

iii) The census gives us information about the occupational, geographical and age distribution of the population. From a local and a central government point of view the census provides information for planning public services such as education, health and housing. The building of new schools, hospitals and roads will be based in part on projections of population growth in different regions. Thus the size and direction of local and central government expenditure can be assessed more accurately. Private sector firms can use information from the census to plan the location of their firms and where new products can be marketed.

STUDENT'S ANSWER TO Q.1 WITH EXAMINER COMMENTS

(i) (a) The diagram shows that there have been fluctuations in the number of people aged sixteen to twenty-nine. Starting in 1951 there are just over eight-million people in that category. Then in the 1960's there is a 'dip' in this age-group but from then on there is a steady but unstable increase to the present time (1990's). Projected figures show a decline, a rise and a further decline of sixteen to twenty-nine year olds.

However, from 1951, the number of people aged seventy-five and over has increased steadily and is shown to increase for another forty years. This shows that at the times when there are fewer sixteen to twenty-nine year olds there will be more people aged seventy-five and over. So by the year 2031 there will be approximately nine million sixteen to twenty-nine year olds compared to just over eight million in 1951 and there would be about six million people aged seventy-five and over in 2031 compared to one and a half million in 1951.

(b) Factors causing 'ageing populations' are things such as low birth-rates and low death-rates. Reasons for low birth-rates are that there are more contraceptives which are widely available which reduce teenage pregnancies. More and more people are concerned with pursuing their careers, therefore, not having children or deciding to have them later.

Death rates are low because of better health care enabling people to live longer. Living standards are also better as there are less people living in poverty now than in 1951.

(ii) There will be a lot of pressure on the housing market as more people will demand smaller houses. Elderly people and people without children will require mostly one to two bedroomed houses therefore causing a decrease in the demand for large houses.

The older generation will become dependant and require better health care. The age of retirement will have to be increased in order to cope with the excess demand for labour as there are fewer young people. Because there are fewer young people there will be less demand for schools. Goods and services will have to be adapted to the needs of elderly people.

(iii) Information collected in a census forecast the likely trends of future populations. From the information people can find out future birth rates and death-rates, and the number of elderly, therefore, being able to plan future needs. Developments in birth control, medicine and food production can also be made. The information is collected every ten years to allow trends to change or maybe not. It also shows the geographical distribution of the population, distribution by sex and also age. This provides the government some idea of how to spend their money. The census shows the likely trends of what sort of jobs people may have, the sort of housing which may later be demanded and what sort of transport people use.

IDEAS FOR COURSEWORK

How has the population of your town or city changed in the last twenty years? You could look at:

- age and sex structure
- inward and outward mobility etc.

You could consider the causes and effects of these changes. Look at the results of the 1981 and 1991 Censuses.

SOURCES OF INFORMATION

See the list at the end of Chapter 4.
Also:

- *Annual Abstract of Statistics*, Central Statistical Office
- *Regional Trends*, Central Statistical Office
- *UN Statistical Yearbook*, HMSO
- *World Development Report*, World Bank
- The UK Census, 1981 and 1991
- Local reference library

R E V I E W   S H E E T

1   Classify the following as land or capital:

   i)   a blast furnace
   ii) a ship-yard
   iii) a natural lake
   iv) a field of wheat
   v)   a deposit of oil.

2   Are some types of land occupationally more mobile than others? Explain your answer.

   _____
   _____
   _____
   _____

3   What factors determine the supply of labour to an economy?

   _____
   _____
   _____
   _____

4   Complete the following sentence.
   Capital accumulation depends on _____ from _____ .

5   What is meant by the term **net investment**?

   _____
   _____
   _____
   _____

6   Explain whether division of labour is possible *within* the following occupations:

   i)   car repair

   _____
   _____

   ii) teaching

   _____
   _____

   iii) construction.

   _____
   _____

7   What is the difference between production and productivity?

   _____
   _____
   _____
   _____

8   Which factor(s) of production *can* be geographically immobile in

   i)   the short run

   _____
   _____

   ii) the long run?

   _____
   _____

9   Complete the following table by obtaining the appropriate values for average and marginal product.

NO. OF WORKERS	TOTAL PRODUCT	AVERAGE PRODUCT	MARGINAL PRODUCT
1	1		
2	3		
3	7		
4	14		
5	12		
6	9		

   i)   What is the marginal product of the fourth worker?

_____

  ii)   What is the average product of the third worker?

_____

iii)   After the employment of which worker does diminishing returns occur?

_____

10   What is the difference between increasing returns and economies of scale?

_____

_____

_____

_____

11   The main reason that there has been a rapid rise in the population of developing countries is that there has been a fall in the_____ _____.

12   An increase in the level of unemployment will have no effect on the size of a country's _____ population.

13   If *all other things remain equal*, an increase in a country's birth rate will always lead to an increase in the country's _____ ratio.

14   Developing countries typically have high _____ and high _____ so that the average age of the population is relatively low.

15   The following table shows the values of output measured in £m that are associated with different levels of population in country X:

Population (millions)	Output (£m)
50	100
60	170
70	280
80	360
90	400

What level of population in country X would be described as the optimum level?

_____

_____

16   Using the *Annual Abstract of Statistics* and *Social Trends*, both of which are available in most central libraries, answer the following question. During the last 50 years the UK has experienced an increase in which of the following?

   i)   the dependency ratio
  ii)   the average age of the population
iii)   the birth rate
iv)   the death rate
  v)   the male activity rate
vi)   the female activity rate

17 What term would you use to describe the difference in numbers between the *workforce* of Great Britain and the *workforce in employment*?

_____

_____

18 If a country has a total population of 150 millions and of these 30 millions are in non-working age groups, what is the dependency ratio?

_____

_____

19 In recent years rural depopulation has occurred in Britain. How do you explain this?

_____

_____

_____

_____

20 Why is the dependency ratio in Asia and Africa likely to fall between 1990 and 2050?

_____

_____

_____

_____

DEMAND, SUPPLY & PRICE

Whatever the term used, *all* the GCSE syllabuses in economics require that you understand how **price** is determined in a **market**. We have already seen in Chapter 4 that in a free market economy the **price mechanism**, that is, changes in the prices of different goods, is used as a means of allocating the scarce resources of land, labour and capital between alternative uses. If you are to understand how price is determined in a free market then you must have a good grasp of the concepts of demand and supply. In particular you must be able to draw and use demand and supply **curves**.

The use of the word 'market' sometimes causes confusion in economics. To economists, a market is simply an arrangement which brings buyers and sellers into contact. Most towns and cities have a local market where buyers of products are brought into direct contact with sellers, but in many of the world's important markets buyers and sellers never meet. This is true of the Stock Exchange (see Chapter 11) and the foreign exchange market (see Chapter 14). In these cases buying and selling is done over direct computer lines, or by using a telephone, telex and fax facilities.

DEMAND

SUPPLY

PRICE DETERMINATION

CHANGES IN PRICE & QUANTITY

ELASTICITY

PRICE ELASTICITY OF DEMAND

CROSS ELASTICITY OF DEMAND

INCOME ELASTICITY OF DEMAND

ELASTICITY OF SUPPLY

ESSENTIAL PRINCIPLES

In economics the term **demand** has a specific meaning. It does *not* simply mean the *desire* to possess something. I might *desire* a stately home to live in, but anyone who knows me would quickly conclude that I lack the **purchasing power** to put that desire into practice! Only when the desire to possess something is backed up by the willingness and the means to pay for it do we speak of demand. To emphasize this point economists often use the term **effective demand**.

However, when considering demand it is also important to relate it to price and to a specific period of time. For example, a statement such as 'Demand for this product is 100 units' is meaningless since it does not tell us over what *period of time* demand is 100 units. It could be a day, a week or even a year! Neither does it tell us the *price* at which 100 units are demanded. The answer to both of these questions is important if sellers are to be persuaded to meet the demand. It is much more meaningful therefore to say that 'At a price of £2 demand for this product is 100 units per week'.

Having defined demand, an important question is why there is any demand at all. It is to an understanding of this that we now turn.

UTILITY

The word **utility** is used by economists to refer to **satisfaction**. The amount of utility or satisfaction gained from consuming a product is, of course, different for different people. Indeed, since there is no such thing as a 'unit of satisfaction' which is common to everybody, it follows that we cannot *measure* utility. Nevertheless it is an important concept since it is assumed that only those products which possess utility, that is, which provide satisfaction, will be demanded.

Economists usually assume that in deciding what to buy, consumers will act **rationally**. This simply means that they will choose between different goods and services so as to maximize (gain as much as possible) total utility. In other words, consumers will change the goods and services they buy whenever this will increase their total utility.

The **law of diminishing marginal utility** simply states that as extra units of a product are consumed, each **extra** (marginal) unit adds less and less to total utility (satisfaction). The second cold drink on a hot day may certainly increase your satisfaction, but *by less* than you gained from consuming the first cold drink! In other words, the marginal utility of the second cold drink was less than the first, and so on.

The law of diminishing marginal utility helps to explain the general nature of an individual's demand for a good or service and the price of that good or service. If each extra unit of a product gives less satisfaction to an individual than the previous unit, then it follows that the individual will often need the incentive of a **lower price** if he or she is to be encouraged to consume an extra unit. Because of this it is reasonable to assume that for an individual, as the price of a good or service falls, the amount demanded will rise.

DEMAND CURVES

A **demand curve** is a picture or graph of the relationship that exists between the **price** of an item and the **quantity** of that item demanded over a certain period of time. We have already seen that for an individual, more will be demanded as the price falls. If we consider the case of an individual household's demand for oranges, we might observe the following relationship:

Price per lb of oranges £	lbs of oranges demanded by the household per week
0.30	3
0.20	4
0.10	5

If we draw this relationship it will appear as in Figure 7.1. It is usual to put **price** on the vertical axis, and **quantity demanded** on the horizontal axis. The line connecting the three observations is called a demand curve, even though in this case it is a straight line (or **linear**) demand curve. In general a demand curve shows us how much of an item is demanded over a given period of time at different prices.

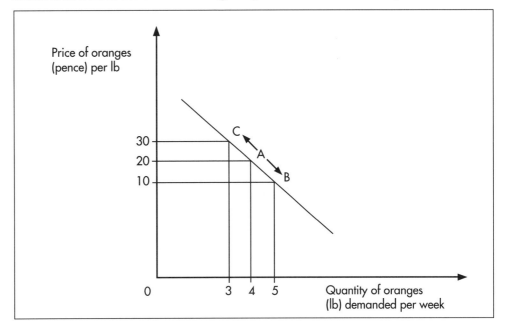

Figure 7.1

While we have concentrated on the individual's demand curve, for most practical purposes we are more interested in the *market* demand curve. However, it is easy to move from the individual's demand curve to the market demand curve. We simply sum (add together) *horizontally* all the individual demand curves. Question 6 on p. 85 provides you with an opportunity to obtain a market demand curve from individual demand curves. The main point here is that a market demand curve, like an individual's demand curve, will slope down from left to right.

MOVEMENTS ALONG A DEMAND CURVE

Figure 7.1 shows the amount of oranges demanded by an individual household at different prices. Of course, many factors other than price will affect the individual household's demand for oranges, including the price of apples, the household's income and so on. We return to these below. Here, for simplicity, we assume that all these other things remain equal; in other words that only the *price* of oranges changes. When we make this assumption we move *along* a given demand curve. This is true for any good or service we consider. Whenever the price of the good or service is the only thing that changes, we move along a given demand curve. It is very important that you remember this!

Suppose we start at point A in Figure 7.2 which shows the market demand for oranges. At a price of 15p per pound, Q pounds are demanded per week. If price now falls to 10p per pound then **quantity demanded** increases to Q_1 pounds, per week – we move to point B on the demand curve. Economists refer to this as either an **increase in the quantity demanded** or an **extension of demand** and you must take great care over the use of these terms.

> Remember to use the words *quantity demanded*, or *extension* or *contraction* for a movement *along* a given demand curve

Returning to point A, if we consider a price rise from 15p per pound to 20p per pound we can see that this will lead to a decrease in the quantity of oranges demanded per week to Q_2 – we move to point C on the demand curve. Again we must be careful how we describe this. It can be referred to as either a **decrease in the quantity demanded** or a **contraction of demand**.

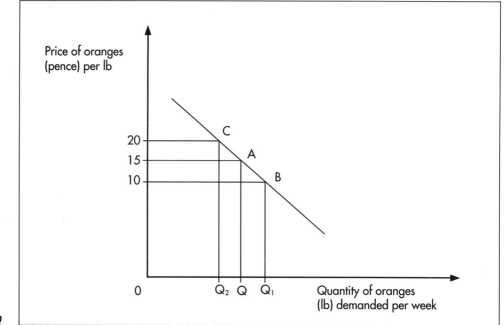

Figure 7.2

SHIFTS IN A DEMAND CURVE

In our analysis above we assumed that of all the factors which affect demand for a product only the price changed. This is a very unrealistic assumption. In practice many factors which affect demand can and do change. These *other factors* which affect demand are referred to as the **conditions of demand**, and a change in any of these will result in a complete **shift** of the whole demand curve. There are two possibilities: either the demand curve shifts to the right or the demand curve shifts to the left. Both of these are illustrated in Figure 7.3.

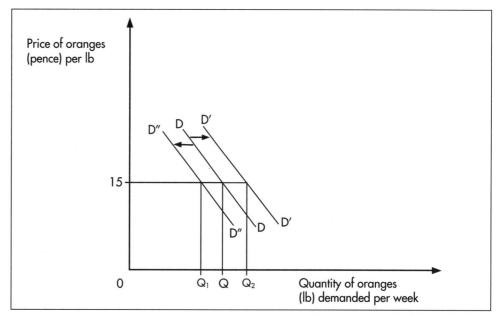

Figure 7.3

Suppose the demand curve for oranges is initially represented by DD and that subsequently the demand curve shifts to D'D'. (We consider the possible causes of such a shift in the next section.) After the shift in demand to D'D' more oranges are demanded at *each and every price* than beforehand. For example, at a price of 15p, Q pounds of oranges are initially demanded. However, when the demand curve shifts to D'D' we find that at the *same price* of 15p, Q_2 oranges are now demanded. In other words, more oranges are now demanded at the same price. Indeed, after the shift in demand, more oranges are demanded at each and every price. For this reason, when there is a shift in the demand curve to the right, we say that there has been an **increase in demand**.

If the demand curve shifts to the left, a shift from DD to D″D″ in Figure 7.3, this is referred to as a **decrease in demand**. The reason for this is clear. Q oranges were initially demanded at a price of 15p, but when the demand curve shifts to the left only Q_1 oranges are demanded. At the same price less is now demanded. Indeed, after the shift in demand, less is demanded at each and every price.

Great care must be taken not to confuse the terms an increase (decrease) in **demand** (shift of the curve), and an increase (decrease) in the **quantity demanded** (movement along the curve). It is clear from the discussion above that they mean entirely different things!

❝❝ The terms *increase* or *decrease*, on their own, mean a *shift* in the demand curve ❞❞

FACTORS CAUSING AN INCREASE IN DEMAND

In this section we consider briefly the major factors that might cause an **increase in demand** for a good or service. For simplicity we look at demand for oranges, but we could apply the same reasoning to demand for any good or service.

● **A rise in the price of a substitute in consumption:** **Substitutes** for oranges might be apples, bananas or pears. If any of these substitutes rise in price, then oranges become more attractive to the household. At any given price the household can be expected to buy more oranges and less of the substitutes.

● **A fall in the price of a complement in consumption:** A **complement** is any product which tends to be bought together with another good. There are many examples of goods which are complements: fish and chips, bread and butter, video recorders and video tapes and so on. In this example suppose our household buys oranges mainly for making (sweetened) orange squash or marmalade, so that it buys sugar whenever it buys oranges. We would then say that oranges and sugar are complements in consumption for this household, i.e. products that are bought together. A fall in the price of sugar, the complement, might encourage our household to buy more oranges, since both orange squash and marmalade would now be cheaper to make. Again the whole demand curve would shift bodily to the right, from D to D′ in Figure 7.3, representing an increase in demand.

● **A rise in income:** Most products are what economists refer to as normal goods, that is, more is bought when income rises. It is quite likely that oranges would come into this category. A rise in income would cause the demand curve for oranges to shift bodily to the right, from D to D′ in Figure 7.3.

● **A change in tastes of the household in favour of oranges:** If the tastes of the household altered so that it now preferred oranges, this would shift the demand curve from D to D′ in Figure 7.3. This is simply because if members of the household began to prefer oranges to other types of fruit, then more oranges would be bought at any given price.

FACTORS CAUSING A DECREASE IN DEMAND

If the demand curve shifts bodily to the *left*, then the demand curve shifts from DD to D″D″ in Figure 7.3, and *fewer* oranges will be demanded *at each and every price*. At 15 pence only Q_1 pounds of oranges are demanded per week instead of the Q pounds initially. We refer to this shift as a **decrease in demand.**

Can you list the factors which might cause a decrease in demand for any product? They are, of course, the opposite to those already mentioned:

● a fall in the price of a substitute in consumption
● a rise in the price of a complement in consumption
● a fall in income, for a normal good
● a change of tastes against the product.

Think carefully through each of these to make sure that you understand why they would shift the demand curve to the left.

THE CASE OF THE 'INFERIOR GOOD'

So far we have referred only to **normal** products, more of which are demanded as income rises, and less as income falls. Of course, most products are like this. However, there are a few exceptions. These are called **inferior** products. They are defined as a cheap, but poor quality, substitute for some other good. An example might be black-and-white television sets for colour television sets.

The inferior product may complicate slightly what we have said so far. What can happen with these goods is that a *rise in income* can lead to a *decrease* in demand for them. With higher income the household might now be able to switch from the cheaper, but poorer quality substitute to the more expensive, but preferred alternative. As a result, *less* of the inferior product is demanded at higher levels of income. Using our example, fewer black-and-white television sets are demanded at higher levels of income as households can now afford the more expensive, but preferred, colour television sets.

2 ⟩   **SUPPLY**

If you have understood the main features of demand then you will quickly grasp those of **supply**. Quite simply, supply refers to the producers' desire and ability to offer a product for sale. This means that we are interested only in **effective supply.**

THE SUPPLY CURVE

This is a picture or graph of the relationship between the price of an item and the quantity of that item supplied over a certain period of time. Figure 7.4 presents the supply curve for wheat of a farm in East Anglia. Clearly, as the price of wheat rises so does the amount of wheat the farmer is willing and able to produce in a year.

There are two reasons why supply curves slope upwards from left to right. When price rises it becomes more profitable for all those firms already producing the product to increase their output. In addition, it also becomes profitable for other firms to start producing that product. For both of these reasons we find that more is supplied at a higher price than at a lower price.

MOVEMENTS ALONG A SUPPLY CURVE

If only the price of wheat varies, that is, all the other things that affect the supply of wheat do not change, then we move *along* a given supply curve. In Figure 7.4 a rise in the price of wheat from £4 to £5 per tonne causes the farmer to produce 15 tonnes per year instead of the original 10 tonnes. Perhaps he is encouraged by the higher price of wheat to produce less barley or rye and more wheat. We move from A to B along the supply curve, and refer to this as an **increase in the quantity supplied** or an **extension of supply.**

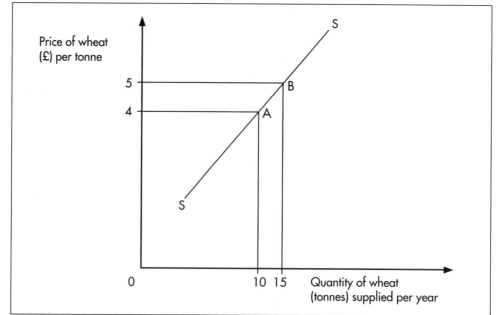

Figure 7.4

If the price of wheat fell then we would move in the opposite direction (e.g. from B to A) and we would call this a **decrease in the quantity supplied** or a **contraction of supply**.

SHIFTS IN A SUPPLY CURVE

If *other things* do not remain equal, then the whole supply curve may **shift** its position. These *other things* might be the prices of other products, the costs of production, the tastes of the consumer, etc. We call them the **conditions of supply**.

If the whole supply curve shifts bodily to the right, as in Figure 7.5, then we call this an *increase in supply*; more wheat is provided for sale at each and every price. At £4 per tonne our farmer now supplies 15 tonnes per year instead of the original 10 tonnes per year (a move from A to A¹).

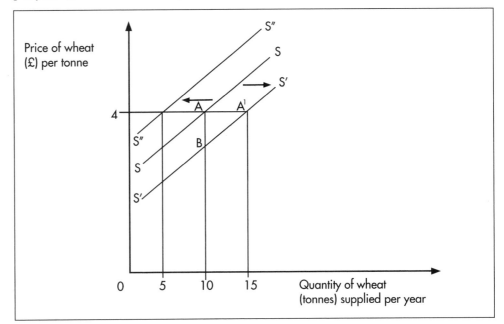

Figure 7.5

FACTORS CAUSING AN INCREASE IN SUPPLY

Let us briefly consider what might have caused this increase in supply.

● **A fall in the price of a substitute in production:** A **substitute in production** is another product which *could have* been produced with the *same resources* of land, labour and capital. In the case of our East Anglian farm this might have been barley, rye or rape seed. If any of these fall in price, then wheat becomes relatively more attractive, and the farmer may choose to grow wheat on land previously used to grow these other products.

● **A rise in the price of a complement in production:** A **complement in production** refers to a **by-product** of our main product. The technology of production will dictate whether or not there are any such by-products. When wheat is harvested the grain is separated from the dried stalks, which are known as straw. The combine harvester threshes and bags the grain as it is cut, leaving the straw behind in the field. Straw is clearly a by-product (complement) of wheat production, and has many uses. It can be used as bedding or fodder for animals, and manure (i.e. fertilizer). If straw rises in price, so that the farmer can sell it for more profit, then this might even encourage him to grow more wheat. In other words, a rise in the price of the complement in production (straw) may lead to an increase in the supply of wheat, more wheat being supplied at each and every price. We sometimes refer to wheat and straw (in this example) as being **jointly supplied** products.

● **A fall in the costs of production:** A fall in the costs of production of wheat could lead to an increase in the supply of wheat. You can think of this in either of two ways: at *any given price* the farmer will now be able to supply more wheat (A to A¹ in Figure 7.5), *or any given quantity* of wheat can now be supplied at a lower price (A to B in Figure 7.5). In other words, a *rightward* shift of the supply curve is the same as a *downward* shift of the supply curve. In both cases supply increases.

● **Changes in the tastes of producers:** There may, of course, be other factors leading to the increase in supply of wheat. The farmer may now *prefer* to produce wheat rather than to engage in other types of farming. We call this a change of the producer's tastes in favour of wheat.

● **The weather:** For most agricultural commodities the weather might have a major influence on supply. In particular, favourable weather conditions will produce a bumper harvest and will tend to increase supply, whereas unfavourable weather conditions will lead to a poor harvest and will therefore tend to decrease supply.

● **Taxes and subsidies:** These might also have a major effect on supply. When the Government removes or reduces a tax on a good, this has exactly the same effect as a fall in the costs of production. A tax cut on products therefore increases supply, that is, shifts the supply curve from SS to S'S' in Figure 7.5.

A **subsidy** has exactly the same effect as a tax cut. It will tend to increase supply, that is, shift the supply curve from SS to S'S' in Figure 7.5. This is because a subsidy of, say, 5 per cent has the same effect as a 5 per cent reduction in costs of production.

Check that you can *reverse* the points we have made to account for a *decrease* in supply, this would be a *leftward* shift in the supply curve, from SS to S''S'' in Figure 7.5.

INDIVIDUAL SUPPLY AND MARKET SUPPLY

To move from an **individual** supply curve to a **market** supply curve, we simply add the individual supply curves *horizontally* – just as we did with demand.

3 ▷ PRICE DETERMINATION

EQUILIBRIUM PRICE AND QUANTITY

We shall assume in this chapter that we have a **free market**, i.e. one in which demand and supply alone determine price. Since our demand and supply curves have the same axes, i.e. price and quantity, we can put them on the same diagrams. We do this in Figure 7.6, and we can see that at price P_1 the demand and supply curves intersect at the same quantity, Q_1. We call this price P_1 and quantity Q_1 the **equilibrium** price and quantity. Equilibrium means 'at rest', with 'no tendency to change'.

> Equilibrium is a state of rest

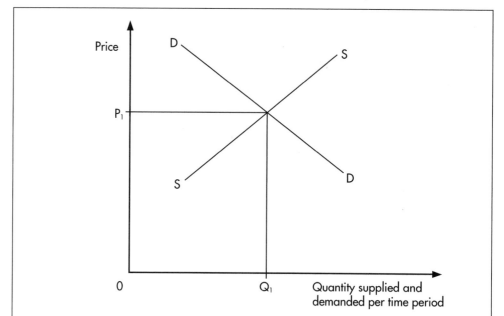

Figure 7.6

At any price other than P_1 there will clearly be a tendency for change. Suppose price is higher than P_1, then supply will exceed demand. At price P_2 in Figure 7.7 there is an **excess supply**. In a free market this excess supply will cause price to fall as suppliers try to dispose of their surplus stock. As price falls we move rightwards along the demand curve D (extension of demand) and leftwards along the supply curve S until we reach price P_1. Here sellers and buyers are in harmony, with all that is offered for sale being purchased, i.e. we have equilibrium in the market.

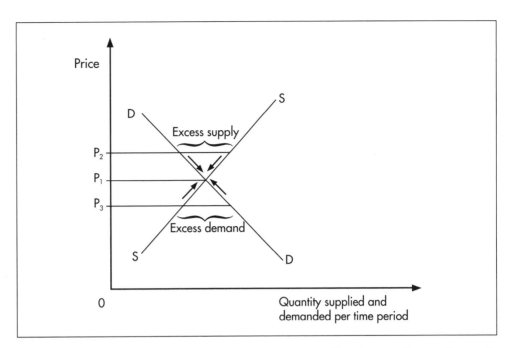

Figure 7.7

At any price below P_1, such as P_3, we have the opposite effect. Demand exceeds supply and price will be bid up in the free market (as at an auction). As price rises, supply will extend and demand contract until we reach the equilibrium price P_1.

---

4 CHANGES IN PRICE AND QUANTITY

We have seen that changes in the conditions of demand or supply will *shift* the demand or supply curves. This in turn will cause changes in the equilibrium price and quantity in the market.

INCREASE IN DEMAND

We have seen that the demand curve may shift to the right (increase) for a number of reasons: a rise in the price of a substitute in consumption; a fall in the price of a complement in consumption; a rise in income for a normal product; a change of consumer tastes in favour of the product, etc.

💬 Get lots of practice in shifting curves and finding the new price and quantity equilibrium 💬

In Figure 7.8 demand increases from D to D′, so that the original equilibrium price–quantity P_1–Q_1 can no longer continue. At price P_1 we now have a situation of **excess demand**. In a free market, price will be bid up. As price rises, supply *extends* along S and demand *contracts* along D′ until we reach the higher price P_2 at which demand and supply are again equal at Q_2. We call P_2–Q_2 the new price and quantity equilibrium.

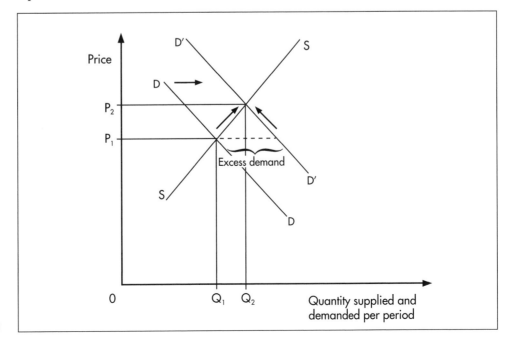

Figure 7.8

- *Prediction*: **An increase in demand will raise equilibrium price and quantity**.

DECREASE IN DEMAND

In the opposite case (Figure 7.9), where demand shifts leftwards from D to D″, we find the new price–quantity equilibrium to be P_2–Q_2.

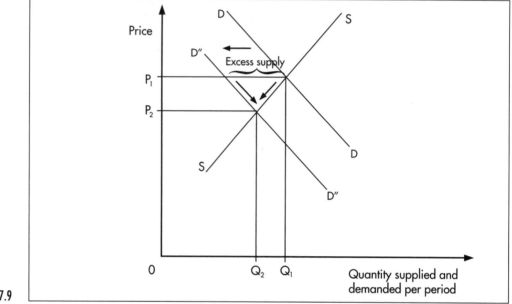

Figure 7.9

- *Prediction*: **A decrease in demand will reduce equilibrium price and quantity**.

INCREASE IN SUPPLY

We have seen that the supply curve may shift to the right (increase) for a number of reasons: a fall in the price of a substitute in production; a rise in the price of a complement in production; a fall in costs of production, etc.

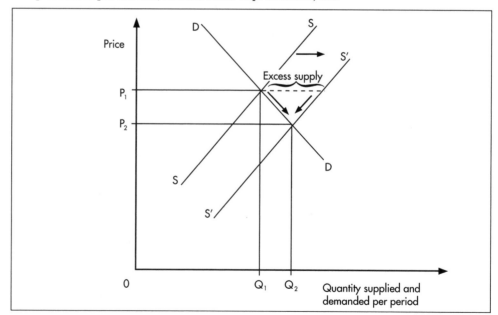

Figure 7.10

In Figure 7.10 supply shifts from S to S′ so that the original equilibrium price–quantity P_1–Q_1 can no longer continue. At price P_1 we now have a situation of **excess supply**. In a free market, price will fall as producers try to dispose of surplus stock. As price falls, supply *contracts* along S′ and demand *extends* along D until we reach the lower price P_2 at which demand and supply are again equal at Q_2. We call P_2–Q_2 the new price–quantity equilibrium.

- *Prediction*: **An increase in supply will lower equilibrium price but raise equilibrium quantity.**

DECREASE IN SUPPLY

In the opposite case (Figure 7.11), where supply shifts leftwards from S to S″, we find the new price–quantity equilibrium to be P_2–Q_2.

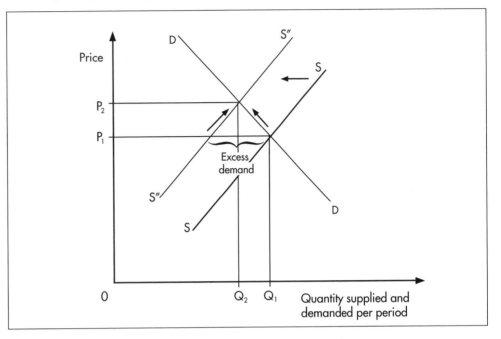

Figure 7.11

- *Prediction*: **A decrease in supply will raise equilibrium price but reduce equilibrium quantity.**

 ELASTICITY

Elasticity is a very important term in economics and is one which is often applied to demand or supply in a market. It is basically concerned with the **responsiveness** of demand or supply to changes taking place in the market, that is, changes in the price of a good, changes in the price of a substitute or complement, or changes in the income of consumers.

ELASTICITY OF DEMAND

 Try to become familiar with these. They will help you in other parts of your economics course

We are interested in how the demand for a product responds to a change in

- its own price – **price** elasticity of demand
- the price of other goods – **cross** elasticity of demand
- the income of households – **income** elasticity of demand.

We shall consider each of these 'elasticities' in turn.

6 PRICE ELASTICITY OF DEMAND

We have already seen that as the price of a product changes and all other things remain equal, we move *along* the demand curve for that product. We called this an extension or contraction of demand. A crucial question to answer is, by how much will demand extend or contract when the price of the product changes?

Economists have worked out a precise measure of the responsiveness of demand to a change in the price of the product. This measure is called **price elasticity of demand (PED).**

$$PED = \frac{\text{percentage change in quantity demanded}}{\text{percentage change in price}}$$

If a 2 per cent fall in price caused a 4 per cent extension of demand, then price elasticity of demand = 4%/2% = 2. Strictly the answer is -2 since the fall in price should be represented as –2 per cent. PED is almost always negative, since price and quantity move in *opposite* directions. However, economists usually ignore the negative sign.

Price elasticity of demand can vary in value (ignoring the sign) from zero to infinity. Figure 7.12 presents a number of widely used values for PED, with associated diagrams.

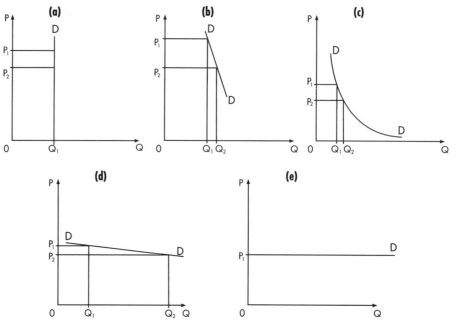

Figure 7.12

● **Perfectly inelastic demand:**   In Figure 7.12(a) the numerical value for PED = 0. Whatever the percentage change in price there is no change at all in quantity demanded. We have the vertical demand curve at some initial quantity Q_1. Demand is **totally unresponsive** to changes in price.

● **Relatively inelastic demand:**   This refers to a numerical value for PED in the range 0 to 1. A given percentage change in price leads to a *smaller* percentage change in quantity demanded.

For instance, if price fell by 2 per cent and quantity demanded rose by only 1 per cent, the PED = 1%/2% = ½ (ignoring sign). In other words, demand is **relatively unresponsive** to changes in price (see Figure 7.12(b)).

● **Unit elastic demand:**   This is an important, but unusual case where the numerical value of elasticity of demand is exactly 1. Here a given percentage change in price leads to *exactly the same* percentage change in quantity demanded (Figure 7.12(c)).

● **Relatively elastic demand:**   This refers to a numerical value for PED in the range 1 to infinity. A given percentage change in price leads to a *larger* percentage change in quantity demanded. In other words demand is **relatively responsive** to changes in price (see Figure 7.12(d)).

● **Perfectly elastic demand:**   In Figure 7.12(e) the numerical value for PED is infinity. The suggestion here is that purchasers will buy all that is available of the product at the existing price, P_1. However, a tiny rise in price above P_1 will cause demand to fall dramatically to zero. In this extreme case demand is **totally responsive** to a change in price.

FACTORS AFFECTING PRICE ELASTICITY OF DEMAND

● **The availability of substitutes:** Where there are few close substitutes in consumption for a product, demand will tend to be less elastic. If you have gas central heating, and the price of gas rises, then it would be inconvenient and expensive to switch to oil or electric central heating. Price elasticity of demand for gas will therefore tend to be low. Consumers may, however, use their gas heating for shorter periods of time, so that there will be some fall in the quantity demanded.

● **Whether the product is a necessity or a luxury:**   Gas is seen by many as a 'necessity' for cooking, heating, etc. Consumers will cut back least on products they consider 'necessities' (low PED) and most on products they consider 'luxuries' (high PED).

● **The proportion of income spent on the product:**   If the proportion of income spent on the product is small, e.g. on salt, then even a substantial change in price may cause little change in quantity demanded (low PED).

● **Whether the product is habit-forming:** Some products, such as tobacco, alcohol and other drugs, are habit-forming. If so, the quantity demanded will tend to be less affected by changes in price (low PED).

● **The period of time:** For most products demand is less elastic in the short run than in the long run. A rise in price of gas over other types of energy, if sustained over a period of time, may indeed lead private households and firms to change to oil or electricity. When new buildings are constructed there will be a tendency to install alternatives to gas for heating and cooking. In the long run there will therefore be a greater change in demand (higher PED) than in the short run. In Chapter 9 we return to price elasticity of demand to consider its links with total revenue.

As we have seen, the demand for a product will change with changes in the prices of other products, if these are substitutes or complements in consumption. The whole demand curve will shift (increase or decrease) as the prices of these substitutes and complements in consumption change. **Cross elasticity of demand (CED)** measures the responsiveness of demand for a product to changes in the prices of other products.

$$CED = \frac{\text{percentage change in quantity demanded}}{\text{percentage change in price of another product}}$$

The firm will be interested in knowing how changes in the pricing policy of its competitors will affect its own demand curve.

● **Substitutes in consumption:** This time we do *not* ignore the sign! Suppose the two products are substitutes in consumption, e.g. apples and oranges. We would then expect a fall in the price of apples to lead to a decrease in the demand for the other product, oranges. If a 2 per cent fall in the price of apples leads to a 4 per cent decrease in the demand for oranges, then the CED for oranges is –4%/–2% = +2.

A **positive** sign for cross elasticity of demand tells us that the products are **substitutes** in consumption. The closer they are as substitutes, the greater the positive value for CED. If a 2 per cent fall in the price of apples led to an 8 per cent *decrease* in demand for oranges, because they were such close substitutes, CED for oranges would be –8%/–2% = +4.

● **Complements in consumption:** If the products are consumed together (e.g. fish and chips), that is, they are complements in consumption, the sign of cross elasticity of demand will be **negative**. A 2 per cent fall in the price of fish might lead to a 4 per cent *increase* in demand for the other product, chips, giving a CED for chips of +4%/–2% = –2. The closer the products are as complements, the greater the negative value for CED.

The firm will also be interested in knowing the likely effect of a change in **income** on the quantity demanded of its product. In other words, how much the demand curve will shift to the right (increase) if income rises in the economy, or vice versa. Again, economists have developed a precise measure for this, namely **income elasticity of demand (IED)**.

$$IED = \frac{\text{percentage change in quantity demanded}}{\text{percentage change in income}}$$

For some products, whether goods or services, income elasticity of demand is relatively high, in that as income rises in the economy, demand for that product increases rapidly. If a 1 per cent rise in income led to a 4 per cent increase in demand for the product then IED = +4%/+1% = 4.

For **normal** products the sign of income elasticity of demand will *always* be positive. For **inferior** products, however, the sign of IED may be negative over some ranges of income. As income rises above a certain level, demand for the inferior good may decrease as consumers switch to the better-quality alternative they can now afford.

This measures the responsiveness of quantity supplied to a change in price. It tells us by how much we will move along the supply curve (extend or contract) when there is a change in the price of the product.

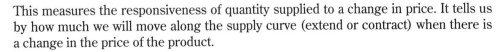

$$PES = \frac{\text{percentage change in quantity supplied of the product}}{\text{percentage change in price}}$$

The widely used numerical values for price elasticity of supply are exactly the same as those for price elasticity of demand. Of course, in this case *all* the values are **positive**, since price and quantity supplied will move in the same direction. An increase in price leads to an increase in quantity supplied and a decrease in price leads to a decrease in quantity supplied.

FACTORS AFFECTING PRICE ELASTICITY OF SUPPLY

● **Factor mobility:**   The easier it is to switch factors of production (land, labour and capital) from one product to another, the higher PES will tend to be. If you could just as easily use your machinery, workers and raw materials to produce boots or shoes, then a *small* change in the price of either product could lead to a *substantial* change in the quantity supplied of that product (high PES). On the other hand, if the factors of production are specific to a product, that is, of little use in producing anything else, even a large change in the price of the product may cause little change in the quantity supplied (low PES). In other words, the more mobile the factors of production, the higher the PES; the less mobile the factors of production, the lower the PES.

● **Availability of stocks:**   An important factor determining elasticity of supply is whether the product can be stored. When it is possible to store a product, a rise in price is likely to have a relatively large impact on quantity supplied. When the product cannot be stored, a rise in price will lead to an increase in quantity supplied only when producers have increased their output.

● **Time:**   It often takes time to change the supply of a product in response to a change in its price. New machinery may have to be installed, new labour recruited and so on. Therefore the longer the time period, the higher the PES is likely to be.

TYPICAL EXAM QUESTIONS

1   Study the graph below for a certain product and answer the questions which follow.

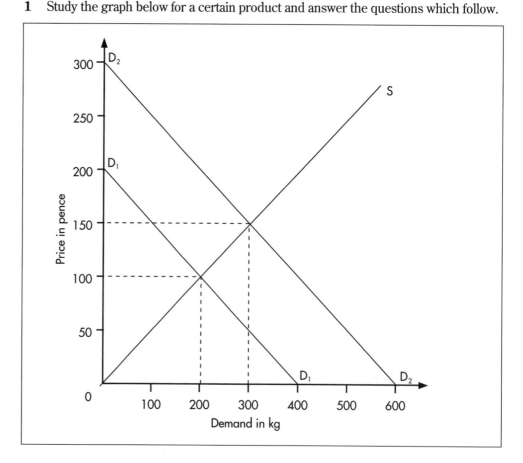

$D_1 - D_2$ is the original demand curve
$D_2 - D_2$ represents the change in damand
$S - S$ is the supply curve

i) Give the price, quantity and the value of sales per week for a) the original equilibrium position, b) the new equilibrium position.
ii) Why might the change in demand for the product shown on the graph have taken place?
iii) Calculate the elasticity of demand at the original equilibrium price from the information shown in the graph.
iv) What use would this information be to the manufacturer who wanted to sell this product?

2   In recent years there have been instances of water shortages in parts of the UK resulting in hosepipe bans. This has come about because demand has outstripped supply.
i) Why is water not a 'free good'?
ii) What factors have led to this imbalance in the market for water?
iii) What policies would you advocate to lower the demand for and raise the supply of water?

3   A student discovers that the demand for bread, cakes, eggs, flour and margarine is affected by the price of butter. The cross elasticities of demand for these goods in relation to the price of butter are shown below.

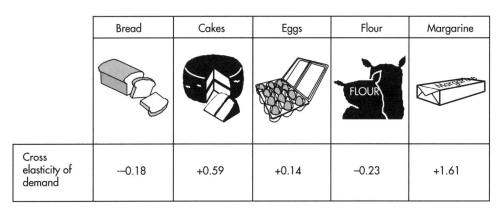

	Bread	Cakes	Eggs	Flour	Margarine
Cross elasticity of demand	--0.18	+0.59	+0.14	–0.23	+1.61

i) a) Define cross elasticity of demand.   [1]
    b) How is it measured?   [1]
ii) a) In relation to demand, explain the difference between a
       complementary good and a substitute good for a product.   [2]
    b) Which of the goods shown above are complementary, and which are
       substitute for butter?   [2]
iii) If the price of butter rose by 10 per cent, what would you expect to
     happen to the demand for each of the goods shown above?
     Explain your answer.   [6]
iv) Why might the information given in your answer to (iii) be useful
    to a shopkeeper?   [4]

                                                                ULEAC, 1991

4   Read the following information and then answer the questions.

A car park in a town centre has 2000 spaces. If the local council fixes the daily charge at £1 the car park is full all day and no drivers seek parking elsewhere. If the charge is fixed at £2 only 1000 spaces are used, and a charge of £1.50 results in 1500 spaces being used. However, if the charge is reduced to 50p per day the car park is full by 10.00 a.m. with 500 drivers having to park elsewhere.

i)   What is the equilibrium price?   [1]
ii) At which price is there excess demand?   [1]
iii) At which price will the local council obtain the highest daily revenue
     from the car park? Show your working.   [2]
iv) What is the price elasticity of demand for car parking spaces when
     the daily charge falls from £2 to £1.50?   [3]

v) Sketch the demand and supply relationship in the car park. [3]
vi) a) What do you understand by the term elasticity of supply? [2]
    b) How might the value of elasticity of supply for spaces in the car park
       change from the short run to the long run? [4]
vii) Which products/services are likely to have a positive cross
     elasticity relationship with the car park charges? Explain your answer. [4]

TUTOR'S ANSWER TO Q.1

i) a) At the original position the price is 100p and the quantity 200 kilos. The value
       of sales is 100p × 200 = £200.
    b) At the new equilibrium position the price is 150p and the quantity 300 kilos.
       The value of sales is 150p × 300 = £450.
ii) The change in demand to D_2 is an increase in demand at all prices. This could
    have been caused by advertising, a rise in incomes, a rise in the price of a
    substitute or a fall in the price of a complement. It is possible that the product may
    have become more popular because it has become more fashionable.
iii) Price elasticity of demand measures the responsiveness of demand to a change in
     price

$$PED = \frac{\text{percentage change in quantity demanded}}{\text{percentage change in price}}$$

Using demand curve D_1, if price rose from 100p to 150p (50 per cent) demand
would fall from 200 to 100 kilos (50 per cent). Thus the price elasticity of demand
would be 1 (unity).

iv) If a firm knows the price elasticity of demand for its products it is able to devise a
    price policy which will maximize sales revenue. If price elasticity is elastic over a
    section of the demand curve the firm should lower its price to increase its
    revenue. If demand is inelastic then the firm would be advised to raise its price to
    increase its sales revenue. If elasticity is unity then revenue will be constant at
    whatever price is chosen by the firm, but if price is increased, *profits* will increase
    (if costs fall because output is less)!

OUTLINE ANSWER TO Q.2

i)   There is a scarcity of water, at least in some regions. More water to some may
     mean less to others.
ii) You could mention **supply** problems, e.g. lack of pipelines to take water from
     regions of plenty to regions of shortage. You could also mention **demand**
     problems, e.g. where no charge for water 'excessive' consumption, etc.
iii) Various possibilities here, e.g. extra pipelines, new reservoirs, metering of water,
     etc.

OUTLINE ANSWER TO Q.3

i)   See page 73.
ii) a) Complementary goods go together, substitutes are alternatives. Give
        examples.
     b) Bread and flour are complements (negative signs for cross-elasticities).
        Others are substitutes.
iii) Decrease in demand for bread of 1.8%, increase in demand for cakes of 5.9%, etc.
iv) Decisions on levels of stock etc.

STUDENT'S ANSWER TO Q.4 WITH EXAMINER COMMENTS

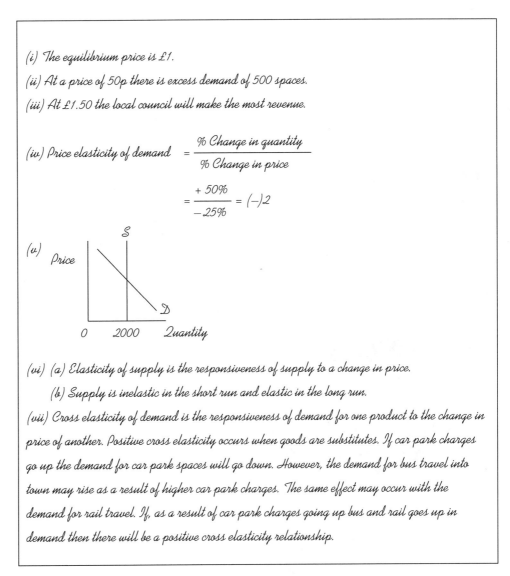

(i) The equilibrium price is £1.

(ii) At a price of 50p there is excess demand of 500 spaces.

(iii) At £1.50 the local council will make the most revenue.

(iv) Price elasticity of demand $= \dfrac{\text{% Change in quantity}}{\text{% Change in price}}$

$= \dfrac{+50\%}{-25\%} = (-)2$

(v)

(vi) (a) Elasticity of supply is the responsiveness of supply to a change in price.

   (b) Supply is inelastic in the short run and elastic in the long run.

(vii) Cross elasticity of demand is the responsiveness of demand for one product to the change in price of another. Positive cross elasticity occurs when goods are substitutes. If car park charges go up the demand for car park spaces will go down. However, the demand for bus travel into town may rise as a result of higher car park charges. The same effect may occur with the demand for rail travel. If, as a result of car park charges going up bus and rail goes up in demand then there will be a positive cross elasticity relationship.

> A fair attempt but you must expand your answers a little and show all your working. Don't assume the examiner knows all your thoughts!

IDEAS FOR COURSEWORK

Try to establish how responsive consumers are to a change in the price of a product, e.g. CDs or cassettes. Construct a questionnaire with a range of realistic prices for CDs asking people how many they would buy per month at each price. CDs have varied enormously in price in recent years, which makes this exercise more interesting.

Try to ask people who are likely to buy CDs regularly. Then construct a demand curve of price plotted against quantity demanded.

APPLICATION OF PRICE THEORY

PRICE CONTROLS

METHODS OF ALLOCATING RESOURCES

EXAMPLES OF PRICE CONTROL

GETTING STARTED

In Chapter 7 we saw how demand and supply together determine price in a free market. Of course, many markets are not entirely 'free'. In particular, governments might intervene to set **maximum** and **minimum prices**. We will consider *how* resources are allocated when the market is *prevented* from reaching an equilibrium because of intervention by the Government or some other agency. We will also consider what happens to a market when an initial equilibrium is disturbed because of a change in demand and/or supply. Will that 'balance' be restored, or will the market become more and more unsettled?

ESSENTIAL PRINCIPLES

1 > **PRICE CONTROLS**

66 Now we are no longer in a *free* market 99

Governments and other organizations often seek to influence the price of products or the price of factors of production. This may be for **political** reasons, such as keeping prices down before an election. It may be for **economic** reasons, such as a belief that only low prices will help Britain to compete effectively in world markets. Of course, the intervention may not always be to keep prices low! For example, the **European Union (EU)** has often tried to keep prices of agricultural products high, in order to encourage production and raise farm incomes. Remember, at higher prices more is supplied. Whatever the motive, attempts to influence price mean that the market ceases to be 'free'. In other words, the market is no longer one in which demand and supply alone determine price.

MINIMUM PRICES

The Government or some other agency may seek to establish a **minimum price** in the market, i.e. a floor below which price will not be allowed to fall. We can use our familiar demand and supply diagrams as in Figure 8.1 to show what will happen in these circumstances. We start off with an initial price–quantity equilibrium in the market P_1–Q_1. Here the price is at a level where all that is offered for sale is purchased by buyers. In other words there is 'harmony' (equilibrium) between sellers and buyers in the market.

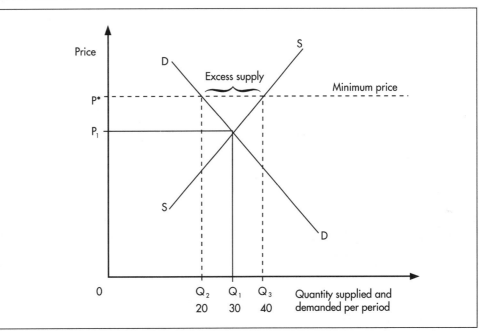

Figure 8.1 A minimum price set above the equilibrium price

Suppose now that the Government imposes a minimum price, P*, below which price will not be allowed to fall. If that minimum price is set *below* the equilibrium price P_1 then there will be no problem. The market will already have reached its equilibrium at price P_1, and there will be no reason for P_1 to change. If, however, the minimum price is set *above* the equilibrium price P_1, then price will have to rise from P_1 to the new minimum, P*. We can see from Figure 8.1 that there will then be an excess supply at P* of Q_3–Q_2 units (here 20 units).

Now if the market had remained free, the excess supply would have been removed by the price system. Price would have acted as a signal to producers and consumers. By falling it would have discouraged some producers, so that supply would have contracted from Q_3 to Q_1. By falling it would have encouraged some consumers, so that demand would have extended from Q_2 to Q_1.

However, the important point here is that the market is not free! Price cannot fall below the minimum that has been set, P*. The excess supply will therefore remain, and the price system will not be able to remove it. Sellers will be unable to dispose of their surplus stocks, which will have to be stored or destroyed.

MAXIMUM PRICES

The Government or agency may seek to establish a **maximum price** in the market, i.e. a ceiling above which price will not be allowed to rise. Again we can use demand and supply diagrams as in Figure 8.2 to show what will then happen.

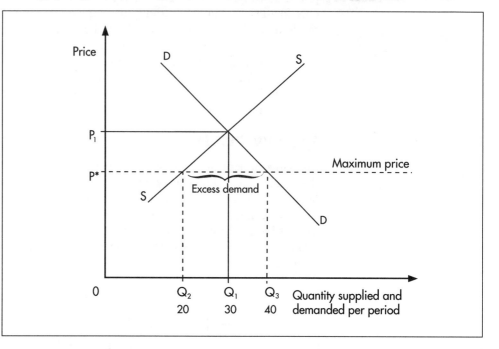

Figure 8.2 A maximum price set below the equilibrium price

We start off with an initial price – quantity equilibrium in the market of P_1–Q_1. Suppose now that the Government imposes a maximum price, P^*, above which price will not be allowed to rise. If that maximum price is set *above* the equilibrium price P_1, then there will be no reason for the equilibrium price P_1 to change. If, however, the maximum price is set *below* the equilibrium price P_1, then price will have to fall from P_1 to the new maximum P^*. We can see from Figure 8.2 that there will be an excess demand at P^* of Q_3–Q_2 units (here 20 units).

| 2 | METHODS OF ALLOCATING RESOURCES |

Since price can no longer play its normal role in bringing harmony between sellers and buyers, some other method will have to be adopted. In Figure 8.2 we have a situation of excess demand at the imposed maximum price P^*. Price can no longer rise to encourage producers to use extra resources to raise output, and to discourage buyers by raising the price of the product. Instead, a method other than price must be used to allocate the restricted output of Q_2 units at P^* between the higher number (Q_3) who wish to buy the product at that price.

What non-price methods are available to allocate resources in this situation?

❝ If *price* is no longer able to allocate resources, we must use *non-price* alternatives ❞

RATIONING

The Government or agency could issue vouchers to ration the limited supply amongst the greater number who wish to purchase. Rationing would at least ensure that everyone got some of the product. The Government could also decide who should get more than the average amount. If petrol were rationed, businesses might be given more vouchers than households, to ensure that products were transported around the country. Of course, rationing has the disadvantage that it is costly to administer: vouchers have to be printed and distributed etc. Rationing was used during the Second World War in Britain when many goods, especially foodstuffs and petrol were in short supply.

FIRST COME FIRST SERVED

This method of allocating resources is often used when there are shortages. The limited supply is allocated to those who come first; this usually means those who are willing to queue longest. In some Eastern European countries such as Russia, where shortages of meat and other foodstuffs sometimes occur, queuing is a major part of the day for many households. Unfortunately this means that other activities are not taking place, because of the time spent in the queues. In other words, this method of allocating resources may have a high opportunity cost (the alternatives forgone – see Chapter 3).

BALLOTS

The limited supply may be shared amongst the potential purchasers by means of a ballot. People may be issued with 'tickets' and a draw made to decide who is 'successful' and can have the product at the price P*. Again, a ballot would be costly to administer. It could also be considered less fair than rationing since those unsuccessful in the ballot receive nothing at all.

3 ▷ EXAMPLES OF PRICE CONTROL

There are a number of well-known examples of price control which we observe in everyday life.

MINIMUM WAGE LEGISLATION

Wages can be regarded as the 'price' of labour. For many years Wages Councils set minimum wages for certain types of industry, but by 1993 they had all been abolished, except one which fixes agricultural wages. In recent years there has been mounting pressure from the Opposition parties for a national minimum wage. In 1994, trade unions campaigned for a minimum wage of £4 per hour. Other suggestions are for a minimum wage on a per industry rather than a national basis. In terms of Figure 8.1, if the minimum wage P* is set above the free market wage P_1, then we will have **excess supply**. In the case of the labour market, *excess supply* can be regarded as *unemployment*: more people offering themselves for work than are demanded by employers.

COMMON AGRICULTURAL POLICY

The European Union (EU) has from the very beginning had a 'managed' market in agriculture. Rather than allow the free market, that is, supply and demand, to set prices, the EU has itself set guaranteed or minimum prices for the whole range of agricultural products within the EU. This attempt to set minimum prices is part of the **Common Agricultural Policy (CAP)**. The idea behind the CAP has been to set guaranteed (or minimum) prices which are high enough

- to encourage stable and high levels of farm output (higher prices encourage supply)
- to give farmers a secure standard of living (higher prices give farmers higher earnings).

Each year a guaranteed or minimum price is set for each agricultural product. For most products this minimum price is set below the equilibrium (or world market) price, P_1 in Figure 8.1, which has not therefore been affected. However, sometimes the guaranteed price has been set above the world market price P_1. We then have the situation of excess supply at the minimum price P* in Figure 8.1. This is, of course, the familiar problem of 'wine lakes', 'butter mountains', etc., with the EU price set too high, encouraging production well in excess of demand.

BLACK MARKETS

A **black market** is usually the result of setting a maximum or *official* price for an item which is such that demand exceeds supply at the price set. We are in the situation of Figure 8.2 above. This is often the case with tickets for the finals of major sports events or for popular concerts. The seating capacity of many stadiums, concert halls and theatres is usually limited to a fixed number. This can be represented as the vertical supply curve S in Figure 8.3, where we suppose a football stadium can take 100 000 people for a game or concert. If the official price for a ticket is set below £10 (P_1), the equilibrium price, then there will be excess demand. In this case 50 000 people are 'disappointed' at a price of £5 per ticket. Those unable to get tickets may be willing to offer more than the official price of £5 (P*) to those who have tickets. Although the official price on the ticket remains £5, tickets may change hands at unofficial prices well above £5. The demand curve (D) indicates the *willingness to pay* of consumers. It tells us that 1000 consumers are willing to pay £20 or more to go to the game or concert. This is, of course, the ideal setting for 'ticket touts' who try to find those people willing to pay more than the official price. (Question 11 on p. 86 provides you with an opportunity to test your understanding of black markets.)

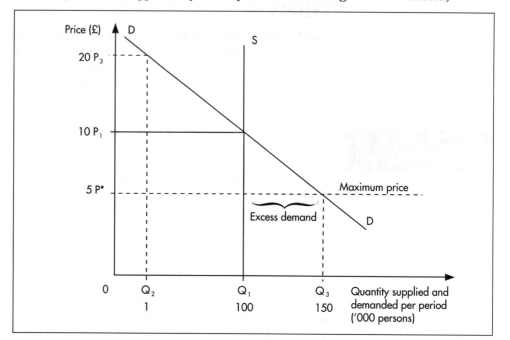

Figure 8.3 The price of weekly tickets is set too low

RENT CONTROLS

Until recently there were limits to the rent that landlords could set in the UK. **Rent controls** now only apply to private tenancies that started before 15 January 1989. If a tenant appeals against a rent they consider is unfair, then a rent officer can set what he or she regards as a fair rent for property of that type, in that location. If the rent control is such that the rent is set below the free market price, P_1 in Figure 8.2, then we will have excess demand, as shown in the figure. This will mean that more people will want to rent accommodation than there is supply available. One of the reasons why the present Government removed many rent controls in the UK was to increase the supply of private rented housing.

TYPICAL EXAM QUESTION

1   i)   Using diagrams, show how a minimum price would affect the market for a product if it is fixed a) below, b) above the free market price.

     ii) How would you support the assertion that the use of maximum and minimum pricing by governments for certain products leads to a misallocation of resources?

TUTOR'S ANSWER TO Q.1

i) a) If a government fixed a minimum price for a product which is below its free
        market price then there would be no effect on demand or supply. The diagram
        below illustrates the position.

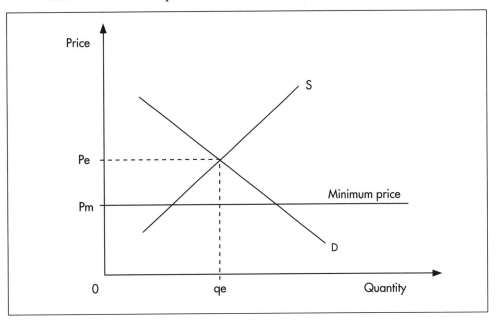

    The free market price Pe is above the minimum price Pm and so there is no
change in the original equilibrium situation.

    b) If a government fixed a minimum price for a product above its equilibrium
        price there would be a problem of excess supply. In the diagram below excess
        supply arises because at the minimum price Pm producers will supply more
        than consumers are prepared to demand.

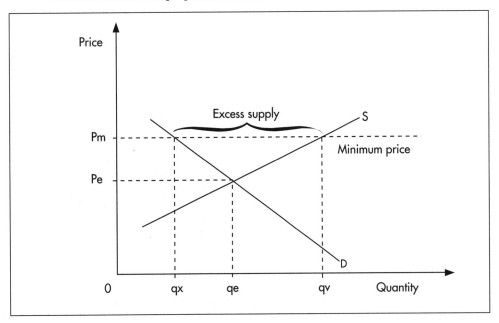

    The excess supply is qx – qv. This arises because at higher prices
consumers demand less and producers supply more.

ii) Maximum pricing by governments will only lead to a misallocation of resources if
     the price is fixed below the equilibrium price. In the diagram below a maximum
     price will lead to an excess demand of qx – qv.

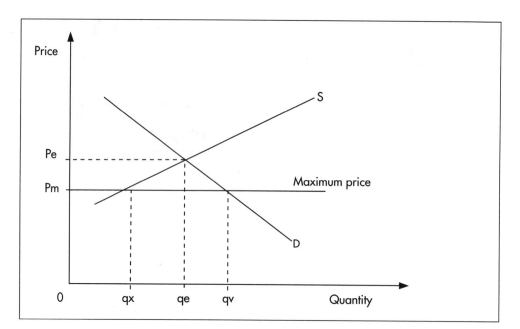

At a lower price suppliers will supply less, and the resulting excess demand could lead to rationing and black markets.

Minimum pricing by governments will only lead to a misallocation of resources if the price is fixed above the equilibrium price. In the diagram below a minimum price will lead to excess supply of qx – qv, because it will encourage over-production leading to unwanted goods at the prevailing price.

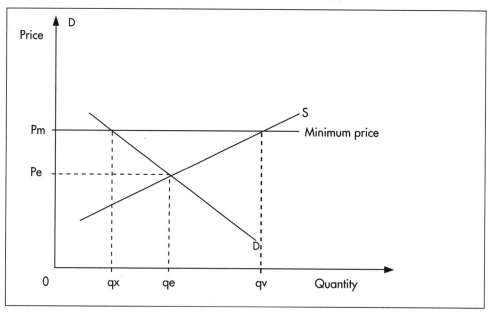

Resources are drawn towards the production of a product that is not wanted by consumers. This problem has occurred for several years in the European Union (EU) with the Common Agricultural Policy (CAP). High guaranteed prices to farmers in the EU have led to enormous food surpluses.

IDEAS FOR COURSEWORK

Examine how the determination of the price of milk in the UK changed following the abolition of the Milk Marketing Board and its replacement by Milk Marque.

REVIEW SHEET

1 Effective demand is the _____ to possess something backed by the _____ and _____ to pay for it. What are the missing words?

2 Why is it misleading to say that demand for good X is 15000?

3 What is the difference between a movement *along* a supply curve and a shift in position *of* a supply curve?

4 The price at which market demand for a commodity exactly equals market supply is known as the _____ price.

5 Show with the aid of a diagram how an **increase in demand** causes an **extension of supply** or **increase in the quantity supplied**.

6 Assume that in a particular market there are only three sellers, A, B and C, and three buyers, X, Y and Z, and that the following information is known:

Price	Units supplied per week			Units demanded per week		
	A	B	C	X	Y	Z
1	–	8	7	11	14	10
2	–	11	9	9	12	9
3	3	12	10	8	10	7
4	6	13	11	6	9	5
5	7	15	13	5	6	4

i) On a sheet of graph paper construct the market supply and market demand curve. Label these curves SS and DD respectively.

ii) What is the equilibrium price and quantity of this product?

iii) What is the price elasticity of demand if price falls from £2 to £1?

iv) What would be the new equilibrium price if demand increased by 20 per cent at all prices?

7   Draw a normal supply and demand diagram such as that shown in Figure 7.6. Use this diagram to illustrate the effects of each of the following. (Draw a new diagram in each case.)

i)   An increase in consumers' incomes.

ii) A sudden discovery that the product illustrated is a health hazard.

iii) An increase in the price of a product which is a substitute in consumption.

iv) A decrease in the price of a product which is a complement in consumption.

v)   A subsidy is granted to producers of this product.

8   You are given the following information on the income elasticity of demand (IED) for two goods, A and B.

Good	IED
A	–2
B	+2

i)   Which good is a normal good and which is an inferior good?

_____

_____

ii) Give a possible example of each good and explain why you have chosen these goods.

_____

_____

9   Why is the income elasticity of a black-and-white television set likely to be different from that of a camcorder?

_____

_____

10 What is likely to be the cross elasticity relationship between rail and bus travel between two major cities?

_____

_____

11 This question is based on the following diagram which shows supply and demand for tickets to a pop concert.

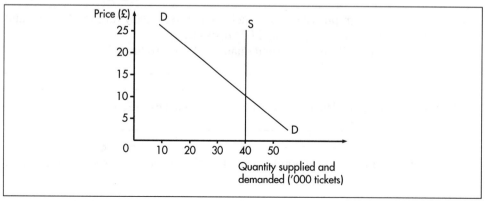

    i)   What is the equilibrium price of tickets to the concert?

_____

    ii) What would be the new equilibrium price if, to satisfy fire regulations, 10,000 fewer places were available at the concert?

_____

    iii) What would be the equilibrium price and the amount sold if the organizers set a maximum price for tickets of £5?

_____

12 If a minimum wage was established in an industry, some workers would probably experience a rise in earnings while others would experience a fall. Why is this?

_____

_____

13 Why do price controls often lead to black markets?

_____

_____

14 Use supply and demand to show why a minimum price which is set above the free market equilibrium price leads to increased production. What problems does this create?

_____

_____

_____

_____

15 What will be the effect of a government setting a maximum price above the equilibrium price for a given product?

_____

_____

16 On which types of goods might a government impose minimum price controls?

_____

_____

17 What is the elasticity of supply of seats in a football stadium?

_____

_____

18 Why might there be fewer houses available for rent if landlords were subject to rent controls?

_____

_____

19 Why is the elasticity of supply of motor cars likely to be higher than that of malt whisky?

_____

_____

_____

_____

20 What is the reason why ticket touts are often seen outside major sporting events?

_____

_____

_____

_____

CHAPTER 9

REVENUE, COST & PROFIT

GETTING STARTED

In Chapter 5 we looked at the way in which the firm's output changed as its inputs changed. Here we look at how the firm's **revenue, cost** and **profit** might change as output rises or falls. We consider in some detail the close relationship between **price elasticity of demand** and **total revenue**. We also examine the effect of economies of scale on the firm's **long run** average cost. Since total profit is defined as total revenue minus total cost, we can turn to profit only *after* a careful look at revenue and cost.

ESSENTIAL PRINCIPLES

1 > REVENUE

There are three type of revenue: **total**, **average** and **marginal**.

TOTAL REVENUE (TR)

Total revenue is simply the amount received by the firm from the sale of its output. If the price is £5 per unit, and it sells 10 units, then its total revenue is £5 × 10 = £50.

total revenue = price × quantity

Total revenue and price elasticity of demand

Total revenue is closely related to price elasticity of demand for the product. To see why, let us consider Figure 9.1 which shows demand for an individual firm's product at various prices. Suppose the firm reduces the price of its product from £10 to £9 per unit. In terms of Figure 9.1 the firm *lost* area A of revenue because it now sells the original quantity at £1 per unit less, that is, a total loss of £1 × 100 = £100. But it *gained* area B of revenue because the lower price encouraged consumers to buy more, that is, a total gain of £9 × 20 = £180. The key question is whether the firm gains more than it loses, that is, whether area B is greater than area A.

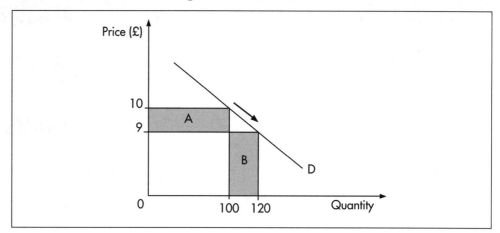

Figure 9.1 Total revenue and price elasticity of demand

⁶⁶ The firm's revenue is closely related to price elasticity of demand for its product ⁹⁹

The relationship between these two depends on **price elasticity of demand** (PED) over the relevant part of the demand curve.

● **If PED is elastic** (greater than 1) then area B is *greater than* area A. We gain more revenue than we lose. A *fall* in price *raises* total revenue, since a more than proportionate number of extra people are encouraged to buy the now cheaper product. Of course, a *rise* in price *reduces* total revenue, since the firm loses area B and gains area A.

● **If PED is unit elastic** (1 exactly) then area B *exactly equals* area A. We gain exactly the same revenue as we lose. A *fall* in price or a *rise* in price will leave total revenue *unchanged*.

● **If PED is inelastic** (less than 1) then area B is *less than* area A. We gain less revenue than we lose. A *fall* in price will *reduce* total revenue, since a less than proportionate number of extra people are encouraged to buy the now cheaper product. Of course a *rise* in price will *raise* total revenue (lose area B and gain area A).

It is very important that you know how price elasticity of demand is related to total revenue. If a firm cuts its price in the expectation that it can sell more and raise total revenue, it must be sure that its demand curve is elastic. If the numerical value of price elasticity of demand is *not* in fact greater than 1, then total revenue will fall as a result of the price cut.

AVERAGE REVENUE (AR)

Average revenue is simply the average amount received by the firm from the sale of each unit of output. Like any average, we divide the total by the number of units. Thus we have:

$$\text{average revenue} = \frac{\text{total revenue}}{\text{total output}}$$

$$AR = \frac{TR}{Q}$$

$$AR = \frac{P \times Q}{Q} = P$$

The average revenue is therefore the **price** of the product, provided that the firm sells all its output at the same price. If we want to find the average revenue from any given level of sales we simply look at the **demand curve**. In Figure 9.1 the firm sold 100 units at a price of £10, which is exactly the same as average revenue. Similarly the price, or average revenue, when the firm sells 120 units in Figure 9.1 is £9. In other words **the demand curve is the average revenue curve**. It tells us the price, or revenue per unit, the firm receives when it sells any given quantity of output.

MARGINAL REVENUE (MR)

Marginal revenue is **the addition to total revenue** gained from selling an extra unit of output. Suppose 5 units can be sold at £100 per unit and 6 units at £90 per unit. The total revenue from 5 units would then be £500, and from 6 units £540, so that the addition to total revenue (MR) from selling the sixth unit would be £40.

Just as the firm is interested in the revenue it gains from selling its output, so it is interested in the **cost** it incurs in producing its output. There are two main types of cost: **direct** or **variable** cost, and **indirect** or **fixed** cost.

2 › COST

DIRECT COST

Direct costs are those which *vary directly* with output; they are sometimes known as **variable costs**. If a firm produces more output, it will need more raw materials and use more energy (electricity, gas, oil, etc.) in production. It might also require more labour. Clearly, when the firm increases the input of these factors of production it will incur higher total costs. It is for this reason that such costs are called direct costs.

INDIRECT COSTS

Indirect costs do *not* vary directly with output; this is why they are sometimes known as **fixed costs**. They are fixed, or constant, as output changes. A firm might be able to produce more output in the same building and by using the same machinery. The associated costs such as rent, rates and the cost of capital equipment might therefore be **unchanged** or **fixed** despite an increase in output.

Because of this, fixed costs are easily recognized. They are the costs the firm incurs even when it produces no output! For example, if a firm closes its factory for two weeks during the summer or over Christmas it still pays interest on loans, rent and rates on premises, insurance and so on, even though no output is produced.

TOTAL COST

Total cost is made up of two parts: the **total fixed cost (TFC)** and the **total variable cost (TVC)**.

Suppose we need to spend £1000 on renting premises and paying rates for one year, and a further £2000 on buying machinery. This £3000 must be paid *before* production can begin, and will not change however many units we produce each week. If these were the only costs which did not change as output changed, we would have £3000 as the total fixed cost.

Table 9.1 shows how **total variable costs** rise with output. To calculate **total cost** we must add together TFC and TVC at each output. For example, the total cost of the third unit is £3000 + £2400 = £5400.

OUTPUT	TFC	TVC	TC	AFC	AVC	ATC	MC
0	3000	0	3000	–	–	–	–
1	3000	1000	4000	3000	1000	4000	1000
2	3000	1500	4500	1500	750	2250	500
3	3000	2400	5400	1000	800	1800	900

Table 9.1

Figure 9.2 plots the TFC and TVC curves of Table 9.1 on the same graph. We add the curves *vertically* to get the total cost (TC) curve.

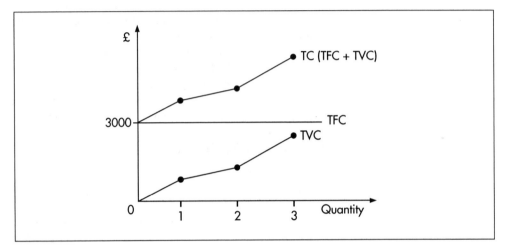

Figure 9.2 Total cost, total fixed cost and total variable cost curves

AVERAGE TOTAL COST

Average total cost is the total cost per unit of output. We simply divide total cost (TC) by total output (Q). Thus:

$$ATC = \frac{TC}{Q} = \frac{TFC + TVC}{Q}$$

i.e. ATC = AFC + AVC

We can see from Table 9.1 that average total cost is found by adding together average fixed cost and average variable cost at each level of output. For example, the average total cost of the third unit is £1000 + £800 = £1800.

Figure 9.3 plots the AFC and AVC curves of Table 9.1 on the same graph. We see that AFC falls continuously as we divide TFC by a greater and greater output. AVC falls at first and then rises because the firm at first experiences increasing returns as output expands, but after a certain point diminishing returns set in (see p. 37).

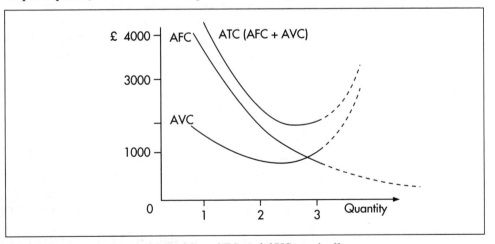

Figure 9.3 Average total, variable and fixed cost curves

The ATC curve is obtained by adding AFC and AVC *vertically*.

MARGINAL COST (MC)

Marginal cost is the addition to total cost from producing an extra unit of output. In Table 9.1 the marginal cost of the third unit is £900. Marginal cost is, of course, entirely **variable cost** since it refers to the *change* in total cost from producing an extra unit.

SHORT RUN COST CURVES

The **law of diminishing returns** has an impact on cost. It means that it eventually becomes more expensive to produce extra units of output. This is because when diminishing returns set in, we are paying perhaps the same wage for extra labour but getting less output from each extra worker. The extra units of output are therefore more costly. Put another way, the **marginal cost** of output will begin to rise.

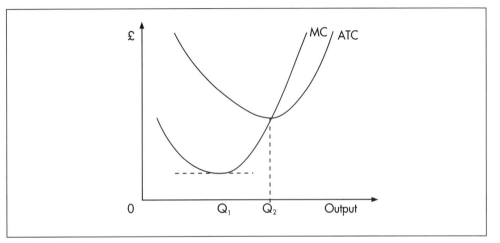

Figure 9.4 The relationship between marginal and average cost

In Figure 9.4 diminishing returns set in at output Q_1 as the marginal cost curve begins to rise. The average total cost curve will still fall *as long as marginal cost is below it*. Just as in a game of cricket, if your score on your last (marginal) innings is *less than* your average, your average will fall. When you score *more* than your average, your average will rise. It is exactly the same relationship between **marginal cost** and **average cost**, as shown in Figure 9.4. Only when the MC curve rises *above* the ATC curve does ATC rise. This must mean that MC cuts ATC at the lowest point of the ATC curve. This must be so because ATC *cannot keep falling*. It must rise when MC is above it. We call the lowest point on the ATC curve the **technical optimum** since average cost is at a minimum. 'Optimum' means 'best possible' output in that it is the output at which the factors of production are combined in the most efficient technical way, giving the lowest possible average cost of production.

> 66 The output at which ATC is a minimum is called the *technical optimum* 99

ECONOMIES OF SCALE

Strictly this term refers to the **long run**: that period of time in which *all* factors of production can be varied. We can change land and capital *as well as* labour in the long run to any level we feel appropriate. Since we no longer add extra units of a variable factor to a **fixed** factor (no factor is fixed in the long run), the law of diminishing returns does not apply. Nevertheless we tend to find that long run average costs fall as output expands. Where this happens the firm experiences economies of scale. However, beyond a certain level of output, long run average costs tend to rise. When this happens the firm experiences diseconomies of scale. The sources of economies and diseconomies of scale are discussed in Chapter 5.

3 ▷ PROFITS

Total profit is defined as total revenue *minus* total cost. In the next chapter we consider whether getting the highest profit is likely to be the firm's major objective. Here we note that if the firm *does* succeed in getting the maximum profit, it will have chosen the level of output at which **marginal cost (MC) equals marginal revenue (MR)**. Only when MC = MR can profits be at a maximum, as we see from Figure 9.5.

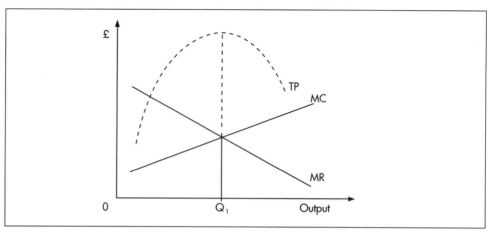

Figure 9.5 The output at which total profit is maximized

At any level of output below Q_1, MR is higher than MC, so that each *extra* unit produced is adding more to revenue than it is adding to cost. In other words, each unit of output up to Q_1 is adding to profit. At Q_1 the last unit adds just as much to revenue as it adds to cost, leaving total profit (TP) unchanged. After Q_1 each extra unit adds less to revenue than it adds to cost. In other words, the firm makes a loss on all units of output beyond Q_1, so that total profit falls. Only at Q_1, where MC = MR, is total profit a maximum.

IDEAS FOR COURSEWORK

Using information from your own family car or from information provided by the Automobile Association (AA), identify the fixed and variable costs of running a car. Try to calculate the total fixed costs and total variable costs per year of running a car.

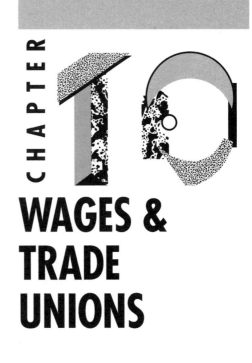
GETTING STARTED

Wages are the reward to the factor of production labour. Indeed, economists refer to wages as the **price of labour**. Like all market prices the price of labour is determined by supply and demand. Since the wages of workers vary, this suggests that there is more than one market for labour. In fact there is a different labour market for each occupation.

Different labour markets give rise to differences in wages between occupations and, to a certain extent, within occupations. Such differences are called **wage differentials**. Any attempt to explain why wage differentials exist must explain why supply and demand conditions are different for each type of labour.

ESSENTIAL PRINCIPLES

1 > DEMAND FOR LABOUR

66 Demand for a factor is always *derived* from the demand for the good or service it produces 99

The demand for labour is a **derived demand**. It is derived from demand for the product that labour produces. Like all normal demand curves the demand for labour in a particular industry slopes down from left to right, so that as the price of labour falls, the quantity demanded increases. The reason is that when the price of labour falls, it becomes more profitable to employ additional workers.

The **elasticity of demand** for labour to any particular industry is determined by many factors. One very important factor is the elasticity of demand for the *product* that labour produces. The less elastic the demand for the product that labour produces, the less elastic will be the demand for labour. This is because an increase in wages which leads to a higher price for the product will not in this case seriously reduce sales. There will therefore be little change in the amount of labour demanded.

2 > SUPPLY OF LABOUR

The supply curve of labour to a particular industry, like all normal supply curves, slopes upwards to the right. This means that as the price of labour increases, the quantity of labour supplied increases. As the price of labour rises, more workers will be attracted into this industry from other occupations. It is also possible that existing workers will be prepared to work overtime at the higher wage rate.

The **elasticity of supply** of labour to an occupation is influenced by many factors. The amount of training required is an important influence on elasticity. The less training required, the greater the elasticity of supply. A small rise in wages can attract lots of extra workers into the industry, since little or no training is needed. More generally, the elasticity of supply will be greater the more *mobile* the population. This includes geographical as well as occupational mobility. Where an industry is highly localized and workers are unwilling to move to that area, the supply of labour to that industry will be less elastic than otherwise.

3 > THE WAGE RATE

IN A PARTICULAR INDUSTRY

The wage rate in a particular industry is determined by the intersection of the demand for labour in that industry with the supply of labour to that industry. Figure 10.1 shows that, with supply and demand for labour represented by SS and DD respectively, the equilibrium wage rate is OW and the number of workers supplied and demanded in equilibrium is ON.

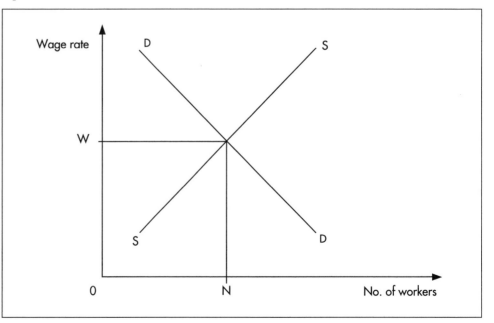

Figure 10.1 Wages of doctors (D) and refuse collectors (R)

DIFFERENCES BETWEEN OCCUPATIONS

Differences in wage rates exist because there are different labour markets with different supply and demand conditions. In Figure 10.2 we consider two separate labour markets, the market for doctors and the market for refuse collectors. Demand for and supply of doctors is shown by D_DD_D and S_DS_D respectively. Demand for and supply of refuse collectors is shown by D_RD_R and S_RS_R respectively.

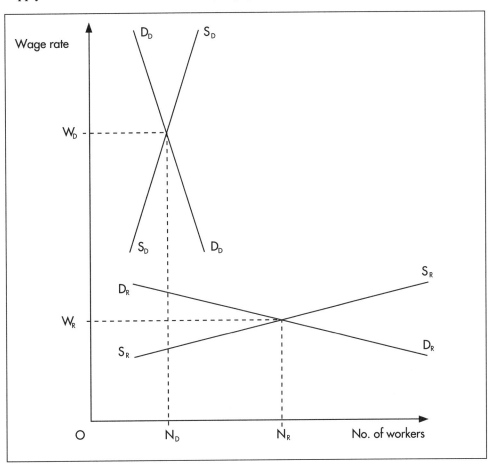

Figure 10.2 Wages of doctors (D) and refuse collectors (R)

The wage rate for doctors in this case is OW_D and the wage rate for refuse collectors is OW_R. The wage rate for doctors is clearly much higher than the wage rate for refuse collectors. Why is this?

One reason is that at higher wage rates, the demand for doctors does not fall off to the same extent as the demand for refuse collectors. Clearly, if the cost of employing refuse collectors increased, more and more people would attend to their own waste disposal. The same is not true of doctors. At times of illness the services of a doctor are indispensable. Therefore the demand for doctors is relatively inelastic, while the demand for refuse collectors is relatively elastic.

However, demand alone does not determine wage rates. Supply is also important. The supply of doctors is restricted by several factors. The limited number of places available annually at medical schools restricts the numbers of people who can be trained. A high level of ability is also required and not everyone has this. There is also a long period of training before qualifying as a doctor. These factors ensure that the supply of doctors is low and relatively inelastic, in that a higher salary will not lead to many extra doctors being available. Refuse collectors, on the other hand, require little or no training, so that most people are capable of carrying out the work of a refuse collector. Supply of labour to this occupation is therefore higher and relatively elastic.

These factors influence the differences in demand and supply conditions for doctors and refuse collectors that are evident in Figure 10.2. They help to explain why doctors are paid about three times as much as refuse collectors (see Table 10.1).

Wages, like any 'price' depend on demand and supply

OCCUPATIONS	AVERAGE GROSS WEEKLY EARNINGS
Medical practitioners	£745.70
Solicitors	£568.60
Building society managers	£537.30
Chemists	£474.20
Primary school teachers	£394.00
Tool fitters	£341.80
Machine operatives	£303.80
Television engineers	£272.30
Assembly line workers	£242.00
Cleaners	£179.90
Sewing machinists	£159.40
Petrol pump attendants	£150.00

Table 10.1

Source: New Earnings Survey, 1994, HMSO

CAUSES OF CHANGES IN THE WAGE RATE

Once the equilibrium wage rate has been established there will be no tendency for it to change unless there is a change in the conditions of demand or supply. Figures 10.3(a) and 10.3(b) illustrate two possibilities.

Figure 10.3

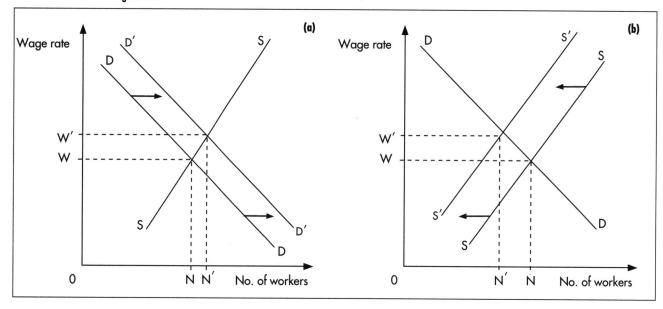

In Figure 10.3(a), the demand for and supply of labour are initially given by DD and SS, and the equilibrium wage rate is OW. Now if there is an increase in the demand for labour, demand will shift to D'D' and the equilibrium wage rate will rise to OW'. Note in this case that an increase in the wage rate is also accompanied by an increase in the number of workers employed.

In Figure 10.3(b), demand for and supply of labour are again initially given by DD and SS, and the equilibrium wage rate is again OW. However, there is now a decrease in supply shown by the movement of supply to S'S'. The result is that the equilibrium wage rate again rises to OW', but this is now accompanied by a reduction in the number of workers employed.

It is clear that the *effect* of an increase in the wage rate depends on its *cause*. It is to an analysis of the causes of changes in labour demand and supply that we now turn.

CAUSES OF CHANGES IN DEMAND FOR LABOUR

● **An increase in productivity:** An increase in productivity means an increase in output per head (see p. 36). When this happens the firm has more output to sell at *any given price* for its product. At any given wage rate the firm will therefore make higher profits than beforehand. Because of this it will demand more labour *at any given wage rate,* that is, there will be an increase in the demand for labour.

- **An increase in the price of the product:** If all other things remain equal, an increase in the price of the product will lead to increased profits for the firm. Since firms produce for profit, they will be keen to increase their output. Therefore *at any given wage rate* there will be an increase in the demand for labour.

CAUSES OF CHANGES IN SUPPLY OF LABOUR

- **Availability of training facilities:** When there is an increase in the availability of training facilities, there will be an increase in the supply of labour to the industry, and vice versa.
- **Removal of barriers to entry:** Barriers to entry into occupations are commonplace, such as the requirement to serve a certain number of years in training as an apprentice. When these barriers are reduced, or removed altogether, there will be an increase in the supply of labour to the industry. One barrier, the **closed shop**, once restricted entry into many occupations. The existence of a closed shop simply means that only members of a particular trade union can be employed. Closed shops are now illegal and therefore the supply of labour to those industries where closed shops were once common has increased or some firms, e.g. Nissan, single Union agreements have become a feature of industrial relations. This means that an employer only recognizes once under for the purposers of collective bargaining (see below).

4 ⟩ TRADE UNIONS

A **trade union** is simply a group of workers who combine together to pursue certain common aims. The main aims are summarized briefly below.

HIGHER WAGES

Trade unions aim to obtain higher wages for their members through **collective bargaining**. This simply means that the trade union negotiates the wages of **all** of its members. The alternative would be for each individual to negotiate his or her own rate of pay. Clearly, any individual would be at a disadvantage when negotiating with an employer. Because the trade union negotiates on behalf of all its members it is in a stronger bargaining position and may be able to obtain a better rate of pay for all concerned.

IMPROVED CONDITIONS

Trade unions attempt to negotiate improved conditions at the place of work for their members. Examples of this might include the provision of canteen facilities, or discounts on staff purchases. However, they also cover such things as hours of work, holiday entitlement and so on.

SECURITY

An important objective of trade unions is job security for their members. They sometimes provide legal advice to employees in cases of suspected unfair dismissal. On occasions a trade union has called a **strike**, that is, members of the trade union withhold their labour and do not attend work, until a sacked member has been reinstated.

THE TUC

The **Trades Union Congress (TUC)** is not a trade union. It is an organization to which all of the main trade unions belong. Representatives of member unions meet annually to decide policy for the union movement as a whole for the coming twelve months. The TUC has little formal power to insist that member unions follow policies agreed at the Congress, but in practice most unions do.

THE CBI

The **Confederation of British Industry (CBI)** is an organization to which many employers belong. Like the TUC it holds an annual conference and represents its members in discussions with the Government.

TYPICAL EXAM QUESTIONS

1 | Trade unions oppose pit closures and give their support to the nine million workers who earn low wages.

   i) Explain the main aims of trade unions. [8]
   ii) Describe how actions taken by trade unions may help them to achieve their aims. [8]
   iii) Why is it argued that the ability of trade unions to achieve their aims has declined in recent years? [8]

WJEC, 1994

2 Would a national minimum wage solve the problem of low pay? What problems would it create?

TUTOR'S ANSWER TO Q.1

i) The main aim of a trade amount is to improve the pay and conditions of its members. Trade unions seek to maintain their members' living standards at the very least by negotiating pay rises equal to the prevailing rate of inflation. Trade unions also seek to improve the conditions their members work under particularly with regard to issues concentring health and safety at work.

Trade unions also aim to protect the employment rights of their members, giving legal help when necessary. This covers issues such as unfair dismissal, discrimination and redundancy. Trade unions may also aim to provide economic and social benefits for their members. This may include discount schemes for purchasing certain products, social clubs and even nursing homes for retired members. Many trade unions have political aims, such as their support for the labour movement through the Labour Party.

ii) Trade unions usually seek to achieve their main aim of improving pay and conditions by negotiation through collective bargaining with their members' employers. If this fails they may start industrial action through an overtime ban or a work-to-rule. The former includes workers only working their contracted hours for their employers. The latter will also reduce output production because workers will carry out their duties strictly to agreed procedures, thereby slowing down activity.

Trade unions, after a ballot of their members, could instruct them to go on strike to support their negotiating partner. Strikes could be just one day, one day per week or indefinite. Workers could picket their workplace to persuade trade unionists not to go into work or to deliver goods at the workplace. Ultimately negotiations may need the help of an distributor to settle the dispute.

iii) The ability of trade unions to pursue their aims has been in decline in recent years due to a number of factors. Union membership has declined because of rising unemployment, particularly in manufacturing, mining and other 'collar' jobs. Changes in the law in the 1980s weakened the power of trade unions in relation to employers. Strike action needs a hallot of members, and secondary picketing is now illegal. Also, closed shops have now no basis in law.

The above factors have shifted the 'balance of lower' in favour of employers who have felt confident to act in a more aggressive manner against trade union action. As a result the level of strike action in the UK has been at its lowest level ever in recent years. The policies implemented by the Conservative government, in power since 1979, have resulted in trade unions having much less influence on economic policy in recent years.

STUDENT'S ANSWER TO Q.2 WITH EXAMINER COMMENTS

Question
Would a national minimum wage solve the problem of low pay? What problems would it create.

A definition of a minimum wage would have been a good start. It reads like a set of brief notes!

It would be good to draw a diagram to explain this.

A good point. Strictly it's the unemployment trap'.

This is probably too low for a National minimum wage nowadays.

It creates some unemployment. National minimum wage has to solve the problem of low pay and prevent poverty. Wether it solves the problem or not depends upon the level of the minimum wage. The government would impose a level and it would be up to individual employers to carry out the minimum wage nationally be law. Any individual working beneath such a level would then prove to be illegal.

It would create some unemployment, employers not being able to afford to keep the number of workers already employed let alone employ more. Along the same line more people would turn to the dole as they would find it more profitable and less time consuming than actually going to work. This is due to the worker recieving more money or slightly less from the social security and family allowance benefits. The poverty trap is where if the national minimum wage causes an individual's wages to rise into a higher tax bracket, then it would have been more profitable for the worker to be below such a level, although the law now prevents this. In some cases we could argue that the National minimum wage does solve the problem of low pay e.g. if the level of minimum wage = £70, then people working in sweat shops + hairdressers etc. would benefit.

Some interesting points, but overall an unconvincing attempt. The points are made too briefly, without a clear structure to the essay. A diagram (same as that for a minimum price in Chapter 8, i.e Figure 8.1) would have helped a lot.

IDEAS FOR COURSEWORK

Examine the changes in trade union membership over the last fifteen years. Give reasons for the changes that you have identified.

SOURCES OF INFORMATION

See the list at the end of Chapter 4. Also:

- *New Earnings Survey*, HMSO
- *Employment Gazette*, Department of Employment

REVIEW SHEET

1 Fill in the missing values to complete the following table.

Output & Sales	TFC	TVC	TC	MC	AFC	AVC	ATC	TR	AR	MR
0	100									
1		25						40		
2		48						78		
3		68						114		
4		84						148		
5		90						180		
6		99						210		
7		120						238		
8		155						264		
9		200						288		

   i) At what level of output is
      a) marginal cost lowest

      b) average variable cost lowest

      c) average total cost lowest?

   ii) At what level of output does the firm make greatest
      a) profit

      b) loss?

2 Classify the following as fixed or variable costs:
   i)   rent
   ii) insurance
   iii) electricity to drive machines
   iv) raw materials
   v) postage costs.

3 Why do marginal costs at first fall and subsequently rise?

4 What is the relationship between marginal cost and average variable cost?

5 Even when average variable cost is rising, average total cost might still be falling. Why is this?

6 What is the difference between the short run and the long run?

7 If the game of professional football were organized regionally rather than nationally how might this affect a football club's costs, revenue and profits?

8 How would you distinguish the terms *sales revenue* and *profit*?

_____
_____
_____
_____

9 How would you calculate the sales revenue for a firm?

_____
_____

10 Why might fixed costs not remain fixed in the long term?

_____
_____

11 Why are some labour costs often treated as fixed costs?

_____
_____

12 What factors influence the supply of teachers?

_____
_____

13 Why is demand for solicitors likely to be less elastic than demand for cleaning staff?

_____
_____
_____
_____

14 This question is based on the following information which shows the supply and demand for labour in a particular occupation at different wage rates.

Wage (£)	No. of workers demanded (00)	No. of workers supplied (00)
100	90	40
110	80	50
120	70	60
130	60	70
140	50	80

i) On a sheet of graph paper construct the supply curve for labour to this industry and the demand curve for labour to this industry.

_____
_____
_____
_____
_____
_____
_____
_____

ii) What is the equilibrium wage rate?

_____

iii) How many workers are employed at this wage rate?

_____

iv) If a trade union negotiated a minimum wage of £140 and all other things remained unchanged, what would be the effect on the number of workers employed in this industry?

_____
_____

    v) In the original situation, if there was an increase in demand for labour at all wage rates of 60 per cent, what would be the new equilibrium wage rate?

_____

_____

15 What is meant by **collective bargaining**?

_____

_____

16 What would be the effect of a government law which abolished wage differentials and created a situation where all workers were paid the same wage?

_____

_____

17 What is a **single union agreement**?

_____

_____

18 If the Government imposed a maximum pay use of £15 per week on all public sector workers, why would low paid workers seem to benefit most?

_____

_____

19 Many professional footballers earn over £2000 per week. If the FA Premier League said that no footballer could earn more than £1500 per week what would be the effect on professional football?

_____

_____

20 i) What is meant by 'an increase in labour productivity'?

_____

    ii) Why does an increase in labour productivity give workers a better chance of a wage increase?

_____

_____

CHAPTER 11

BUSINESS ORGANIZATION & FINANCE

In Chapter 5, we saw that one way of classifying the different types of business organization in the economy was in terms of **activity**. In particular we identified **primary, secondary** and **tertiary** production. However, business organizations can also be classified according to **ownership**.

Those organizations that are owned and controlled by private individuals operate in the **private sector** of the economy. This does not mean that an organization can operate in the private sector only if it is owned and controlled by a single person. As we shall see later in this chapter, some organizations are, but where groups of private individuals jointly own and control a business organization, it still operates in the private sector of the economy.

However, some organizations are not owned and controlled by private individuals. In particular some are owned by the nation as a whole and are controlled by people appointed by the Government. Such organizations operate in the **public sector** of the economy. In a mixed economy such as the UK we find organizations in both the private sector and the public sector.

In recent years a third sector, neither public nor private, has been identified. The central purpose of organizations in this third sector is not to generate profits but to provide a service. They have no shareholders, but on the other hand are not controlled by the Government. Organizations in this third sector, the **social economy**, include the AA, BUPA, the Co-operative Wholesale Society and Eton College.

ESSENTIAL PRINCIPLES

The **firm** is the basic production unit. It is an organization which transforms, or changes, inputs into output. An **industry**, on the other hand, is all the firms in a country that are engaged in a particular productive activity. For example, C is a **firm** which manufactures chemicals in the UK, whereas the chemical **industry** in the UK consists of *all* the firms which manufacture chemicals in the UK.

There are several different types of business organization. Each of these is now considered.

1 ▷ THE SOLE TRADER OR SOLE PROPRIETOR

This is the simplest form of organization. A single person owns and controls the business. Success or failure of the business rests entirely on the ability and efforts of this individual and it is he or she who reaps the profits from success or bears the loss of failure.

Sole trader or proprietorship is still the most common form of business organization in the UK. They are common in farming, certain professions such as accountancy, certain manual occupations such as window cleaning and car maintenance, and the retail trade where 'corner shops' still flourish.

The term 'sole trader' does not mean that only one person works in the business. Sometimes the owner is the only person who works in the business, but sometimes the sole proprietor employs several people. In fact there is no limit on the number of people a sole proprietor can employ. As long as only one person owns the business, it is a sole trader.

ADVANTAGES OF SOLE TRADERS

- **Self-interest:** Since all the profits of the business go to the owner, this gives the sole trader great incentive to make the business successful. This can be very beneficial for consumers because it means that sole traders are often willing to work long and inconvenient hours.
- **Flexibility:** Because only one person owns the business, decisions can be taken quickly and flexibly. This is very important in some business activities where consumer demands change quickly or where each consumer's requirements are different.

DISADVANTAGES OF SOLE TRADERS

- **Unlimited liability:** Undoubtedly the main disadvantage for the sole trader is that the owner of the business is *personally* liable for all the debts arising out of the business. This means that if the business is unprofitable and the owner has to cease trading, or close down, any debts from the business must be paid by the owner. There is no kind of insurance a sole trader can take out against this. If there are business debts when the business closes down, the owner can be compelled to sell his or her private possessions to raise money to pay off these debts.
- **Problem of raising finance:** The finance used to start or expand the business is provided by the owner either from savings or from what can be borrowed. Because of this, sole traders are usually relatively small businesses since the amount of finance that can be raised by one person is strictly limited. This means that sole traders will usually find it difficult to grow and so will not reap the economies of scale (see pp. 38–9) that are available to many large businesses.
- **Continuance of the business:** One problem with sole traders is that the success of the business depends on the ability, skill and energy of the owner. If this person becomes ill and is unable to run the business then the continued existence of the business can be threatened. Of course, it is possible for someone else to take temporary control but this person might not have the same ability as the owner nor the same incentive (remember, the owner keeps all the profits).

2 ▷ PARTNERSHIPS

One of the main ways in which a sole trader can grow is to cease being a sole trader and form a **partnership** with one or more partners. In most cases the size of a

partnership is limited to between two and twenty individuals, or partners, but over the years the law has been changed to allow some exceptions to this rule. For example, stockbrokers, solicitors and accountants can all form partnerships of more than twenty partners.

Usually a business can be recognized as a partnership from its name. For example, 'Jones & Son', 'Day, Boot and Willett, Solicitors', are typical partnership names.

In very rare cases, there might be a 'limited' partnership, where *some* partners in a business have **limited liability**. When a person has limited liability this simply means that in the event of the business closing, that person is liable for any debts that remain only up to the amount he or she has agreed to contribute to the business. Once this is paid, a limited partner cannot be held responsible for any remaining business debts. However, even in limited partnerships at least one partner must have unlimited liability. Usually partners whose liability is unlimited have a greater say in the running of the business and take a greater proportion of the profits.

ADVANTAGES OF PARTNERSHIPS

● **Scope for specialization:** One of the main advantages of a partnership is that it becomes possible for partners to specialize in different aspects of the business. In a partnership involved in some manufacturing activity, for example, it might be possible for one partner to specialize in the production of output; another partner might specialize in sales; while another might specialize in the administration of the business and so on.

● **Limited liability:** One advantage partnerships have over sole traders is that it is possible for some partners to be given **limited liability**. However, as we have seen above, it is not possible for *all* partners to be given limited liability. Under the law as it stands, *at least one* partner must remain personally liable for the debts of the business.

● **Greater access to finance:** Because of the greater number of people in partnerships compared with sole traders, a partnership will almost certainly have greater financial resources than a sole trader. Consequently it will be easier for a partnership to grow. This means that where there is scope for economies of scale, partnerships are more likely to experience them.

DISADVANTAGES OF PARTNERSHIPS

● **Business decisions:** Any partner who does not have limited liability is able to bind the partnership to a decision *without* consulting the other partners. This might lead to serious disagreement within the partnership. Of course, it is more likely that partners will consult over decision-making, but even then there might be disagreements that take time to resolve. Partnerships are therefore often less flexible in decision-making than the sole trader.

● **Lack of continuity:** As with the sole trader, the partnership lacks continuity of existence since the death of a partner automatically brings the partnership to an end.

3 **THE JOINT STOCK COMPANY**

❝❝ Do you know the *differences* between public and private limited companies? ❞❞

Sole traders and partnerships make up the majority of businesses in the UK, but **joint stock companies** are far more important in terms of the number of people employed and the value of output produced. The term 'joint stock' means that the company is jointly owned by individuals who hold shares in it. There are two types of company: a **public company** and a **private company**. In both of these there must be a minimum of two shareholders, but there is no maximum.

In both types of company the shareholders elect a **board of directors** to run the company for them. Each director who is a member of the board of directors also has responsibility for managing a part of the company. One manager might be responsible for marketing, another for production and so on. In large companies, and especially in public companies, the directors are not necessarily shareholders. All shareholders have the right to attend the company's **annual general meeting (AGM)** where the policy of the board of directors and their future plans are discussed. It is also the occasion when some or all of the directors must stand for re-election.

ADVANTAGES OF JOINT STOCK COMPANIES

● **Limited liability:**   In a joint stock company all shareholders have limited liability.

● **Finance:**   Because there is no limit on the number of shareholders in a company they are able to raise considerably more funds than either sole traders or partnerships. In addition, because all shareholders have limited liability many people are willing to contribute funds for investment in companies. This gives joint stock companies considerable advantages in terms of size over other types of business organization.

● **Continuity of existence:**   Any individual owning shares in a public company can dispose of them as he or she wishes. In the event of the death of a shareholder, the company does *not* come to an end.

DISADVANTAGES OF JOINT STOCK COMPANIES

● **Separation of ownership and control:** In all joint stock companies the shareholders are the owners, but control of the company is often in the hands of salaried managers. It is possible for both of these groups to have different aims. For example, shareholders might want their company to be as profitable as possible, while managers might be more interested in increasing sales as much as possible. They might believe that if sales are greater their own salaries and status will be greater.

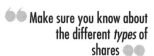

4 ⟩ TYPES OF SHARE

In all cases the owners of a company are the shareholders. However, there are different types of **share**. The main distinction is between **ordinary shares** and **preference shares**. Individuals who own shares will receive a share of the profits when profits are made. The share of the profits that individuals receive is called a **dividend**.

ORDINARY SHARES

Ordinary shareholders can vote on company policy at the annual general meeting (AGM) and it is they who elect the board of directors. Shareholders have one vote for each share they own.

❝❝ Make sure you know about the different *types* of shares ❞❞

The dividend which ordinary shareholders receive is not in any way fixed. Indeed, in years when profits are relatively low it might not be possible to pay any dividend at all to the shareholders. On the other hand there is no maximum on the amount that can be paid as a dividend, and ordinary shareholders sometimes receive relatively high dividends.

One risk that ordinary shareholders take is that no dividend is ever paid to them until interest on any loans has been paid and until any preference shareholders have received their dividend. Similarly, if the company is wound up (i.e. 'goes bust'), before the ordinary shareholders receive any of their money back all loans must be repaid and all preference shareholders must receive the full face value of their shares.

PREFERENCE SHARES

These carry the right to receive a *maximum* rate of dividend, but there is no minimum that must be paid. They are called **preference shares** because they take preference over ordinary shareholders in the payment of dividend. In other words, preference shareholders must receive full payment of dividend up to the maximum rate before ordinary shareholders receive anything. They also take preference over ordinary shareholders if the business is wound up. This simply means they receive the full face value of their shares before the ordinary shareholders receive anything.

Clearly preference shares carry fewer risks. However, preference shareholders also have less influence on company decisions. Usually preference shareholders are not allowed to vote at the AGM except when they do not receive their maximum rate of dividend.

5 ⟩ MULTINATIONAL COMPANIES

A **multinational company** is one which owns and controls firms in several different countries. The head office of a multinational company is usually based in a developed country. For example, the head office of ICI is based in the UK, but it owns and controls firms which operate in many parts of the world. The same is true of BP. Examples of foreign-owned multinationals located in the UK include Nissan, Kodak, IBM and so on.

Multinational companies are very large and collectively account for a vast amount of output. In fact, they are currently responsible for over a third of total world production of goods and services. In recent years the activities of multinational companies have attracted a great deal of attention. One reason for this is that they are able to increase or reduce production in different countries so as to take advantage of cheap labour or to avoid restrictions on imports.

However, they are also very powerful organizations and it has been suggested that it is sometimes difficult for governments to control their activities. It has also been suggested that by cutting back or expanding production in different countries, multinational companies can increase or reduce the popularity of governments.

It is difficult to know how far this is true, but there is no doubt that multinational companies also bring benefits to those countries in which they locate. One benefit is that they create jobs in different countries. The profits made in different countries are also taxed by those countries. Multinationals therefore provide governments with revenue.

6 > HOLDING COMPANIES

A **holding company** is a company that controls one or more other companies by holding a majority of the ordinary, or 'voting' shares in these other companies. The companies that are controlled by the holding company are called **subsidiaries** of the holding company. Most large companies in the UK control subsidiaries.

One advantage of holding companies is that they are sometimes able to gain economies of scale which improve the efficiency of their subsidiaries. In particular there might be financial, managerial or marketing economies that a holding company can exploit. With respect to finance, for example, a holding company might be able to borrow at a lower rate of interest than is available to an individual subsidiary.

7 > COOPERATIVES

There are two types of **cooperative**: **worker cooperatives** and **retail cooperatives**. In the UK we are most familiar with the retail cooperative and each part of the country has its own retail society. However, in many other countries worker cooperatives are more common. Even in the UK there are examples of worker cooperatives in agriculture, printing and certain manufacturing activities, including denim jeans.

WORKER COOPERATIVES

The basic principles of **worker cooperatives** are worker ownership and worker control. This means that the people who work in such a cooperative are the owners of the cooperative. All workers contribute to the finance of the business and each has a single vote on matters that affect the business. In particular, the workers elect a management committee to run the cooperative on a day-to-day basis.

In the UK, although their share of the total economy is small, worker cooperatives and employee-owned businesses do tend to be extremely efficient (perhaps because they are better motivated than mere employees) and have shown a good track record of survival during times of economic recession. Several bus companies have recently transferred from municipal ownership to employee-owned status, so the sector is growing.

RETAIL COOPERATIVES

Originally, retail cooperatives were owned by their customers, but nowadays anyone can buy shares in a **retail or consumer cooperative**. Each share costs £1 and no one is allowed to own more than 20000 shares. Shareholders cannot sell their shares to another person but the cooperative society will always redeem shares at their face value of £1.

Despite an individual investment limit of £20000, all shareholders are allowed only one vote at the AGM regardless of the number of shares owned. At the AGM shareholders elect a management committee (usually volunteers) to decide cooperative policy and to appoint salaried managers to run the retail outlets.

The cooperative movement is about to revive the dividend which was formerly given to shareholders in proportion to expenditure on goods and services. Some cooperative societies pay dividends using 'smart card' technology when shareholders' purchases are recorded on magnetic tape which can be then given as a dividend.

THE PUBLIC CORPORATIONS

All of the organizations considered so far are private sector organizations, that is, they are owned by private sector individuals. However, there are other organizations which are not owned by private individuals. Instead they are owned collectively by the state. Such organizations operate within the public sector, and these are called **public corporations** or **nationalized industries**.

Nationalized industries are the responsibility of a Minister in Parliament. For example, the Post Office is the responsibility of the Industry Minister and Railtrack, which operates the UK's railway infrastructure, is the responsibility of the Transport Minister. The relevant minister appoints a board to be responsible for the day-to-day running of the industry. The board of a nationalized industry therefore functions like the board of a joint stock company. If the current Government policy of privatization continues, few, if any, nationalized industries will remain by the end of the 1990s.

REASONS FOR NATIONALIZATION

Different industries might be nationalized for different reasons, but some of the main reasons for nationalization include the following.

 Remember that reasons for nationalization are reasons *against* privatization and vice versa

● **Natural monopolies:** In some industries there is great scope for economies of scale so that the *minimum* efficient size of the organization is very large indeed. In these cases massive capital investment is necessary and if more than one organization undertakes supply there will be wasteful duplication of this capital equipment. For example, it would not be efficient to have more than one national railway network. Neither would it be efficient to have two national grids to distribute electricity.

These organizations are examples of natural monopolies, and it could be argued that public ownership or nationalization of natural monopolies would prevent the consumer from being exploited. In other words, it is suggested that consumers might have to pay higher prices if these industries were *not* nationalized.

● **Reorganizing an industry:** When demand for an industry's product declines continuously over time, it will be difficult for the industry to attract the funds it might need for reorganization. Where the Government thinks the industry is sufficiently important and where it believes additional cash would enable the industry to survive, it might bring the industry into public ownership. It is sometimes suggested that when an industry is nationalized the Government is able to reorganize production in a planned manner so that production is concentrated in the most efficient plants or production units.

● **Economic management:** One reason sometimes suggested for nationalizing large and important industries is that this will enable the Government to manage the economy more effectively. It will now be possible for the Government to influence location decisions, expansion plans and prices directly, through control of the nationalized industries.

● **Social costs and benefits:** It has been argued that industries should operate in the *public interest* instead of simply considering profit. Indeed, many of the Acts of Parliament which have brought industries into public ownership have made specific mention of the public interest. This has been taken to mean that nationalized industries should take the full social costs and benefits of their decisions into account. For example, an underground rail line might make a financial loss but might still be beneficial to the community by reducing congestion on the roads. If this is the case then granting a subsidy to the loss-making line might benefit society by more than the cost of the subsidy.

It has been argued that if the Royal Mail and the railway system are privatized and left entirely to market forces, then services which provide social benefits only would disappear. Deliveries of letters to remote areas could cost more, and unprofitable rail services could be discontinued.

Any industry which is in private hands will not accept a loss indefinitely. Nationalized industries, on the other hand, can accept losses indefinitely because they are financed by the Government. They are therefore able to take the full social costs and benefits of their activities into account.

PRIVATIZATION

Despite these arguments in support of nationalization, the current emphasis is on **denationalization**, that is, selling public sector industries to the private sector. This again requires an Act of Parliament to create a joint stock company whose shares can then be sold to the general public.

Denationalization is more generally referred to as **privatization**, although privatization in fact means much more than just denationalization. For example, it also includes privatizing goods and services provided through local authorities, such as refuse collection or the sale of council houses. Many of the arguments in favour of privatization can be thought of as arguments against nationalization.

ARGUMENTS FOR PRIVATIZATION

● **Nationalized industries often make losses:** A major criticism of many nationalized industries is that they make repeated losses. One reason that these may arise may be that the board of the nationalized industry tries to take social costs and benefits into account.

However, there is another problem. When a nationalized industry makes a loss this means that it receives a subsidy. In order to provide this subsidy the Government must tax other organizations and people. It has been suggested that because of this, taxes are higher than they otherwise would be. The argument is that these higher taxes have led people to reduce the level of their effort, because they receive a smaller reward for doing so. Consequently the nation produces less than it is capable of producing and this reduces the growth of living standards.

● **Management of nationalized industries might be inefficient:** It has been suggested that because nationalized industries do not have to earn a profit, they have sometimes been poorly managed. When an organization has to make a profit to survive, there is likely to be much less waste and much more emphasis on the best use of manpower. Because privatized companies cannot survive unles they make a profit, the argument is that they will be more efficiently managed than nationalized industries.

● **Privatization raises revenue for the Government:** When a nationalized industry is privatized, this raises a substantial sum of money for the Government. For example, the sale of British Telecom raised about £4000m, while the sale of British Gas raised over £6000m. This money could be used to finance government expenditure and/or reduce taxes.

● **The benefits of competition:** Nationalized industries were initially granted sole rights to supply a particular good or service. The Royal Mail still has a legal monopoly for the letterpost service. This means that no competition exists from other suppliers. If privatization allows other organizations to compete, then this might lead to lower prices and a greater choice for consumers. (British Telecom now competes with Mercury and the cable companies.)

● **Wider share ownership:** A major political argument for privatization is that it allows more individuals to own shares. It is argued by some politicians that this gives more people an interest in improving the efficiency of business.

Firms require finance to meet their fixed and variable costs of production. They obtain this finance in a variety of ways.

RETAINED PROFITS

When firms make a profit they might retain part or all of this within the business. Sometimes we describe this as **ploughing back** profits into the business. For most firms, **retained profits** are the most important source of **additional** finance.

SHARES

These have already been discussed on p. 110

DEBENTURES

These are long-term loans to a company and carry a fixed annual rate of interest. Debentures are very secure loans because if a company fails to pay its debenture holders their interest annually, they can force the company to sell some of its assets to meet both interest and loan repayment.

BORROWING FROM COMMERCIAL BANKS

One function of a commercial bank such as Lloyds or Barclays is to make loans. Banks are prepared to make loans in a variety of ways, but we concentrate here on only three.

● **Term loans or fixed-period loans:** Here banks lend a specific sum for a fixed period of time. Interest is charged on the full amount of the loan for the period it is granted. Firms would use this type of loan to make specific purchases, such as a new machine.

● **Overdrafts:** Here banks agree to lend *up to* a fixed amount and charge interest on the day-to-day amount an account is overdrawn. In other words, the amount of interest firms pay on an overdraft is calculated daily and depends on how much they are overdrawn each day. Overdrafts also differ from term loans in that they are usually repayable on demand.

All firms have an overdraft facility at a bank and use this as part of **circulating capital**. In other words, overdrafts would commonly be used to purchase additional supplies of raw materials and be repaid from the proceeds of sales of the finished product.

● **Discounting commercial bills of exchange:** A **commercial bill of exchange** is simply a promise by one person or firm to pay a fixed sum of money to another person or firm on a particular date. If the holder of the bill wishes to have immediate cash instead of waiting until the bill matures, that is, falls due for repayment, he or she can discount it at a commercial bank. This simply means that a commercial bank buys the bill for less than its face value and holds it until it matures. By discounting bills, commercial banks in effect make short-term loans to the individuals or firms who draw up the bills.

THE GOVERNMENT

The Government provides finance to firms in a variety of ways, but the most important is through its **regional policy**.

Certain parts of the country which have persistently high levels of unemployment qualify for regional assistance. This simply means that firms which set up (or expand their employment) in these areas qualify for a grant. The amount of grant a firm receives depends on the number of new jobs it creates.

Other kinds of assistance might also be available to firms which locate or expand in the assisted areas. For example, the Government will sometimes make rent-free factories available for a limited period.

The Stock Exchange is basically a market in securities, such as shares in joint stock companies, debentures and government bonds. In other words it is an organization which brings buyers and sellers of securities into contact. However, this does not mean that buyers and sellers actually meet. Instead, buyers and sellers contact brokers or dealers to buy and sell on their behalf.

For example, if someone wishes to buy shares they will contact a broker who will consult a SEAQ (Stock Exchange Automated Quotations) screen. This is linked to a computer and is able to list the different prices that 'market makers' in the particular share are currently charging. The dealer is then able to select the lowest price and buy on his or her client's behalf.

TYPICAL EXAM QUESTIONS

1   i)   What are the economic advantages of the public joint stock company as compared with a private company, a partnership and a sole trader?
    ii) Who are the entrepreneurs in a joint stock company?
2   Large firms have many advantages over small firms and yet small firms continue to survive and grow. Why is this?

3 i) What are the differences between a public corporation and a public company from the points of view of
   a) aims
   b) ownership
   c) management
   d) finance?
   ii) What is meant by the term 'privatization'?
   iii) Examine the main economic arguments for privatization.
4 i) How are the prices of securities determined on the Stock Exchange?
   ii) What is the main economic function of the Stock Exchange?

OUTLINE ANSWERS TO Q. 1 AND Q.2

1 i) It is best to begin by giving clear *definitions* of the different business organizations you intend to consider. These are set out earlier in this chapter.

The main advantages of a public joint stock company that you should consider are discussed below.

Since it can appeal to the general public when selling its shares it can raise comparatively large amounts of finance. This makes possible larger-scale production. Consequently joint stock companies are able to gain economies of scale that are unlikely to be available to other forms of business organization. For example, they will be able to recruit experts to manage the different parts of the business. They will also be able to bulk-buy many of their inputs and so on.

The shares in public joint stock companies are attractive to the public because investors can sell their shares at any time and do not need to obtain the company's permission for doing so. Shares in private companies cannot be sold without the company's permission and in general this is why public companies are bigger than private companies.

Public joint stock companies must publish more information about themselves and their activities than other forms of business, and this again gives shareholders more confidence.

Both types of joint stock company offer their shareholders limited liability. This means that the maximum amount a shareholder can lose if a company is forced to close is the value of the shares held in the business.

Joint stock companies also have an advantage over other forms of business organization in that the death of a shareholder, or anyone else connected with the company such as a director, does not bring the business to an end. Unlike the sole trader and the partnership, the life of a company is independent of the lives of the owners or employees.

ii) It is best to begin by defining the term 'entrepreneur' (see p. 33). In a joint stock company the functions of the entrepreneur are divided between the directors and shareholders. Directors carry out the management and decision-making functions, and shareholders carry out the risk-bearing function.

In fact, joint stock companies enable the interests of different groups of people to be harnessed and used for economic activity. There is a group of people who have financial resources, but may have neither the desire nor the expertise to take part in business management. On the other hand there is a different group who have the ability to run a business, but no financial resources. A joint stock company enables the former group to become shareholders, and the latter to become managers.

2 In some British industries we find that most of the firms are small or medium-sized, in others there are a few giant firms and many small firms, while in other industries there are a few very large firms and few, if any, small firms. The fact is that, in spite of the much publicized advantages of large-scale production and mass-production methods, many thousands of small firms continue to survive and grow.

The advantages of large-scale production can be gained only when there is a large market for a standardized product. When these conditions do not prevail, we find that small firms are able to operate very successfully.

This contrast is easily observed. For example, there is a large standardized market for motor cars, cigarettes, petrol and many electrical goods in the UK. Firms producing these goods can gain important technical, financial, managerial and marketing economies of scale. (Examples should be included to illustrate the importance of these. See pp. 38–9.)

However, in other cases the size of the market might be limited. Where consumers demand a variety of products it is not possible to mass-produce output and so we find small firms in the jewellery, clothing, furniture and other such industries.

The market is often limited because the consumer requires some kind of personal service, and so again we find small firms in the professions such as accountancy, architecture and dentistry. Sometimes the nature of the activity limits the size of firms. Restaurants and hairdressers, as well as all kinds of repair work, provide examples of this.

Even in industries such as motor car manufacture, where a few very large firms produce most of the industry's output, it is possible for small firms to survive. They do so because they specialize in the production of a single component for the major producers. In the UK there is a small number of firms who make custom-built cars, and these also are relatively small producers.

When market conditions change rapidly it is possible that small firms will have an advantage over larger firms. They have a more flexible structure and are capable of changing their products and methods more easily than larger firms.

The small firm might also have advantages in labour relations, because it is possible to have a closer relationship between management and workers. In large firms this is more difficult and may be one reason why some firms have a poor industrial relations record.

Nevertheless, large firms have more security and more resources to withstand recessions. They are often able to produce a range of goods and services so that a reduction in demand for one item will not threaten the firm with closure, unlike smaller firms which typically produce only one good or service. Again, modern research is often a costly business and much of it is now done within larger firms. These firms then obtain all of the benefits of the improvements developed in their research laboratories.

i) Prices of securities on the Stock Exchange are determined by supply and demand. The Stock Exchange does not fix, or in any other way influence, security prices. It is simply a market which brings buyers and sellers of securities into contact. The price of any individual security depends on the demand for it relative to the supply. Changes in demand and/or supply for any security will lead to changes in the price of that security, and its price will go on changing until supply and demand are brought back into equilibrium.

ii) The main economic function of the Stock Exchange is that it provides a market in securities. In other words, it brings buyers and sellers of securities into contact. This is very important because if there wasn't a ready market in securities, people who bought shares in public companies would not be able to get their money back when they wanted it. A market in securities makes this possible because investors simply sell their shares to someone else.

Because there is a ready market in securities, people are willing to buy shares in companies. This makes it possible for public companies to raise much larger sums of money than would otherwise be possible.

STUDENT'S ANSWER TO Q.3 WITH EXAMINER COMMENTS

Good points. Of course a public corporation might have *social* objectives as well.

(i) a) aims:

Public corporations – The aim is to move towards a surplus of income over expenditure and this will allow them to finance their own plans for long-term development without having to rely so heavily on money from the state.

Public Limited Companies – The aim is to make profit and this is a good thing for shareholders in the company because they recieve some of the companies' profit.

A plc might also have objectives *other than profit*, such as growing in size, market share or turnover etc.

b) ownership:

Public corporations – These are owned by the state because they have no shareholders.

Good

Public Limited Companies – these are owned by the shareholders of the company. This is done when the shareholders buy the shares from the stock exchange. The shareholder would provide capital by buying shares and agreeing that profits may be kept and used in business.

Only second hand shares. Small shareholders may have little actual say in running the

c) Management:

Public corporations – these are managed by the government and the government appoints a board to manage the public corporation on a day to day basis because there are no private shareholders to elect a board.

Again some good points. What you mean is that only the ordinary shareholder can vote at the AGM, and therefore influence management policy etc.

Public limited companies – these are managed by the shareholders of the company but only if they have an ordinary share. They manage the company by electing a board of directors at the annual general meeting. This board of directors will then appoint a professional manager.

d) Finance:

Perhaps a little more detail here, e.g. 'ploughing back profits', loans (debentures etc.) for plc and so on.

Public corporations – these are financed by the government through taxes.

Public limited companies – these are financed through the private shareholders, when the shares are sold on the stock exchange.

Brief, but to the point!

ii) The term privatization means to place back into private ownership business activities which have previously been in public ownership or under public control eg British Telecom.

Weak! You could have said much more here.

iii) The main argument for privatization is that it is a economic and political issue and so there are arguments over which part of the economy should be in public control and which should be in private control.

IDEAS FOR COURSEWORK

The different types of business organization are common in every town and city. In retailing, sole proprietors as well as joint stock companies are common. In the professions, such as the legal profession or medicine, partnerships are common.

You could investigate the growth of any one of these business organizations. For example, in the case of a sole proprietor you could investigate how the firm started and any problems it faced at the outset; how it dealt with these and the sources of assistance currently available. What does the firm produce and how does it organize production and distribution? Where and how does it advertise its product(s)?

A different project might be to investigate the capital structure of a joint stock company. Such companies publish annual reports which contain a great deal of useful information. As well as investigating the nature of production, distribution and so on, you might investigate the methods by which the company has raised finance and what it has used this finance for. You might go on to look at how the value of its shares has changed over time and what might have caused such changes. It is often a good idea to choose a company whose name is in the news, such as Eurotunnel. You will find a lot of information in quality newspapers covering larger joint stock companies.

SOURCES OF INFORMATION

- *Annual Reports and Accounts*, Various
- *Monthly Digest of Statistics*, Central Statistical Office
- *Financial Times, The Times, Daily Telegraph, Independent, The Guardian.*

CHAPTER 12

GROWTH, LOCATION & MARKET STRUCTURE

GETTING STARTED

A firm can be loosely described as an organization which transforms inputs into output. However, a much more difficult problem exists when we try to define what is meant by a *small firm* or a *large firm*, since the terms 'small' and 'large' have no precise meaning.

Nevertheless, we can measure size. In fact size can be measured in any one of three ways. A firm's size can be measured, first, in terms of the number of workers employed; second, in terms of capital employed; and third, in terms of **turnover** or **total revenue** over some period of time.

We have already looked at the advantages and problems of small firms in Chapter 11. However, firms with more than 1000 employees provide around 27 per cent of employment. In this chapter we consider how firms can **grow** into larger units. We then look at the factors influencing the **location** of firms. We conclude by considering the **structure of the markets** in which firms operate, taking the two extremes of perfect competition and monopoly.

METHODS OF GROWTH

INTEGRATION

REASONS FOR GROWTH

CONTROL OF MERGERS

MONOPOLIES

LOCATION OF INDUSTRY

MARKET STRUCTURE

ESSENTIAL PRINCIPLES

METHODS OF GROWTH

Firms can grow in any one of three basic ways:

- **Internal growth:** Here firms grow simply by reinvesting or **ploughing back** profit into additional assets.
- **Takeover:** Here one firm acquires a majority of the **voting share capital**, that is **equity**, in another firm. A firm attempting to do this is said to be staging a **takeover bid**.
- **Merger:** A merger occurs when two or more firms are combined to form a single firm. Shares in the existing firm(s) are exchanged for shares in the newly formed firm. Mergers are sometimes referred to as **amalgamations**.

2 > INTEGRATION

Integration simply refers to the fact that one firm has merged with another. However, firms can integrate in different ways.

VERTICAL INTEGRATION

❝❝ Make sure you know the different types of integration, and can give *examples* ❞❞

In the case of **vertical integration** a firm merges with another firm or takes over another firm involved in the production of the same good but at a different stage in the chain of production. Vertical integration can be either **backwards** or **forwards**. Vertical integration backwards occurs when a firm merges with, or takes over, another firm which is closer to the source of raw materials. Vertical integration forwards occurs when a firm merges with, or takes over, another firm which is closer to the retail outlets. A car manufacturer taking over a component supplier is *backward* vertical integration; taking over a chain of garages would be *forward* vertical integration.

HORIZONTAL INTEGRATION

In this case firms in the same industry and at the same stage of production merge. For example, one retail chain might merge with another retail chain, or a manufacturer might merge with another manufacturer. The takeovers of British Caledonian and Dan Air by British Airways are examples of **horizontal integration**.

CONGLOMERATE INTEGRATION

In this case firms merge with others in completely different industries. For example, a clothes manufacturer might merge with a chocolate manufacturer. The existence of companies such as Lonrho and Trafalgar House is evidence of conglomerate integration in the UK.

3 > REASONS FOR GROWTH

Different firms might grow for different reasons, but we can identify three factors that explain why a great many firms grow.

ECONOMIES OF SCALE

When firms gain *economies of scale*, average costs fall. This is a particularly important reason for horizontal integration. Where there is scope for economies of scale, horizontal integration will enable firms to exploit them because all firms which integrate horizontally are at the same stage of production. In these circumstances it might be possible to exploit all of the economies of scale discussed on pp. 38–9, and especially the technical economies. A bigger production unit may allow more specialization of labour and machinery, thus raising productivity.

When firms integrate vertically there is not the same scope for economies of scale. It might be possible to exploit certain economies such as managerial and financial economies, but there is less scope for technical economies than when firms integrate horizontally.

MARKET SHARE

Another reason why firms might integrate horizontally is to gain a greater **share of the market**. When firms have a greater share of the market they might be in a position to increase their profits. In particular when a firm has a monopoly, that is, a single firm controls the entire market supply, it might be able to charge consumers higher prices than it would if there were competitors. In general the greater the market share, the greater the influence firms have on price.

SECURITY

Security is likely to be a motive for *vertical* integration. Firms might integrate vertically backwards so that they have control over the supply and quality of inputs. On the other hand they might integrate vertically forwards to have control over the distribution of their product. For example, if firms control the retail outlets they have security that their product(s) will be available to consumers. They can also influence the way in which their product is sold, and the price charged to customers. This might also help them to increase sales and profitability.

Security might also be a motive for *horizontal* integration. If firms control a larger share of the market, there is less likelihood that they will be forced out of business by competition.

Conglomerate integration may also take place for reasons of security. If firms diversify, by merging with firms in entirely different industries, they have more protection against a slump in their initial product line. Many cigarette manufacturers are merging with companies in other industries to protect against the continued drop in the number of smokers. Lonrho, which has mining and leisure interests, is a conglomerate.

4 ▷ CONTROL OF MERGERS

In the UK firms do not have complete freedom to merge. The Government has the power to prevent a merger or break up a merger that has already taken place. The Office of Fair Trading was established in 1973 and the head of the organization, the Director General of Fair Trading, can refer certain proposed mergers to the Monopolies and Mergers Commission (also established in 1973) for investigation. Cases which can be referred are those where the merger would lead to the creation of a firm which would have control of 25 per cent or more of the total market, or where the value of the assets acquired exceeds £70m.

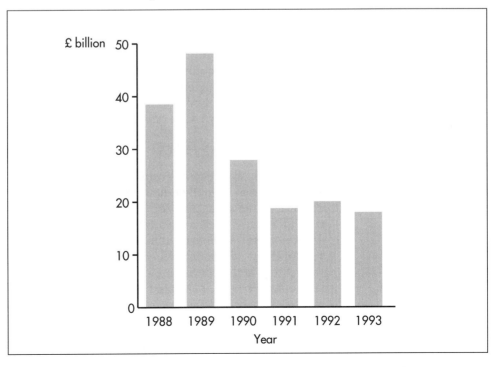

Figure 12.1 UK mergers and acquisitions, 1988 to 1993

Source: Acquisitions Monthly

The Monopolies and Mergers Commission is an independent body which investigates whether a proposed merger is likely to benefit or harm the public. It can investigate only those cases referred to it either by the Director General or by the Secretary of State for Industry. It has no power other than the power to investigate, although at the conclusion of its investigation it can make **recommendations** that a proposed merger should be allowed or disallowed. The Secretary of State for Industry must decide whether to accept or reject these recommendations.

5 ⟩ MONOPOLIES

Monopolies are not illegal in the UK. Where it can be shown that a monopoly operates in the public interest, it is allowed to continue. One obvious way in which a monopoly might operate in the public interest would be if there were substantial economies of scale. The lower costs from large-scale production might then be reflected in lower prices charged to consumers.

For legal purposes firms are considered to have monopoly power when they control 25 per cent of the total market supply of a particular good or service. Where such cases exist they can be referred to the Monopolies and Mergers Commission for investigation.

6 ⟩ LOCATION OF INDUSTRY

Firms are located in different places for a variety of reasons.

TRANSPORT COSTS

This is an important factor in the location of certain industries. Some industries are **weight-** or **bulk-reducing**, i.e. the raw materials lose weight or bulk rapidly when they are processed or refined. In such cases, locations close to the raw material site will be preferred. This is simply because it will be cheaper to transport the finished product to market than to transport the raw materials. This explains the coalfield locations of the iron and steel industry. It also explains the location of the pottery industry around Stoke-on-Trent.

For industries which are **weight-** or **bulk-increasing**, the opposite is true. Baking and brewing are obvious examples of such industries, and these tend to locate close to the market. Many industries which produce bulk-increasing, *consumer durables* are also located near the market. The furniture industry is concentrated heavily around London, because this is the major market.

LABOUR

The availability of labour is an important factor in the location of industry. Even in times of heavy unemployment there might be shortages of labour in certain areas and this might influence firms to locate in areas where labour is more plentiful. Some high-technology firms require highly skilled labour, and may look to university cities, such as Cambridge, and **science parks** for their location. Firms which are more labour-intensive may be interested mainly in keeping the wage bill down. They will look closely at areas where wage rates are relatively low, such as Wales.

ACQUIRED ADVANTAGES

Once an industry becomes established in a certain area, that area tends to acquire advantages that encourage new entrants to the industry to locate in the same area. These acquired advantages are sometimes referred to as **economies of localization**, and, if they exist, they are available to the whole industry rather than just to individual firms. Acquired advantages can take many forms.

● **Ancillary services:** When an industry is highly localized, other industries specializing in the provision of some necessary input will develop. For example, the lace industry is concentrated in Nottingham and is serviced by a host of other industries specializing in the provision of packaging for lace products, repairing lace-making machinery, etc.

● **Labour:** When an industry is highly localized it has easier access to a labour force possessing the skills it needs. One reason for this is that local tertiary colleges will run courses aimed at training local people in the skills which match the local industry. Families build up a tradition of working in certain occupations and also help to pass these skills down to younger people.

● **Commercial facilities:** The localization of an industry creates a situation where banks and insurance companies become more familiar with the needs of the industry than would otherwise be the case. This might also lead to cheaper rates being quoted.

THE GOVERNMENT

The Government takes an interest in the location of firms. In particular, its **regional policy** aims to encourage firms to locate or expand in certain areas. These areas are referred to as the **assisted areas** because financial assistance is available to firms which locate or expand within them. This assistance depends on the firms showing that jobs have been created as a result of the move or expansion, or that jobs have been saved that would otherwise have been lost. Figure 12.2 below shows that rates of unemployment differ across the UK. Many of the regions with unemployment above the UK average are assisted areas.

% of workforce (seasonally adjusted)

Region	%
Northern Ireland	12.7%
North	11.0%
North-West	9.2%
Yorks & Humber	9.2%
West Midlands	9.1%
Wales	9.0%
Scotland	8.8%
South-East	8.7%
Greater London	10.4%
East Midlands	8.4%
South-West	8.0%
East Anglia	6.8%
UK	8.9%

Figure 12.2 Unemployment in the UK: October 1994

Source: Department of Employment

REGIONAL AND URBAN ASSISTANCE

There are two kinds of assisted area: **intermediate areas** and **development areas**. Assistance is available in these areas because they have high unemployment rates compared with the national average, with a high proportion of long-term unemployed.

Financial assistance to the assisted areas is mainly in the form of grants. **Regional Enterprise Grants** are available in development areas for firms with fewer than 25 employees. There are two elements within the scheme: **investment grants** of 15 per cent towards the cost of fixed assets up to a maximum grant of £15000; and **innovation grants** of 50 per cent up to a maximum of £25000 to support product and process development. **Regional Selective Assistance** is available in both development and intermediate areas. This is an investment grant based on the fixed capital costs of a project and the number of jobs expected to be created or safeguarded. Regional Selective Assistance is often used to attract investments by multinational companies into the UK.

In addition to these policies, the Government has also set up **enterprise zones**. These are usually in small urban areas with particularly heavy rates of unemployment. For example, there is an enterprise zone in Newcastle and another one in Glasgow. Assistance of a different type is available to firms which locate within these. In particular, firms locating here are exempt from local rates for ten years. However, they are also given exemption from many of the restrictions faced by firms in other areas. For example, it is much easier for them to obtain planning permission for expansion.

The type of market in which the firm operates will have an important impact on the firm's price and output.

PERFECT COMPETITION

In a **perfectly competitive** industry:

- there are a large number of small producers
- all these firms produce an identical (homogeneous) product
- there are no barriers to entry: new firms can easily set up in the industry (and existing firms leave the industry)
- there is perfect information: all firms can easily acquire the same information about techniques of production, market trends, etc.

In a perfectly competitive industry the individual firms will have *no influence* at all on the **price** of the product. The intersection of market (industry) demand and market supply curve will determine the price of the product (see Chapter 7). In other words the firm will be a **price taker**: it takes the price as *given by* the demand/supply situation in the market as a whole. Being an insignificant part of market supply, the small firm can safely assume that it can sell *as much as it wants* at the going market price.

Of course, the small firm can decide on the **quantity** of the product it will produce at the current price. If it is mainly interested in profit, the firm will produce that output at which its total profit is at a maximum.

Advantages of perfect competition

Efficiency in production The pressure of competition will force the individual firm to be as efficient as other firms in the market, i.e. to produce at the same cost per unit.

All firms face the *same market price* for their (identical) product. There is no way a high-cost producer can raise its price to compensate for its inefficiency in production. A high-cost producer will therefore receive *less profit* on each unit (price minus average cost) than will other firms.

Since the typical firm in the industry will earn only *normal* profit (see below), i.e. *just enough* to keep it in the industry, the inefficient firm will earn *below normal* profit. This will *not* be enough to keep it in the industry, and so it will go bankrupt or withdraw from this industry. A perfectly competitive industry will therefore squeeze inefficient firms out of existence.

The mechanism by which only normal profits will be earned even by efficient firms is as follows. Suppose profits were *above normal*; with the ease of entry into the industry, new firms would have been attracted, increasing market supply and lowering price and therefore profit. Only when profit has returned to *normal* will there be no more incentive for new firms to enter the industry. An inefficient, high-cost producer will therefore earn *less* than the normal profit earned by other producers, and will go out of business.

- **Low prices for consumers:** We have noted that prices will stabilize at the level at which firms earn *just enough* (normal) profit to keep them in the industry. In other words, perfect competition will bring about the lowest price it is possible for consumers to pay while still receiving supplies of the product.
- **More choice for consumers:** With many small producers, the consumer can always switch to alternative sources of supply if not satisfied with a particular producer.

Disadvantages of perfect competition

For these, see also the discussion under the heading 'Advantages of monopoly' below. Two particular problems of perfect competition can be mentioned briefly:

- economies of scale may not be fully exploited, since firms are small
- investment may be discouraged since any *extra* profits created will tend to be competed away.

MONOPOLY

At the other extreme from perfect competition is **pure monopoly**. Here there is a *single firm* supplying the market with the product. In this 'pure' form of monopoly, the

> ❝ Perfect competition is an *extreme* form of market structure. But it helps us *predict* how some markets will behave ❞

> ❝ The arguments in *favour* of competition are *against* monopoly, and vice versa ❞

firm *is* the industry. This, of course, gives the firm considerable control (power) over price *or* quantity. We should remember that even a pure monopoly cannot dictate price *and* quantity! If the firm sets the *price*, the market demand curve will determine *how much* it can sell (quantity). If, on the other hand, the firm sets the *quantity* it will supply, the market demand curve will determine the *price* at which it can be sold. Even a pure monopoly can determine only price *or* quantity, it cannot decide both!

Sources of monopoly power

There are a number of **barriers to entry** into an industry which help a monopoly to exist.

● **Legal barriers:** The monopoly may be the result of **law**. Laws also give **patent rights** to inventors of processes (e.g. Pilkingtons' floating glass process) and products (e.g. Beechams' drugs for arthritis), whereby the inventor has sole rights for a fixed period of years. The letterpost division of the Post Office has a legal monopoly on postage rates of less than £1.

● **Economies of scale:** The most efficient (least cost) size for production may be very large. In the car industry, some analysts reckon that only when 1 million vehicles are produced per year does the average cost per vehicle reach a minimum. In other words, there are substantial economies of scale (see Chapter 5) which carry on up to a high volume of output. It will clearly be difficult for a new competitor to stay in business if the existing large competitor has much lower costs. It can undercut the price of the new competitor and 'strangle it at birth'.

In some cases only *one* firm could fully benefit from the economies of scale available. It is often argued that to have *more than one* railway operator, or provider of electricity, gas, cables, etc. would be inefficient. The duplication of provision would (it is alleged) inevitably create confusion and raise costs. Such industries are said to be **natural monopolies**. The privatizations of British Gas and British Telecom have led to these natural monopolies being opened up to competition. In the latter case by both Mercury and cable television companies.

● **Geographical barriers:** The monopoly may be the result of geographical barriers. For instance, an overseas producer may not be able to compete in the home market because of transport costs or customs duties placed on its product.

● **Marketing barriers:** The producer may spend considerable amounts on advertising and promoting the product, thereby developing a strong **brand image**. Customers may become so attached to the existing product that a new firm would have to spend large sums on advertising etc. to gain a foothold in the market. This would clearly discourage new entrants.

Whatever the source, a monopoly can continue only as a result of such *barriers to entry*.

Advantages of monopoly

● **Economies of scale can be fully exploited:** This may be particularly important if the country wishes to compete on world markets. Only if the domestic firms are large enough to benefit from *all* the economies of scale available will they be able to compete with other international giants.

● **Investment may be encouraged:** Any extra profits from lower costs and control over prices can be reinvested in the industry. With monopoly control, the firm can be more confident that it will reap the benefits of such investment. Research and development into new products and processes and investment in new equipment are costly activities, yet ones which are vital if a firm is to remain at the forefront of national and world industry. In perfect competition, any *extra* (above normal) profits from such investment would be **competed away**. This is not the case with monopoly since barriers to entry exist. Under monopoly, therefore, the firm will have more incentive to undertake the costly activities of research, development and investment, as it can keep the extra profit that such activities help to create.

Disadvantages of monopoly

● **Inefficient firms can stay in business:** The barriers to entry prevent competition, so that inefficient, high-cost firms can stay in business. Under competitive conditions these would go bankrupt.

● **Excess profits may be made:** The monopoly can exploit its market power to charge high prices and make excess profits. Of course, the Monopolies and Mergers Commission (see above) can investigate cases of excess profit, as it did for Barclaycard and Access in 1987. Nevertheless many monopolies will face no challenge to the size of the profits they make.

● **Consumers may face high prices:** Both the points mentioned above would tend to result in high prices to the consumer. Inefficient monopolies will charge high prices to cover their high costs. Monopolies making excess profits will have been *able* to charge high prices because there is no competition. They will have *chosen* to charge high prices because demand for their product is price inelastic (see Chapter 7), so that a higher price raises total revenue.

● **Consumers have less choice:** By definition there will be no alternative sources of supply, at least in the case of pure monopoly.

Despite all the criticisms of monopoly, there are undoubtedly some industries where firms need to be large in order to compete effectively in world markets.

TYPICAL EXAM QUESTIONS

1 | British Airways takes over Dan Air and British Caledonian in bid to challenge world's leading airlines.

i) Explain what is meant by horizontal and vertical take overs/integration.   [8]
ii) How may the above processes of take over/integration help to reduce a firm's costs?   [8]
iii) Why may horizontal and vertical take over/integration between firms bring disadvantages to consumers?   [8]

WJEC, 1994

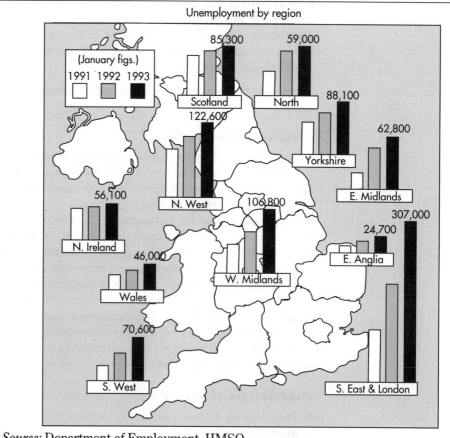

Source: Department of Employment, HMSO

Figure 12.3

2

	1990	1993		1990	1993
North	9.1%	12.2%	W. Midlands	6.1%	11.7%
Scotland	8.7%	9.9%	E. Midlands	6.1%	9.7%
North-West	7.8%	10.9%	South-West	4.4%	10.0%
Wales	6.9%	10.3%	East-Anglia	3.7%	8.6%
Yorkshire & Humberside	7.2%	10.6%	South-East	3.8%	11.7%

Source: Department of Employment

    i) Using the table, identify the regions which had the
      a) highest level of unemployment in 1990, [1]
      b) lowest level of unemployment in 1993. [1]

    ii) Using the map and the table identify information which supports the view that the South-East has been more badly affected by the rise in levels of unemployment than Wales. [3]

    iii) Since 1990 unemployment in the UK has been rising. Explain how this problem has affected both government spending and taxation revenue. [6]

    iv) From the passage below identify *two* measures which may help to reduce unemployment in the South Wales Valleys. [2]

Village for Garden Festival site

THE five-year package worth over £1 billion to promote regeneration of the South Wales Valleys was announced last week by the Welsh Secretary, David Hunt.

The programme is designed to replace the heavy industries, not merely with greenery but with jobs and other economic improvement. It includes the creation of industrial villages, road and rail improvements, new community hospitals at Ebbw Vale and Torfaen, and the development of an "urban village" on the Garden Festival site.

Earlier Valleys initiatives have helped reduce unemployment by 5 per cent, but male unemployment in some areas is still 25 per cent.

Source: Daily Telegraph

    v) Why is unemployment in the South Wales Valleys, which 'in some areas is still 25 per cent', much higher than the average for Wales as a whole? [4]

WJEC, 1994

3 Study Figure 12.3 which shows the market share of three manufacturers of sports shoes.

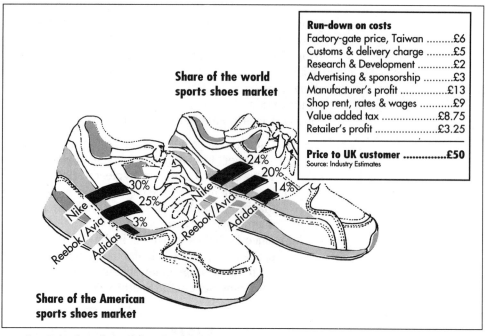

Run-down on costs
Factory-gate price, Taiwan £6
Customs & delivery charge £5
Research & Development £2
Advertising & sponsorship £3
Manufacturer's profit £13
Shop rent, rates & wages £9
Value added tax £8.75
Retailer's profit £3.25

Price to UK customer £50
Source: Industry Estimates

Share of the world sports shoes market

Share of the American sports shoes market

Figure 12.5

i)   Calculate the total profit made on a pair of sports shoes sold in the UK.   [1]
ii)   List in order of size, starting with the biggest, the makers of sports shoes in the world market.   [1]
iii) How much of the American market is controlled by the three manufacturers?   [1]
iv)   Explain briefly how much economic power, in your opinion, these three manufacturers have over the market.   [2]
v)   Suggest *two* ways in which one of the manufacturers could increase its share of the market.   [4]
vi)   Why might one of the manufacturers want to expand a) its share of the sports shoe market, b) into other products?   [7]

ULEAC, 1994

TUTOR'S ANSWER TO Q.1

i)   Horizontal integration occurs when two firms merge that are in the same industry and at the same stage of production. Examples of horizontal mergers are BMW taking over Rover Group and British Airways taking over Dan Air. Following horizontal integration, a larger share of output will be controlled by fewer firms.

Vertical integration occurs when a firm takes over another firm which may supply it with raw materials. For example, a company which owns an oil refinery buys an oil well. This is called backward vertical integration. Vertical integration can also occur when a firm takes over outlets which sell its final product, for example when a brewery buys a chain of public houses. This is called forward vertical integration.

ii)   Horizontal integration leads to a reduction in costs because of the benefits of economies of scale. A larger company will enjoy the benefits of technical, marketing, financial, managerial and research economies of scale. This means that production costs per unit will fall for the newly integrated company.

If backward vertical integration occurs a company will be able to obtain cheaper supplies of raw materials. The mark-up or profit margin from the supplier will no longer be charged following integration, thus lowering input costs.

iii) Once horizontal integration has occurred there are fewer firms in an industry, which may mean less competition, less choice of products and higher prices. A firm which takes over many of its competitors may have a significant degree of monopoly power, which may lead to consumers facing higher prices and lower quality products. The takeover of British Caledonian and Dan Air by British Airways has given the latter a large share of the domestic air travel market in the UK.

If a firm is in control of its raw material supplier it could refuse to allow its competitors to buy from this supplier. If a firm controls the retail outlets for its products it could prevent these outlets from stocking its competitors' products. Vertical integration could thus lead to higher prices or restricted choice for consumers.

STUDENT'S ANSWER TO Q.2 WITH EXAMINER COMMENTS

(i) (a) North

(b) East Anglia

(ii) The table shows and the graph (map) shows that the south-east has been effected much more than Wales by unemployment levels. In 1993 you can see by the map that in Wales 46,000 people were employed opposed to 307,000 unemployed in the South-east. This shows far more people are unemployed in the South-east than in Wales.

(iii) The rising unemployment rate has meant it has affected the government in different ways. The government spending would be allocated in different areas to try an decrease the unemployment rate. It could spend more money on training schemes to make people more skilled in particular areas of work espiecally in areas where there is more employment avaliable.

The taxation revenue would decrease as if people are unemployed they will not pay tax on their earnings. This would lower the tax revenue.

(iv) 1) The creation of industrial village – creation of jobs in villiage.

2) new community hospitals – creating jobs for nurses etc.

(v) The South-wales valleys are not in towns where there is more jobs avaliable. In towns there is more shops, busniess', leisure parks etc. where there is a good amount of jobs avaliable. In the valleys there will not be many jobs avaliable because of this problem of not many busniess', shops etc.

> 💬 You have *not* noted that unemployment in the South-East rose threefold whereas Welsh unemployment didn't even double between 1990 and 1993. 💬

> 💬 Benefits spending would rise with higher unemployment. 💬

> 💬 The Government's budget position would worsen with rising spending and falling tax revenue. 💬

> 💬 In the Welsh Valleys there has been little alternative employment to old industries, i.e. coal. In the rest of Wales there is much more alternative employment. 💬

💬 What you have written is quite good but you leave out too much which has lost you marks. 💬

IDEAS FOR COURSEWORK

Over the last few years there have been many takeovers or mergers, British Airways of Dan Air, BMW of Rover Group, Lloyds Bank of Cheltenham and Gloucester Building Society etc. Investigate, with the aid of newspaper articles, the reasons for and results of a recent merger.

R E V I E W   S H E E T

1   What is the main difference between the **public sector** and the **private sector?**
_____
_____

2   If the name of a business is 'Smith & Son Limited'
    i)   what kind of organization is this
_____

    ii) what does the term 'limited' mean?
_____

3   Give one **advantage** of limited liability.
_____

4   When an industry is privatized, ownership is transferred from the _____
    to _____.

5   What is an organization which is owned by its own workforce called?
_____

6   If a business wished to increase temporarily its stock or working capital, how might it do this?
_____
_____

7   This question is based on the following securities:
    a) a debenture; b) a preference share; c) an ordinary share.
    Which security has
    i)   a guaranteed annual return
    ii) the most variable annual return?

8   What term is used to describe the payment which shareholders receive on their share?
_____

9   Name *two* types of security traded on the Stock Exchange.
_____
_____

10 What is meant by SEAQ and what is its purpose?
_____
_____
_____

11 What is a 'bull', a 'bear' and a 'stag'?
_____
_____

12 Identify *two* financial benefits to an individual from owning shares in a PLC such as ICI?
_____
_____

13 What is backward vertical integration?
_____
_____
_____

14 What is diversification?
_____
_____
_____

15 What are the main functions of the Monopolies and Mergers Commission?

_____
_____
_____

16 What is a weight-losing industry?

_____
_____
_____

17 What is an assisted area?

_____
_____
_____

18 What are the characteristics of a perfectly competitive industry?

_____
_____
_____

19 What do you understand by the term 'monopoly'?

_____
_____
_____

20 A monopoly can only exist if there are _barriers to entry_. Explain, with examples, what is meant by the term 'barrier to entry'.

_____
_____
_____
_____
_____

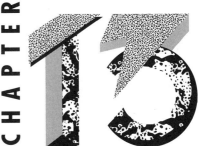
GETTING STARTED

National income refers to the total value of goods and services produced in the country in the year. From this production we obtain incomes which we then spend. So **output** (production), **income** and **expenditure** are all involved when we consider national income.

In this chapter we look at the way in which income **circulates** in the economy. We then define carefully the **measures** of national income that are widely used. We see that the measures are useful in comparing the standard of living between different times and between different countries.

ESSENTIAL PRINCIPLES

1 ▷ THE CIRCULAR FLOW

The **circular flow** of income shows how income *circulates* in the economy. In fact, more than income is involved, as we can see from Figure 13.1

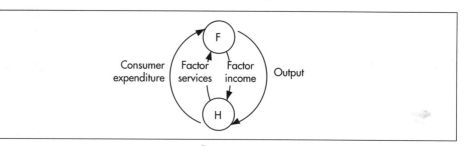

Figure 13.1 The circular flow

Households (H) provide firms (F) with **factor services** (or inputs), such as their **labour, land** for buildings, **capital** for investment and so on. The firms use these factor services to produce output of goods and services for sale. The firms must of course pay for these factor services – **wages** for labour, **rent** for land, and **interest** and **profit** for capital invested. These payments provide the factor inputs with income. Some of this income will be spent on the output produced by the firms (consumer expenditure). So producing output results in income, which leads to expenditure on that output.

In fact, if there were no leakages from, or injections into, this simple circular flow, it could go on at the same value for ever. Suppose *all* the firms in the economy produce £1 million of output, and pay £1 million to the factor inputs in the form of wages, rent, interest and profit, including of course profit to themselves or their shareholders. This £1 million of factor income is then spent on the goods and services produced by these firms.

So, in our simple economy, with no leakages and no injections:

national output	=	£1 million
national income	=	£1 million
national expenditure	=	£1 million

We have here the reason why we can measure national income by three alternative methods – **output, income** and **expenditure** methods – all of which should give the same answer.

2 ▷ INJECTIONS AND LEAKAGES

The simple economy we have described could carry on with a value of £1 million for national income for ever! This is because nothing is being added to, or taken away from the system. Of course, a real economy will have **injections** and **leakages**. Before we go further, we need to define our terms in a little more detail:

● **H**	=	domestic households, i.e. those located in the UK
● **F**	=	domestic firms, i.e. those located in the UK
● **Injections**	=	any income received that is *not* from a domestic firm or a domestic household
● **Leakages**	=	any income received that is *not* passed on to a domestic firm or a domestic household

Can you think of any injections or leakages? Figure 13.2 gives a useful summary of injections and leakages.

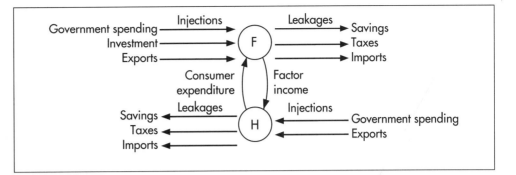

Figure 13.2 Injections and Leakages

INJECTIONS

Read the definition for injections again. The different types of injections are discussed below.

● **Government spending:** Domestic households may receive income from the Government and not from domestic firms. For example, the Government pays the wages of teachers, nurses, doctors, civil servants, etc. Again, domestic firms may receive income from the Government and not from domestic households. For example, the Government puts large contracts with building and construction firms and with suppliers of medical products, office equipment, etc.

● **Investment:** Domestic firms may buy capital equipment, such as machinery, from other domestic firms. Since domestic firms are receiving income that is not from domestic households, then investment is an injection.

● **Exports:** Domestic households and domestic firms may receive income from *overseas* households or firms. So exports are also an injection.

LEAKAGES

Read the definition for leakages again. The different types of leakages are discussed below.

● **Savings:** If domestic households or domestic firms save, they cannot pass the income on, so savings are a leakage.

● **Taxes:** Taxes are taken by the Government from domestic households and firms, so they cannot pass this income on. Taxes are therefore a leakage.

● **Imports:** If domestic households or firms spend money on imports, it goes overseas, so *not* to domestic firms or households. Imports therefore meet our definition of a leakage.

So, in practice, our economy might start at a value of £1 million, or any other given amount, for the circular flow, but it will not stay there. If injections are *bigger* than leakages, then the value of the circular flow will *rise*. If injections are *smaller* than leakages, then the value of the circular flow will *fall*.

In a bath, if more is coming in through the taps than is going out through the plug, the level of water will rise, and if the converse is true, the level will fall. So it is with the value of the circular flow, i.e. national income.

3 ▷ EQUILIBRIUM

❝❞ Equilibrium is a state of balance or rest ❝❞

Equilibrium means balance or rest. If the national income is in equilibrium it means that injections *exactly equal* leakages, so that there is no tendency for change. If the inflow into the bath through taps exactly matches the outflow through the plug, then the level of the bath water would stay the same.

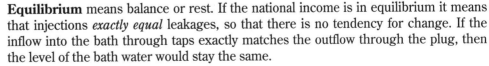

4 ▷ NATIONAL INCOME TERMS

You need to be familiar with the different definitions of national income.

GROSS DOMESTIC PRODUCT (GDP)

This is the value of all the goods and services *produced within the country* during a particular year. It doesn't matter if the firms producing these goods and services come from overseas, as long as they are *located* in the UK. (see Figure 13.3)

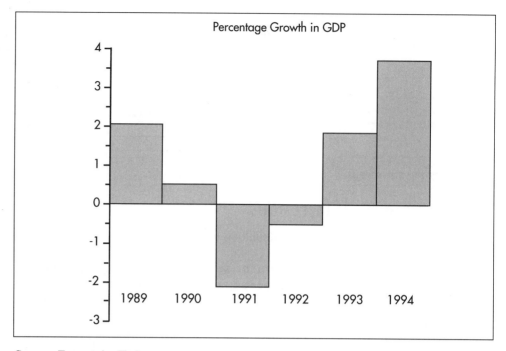

Figure 13.3 Gross domestic product

Source: Economics Today

GROSS NATIONAL PRODUCT (GNP)

This is the value of all the goods and services *produced by UK-owned resources*, wherever they are located. So we must *add* to GDP the income earned by UK-owned resources abroad, such as interest and profit on assets held overseas. But we must *subtract* from the GDP the payments made to foreigners who own assets in the UK. The *difference* between what we add and subtract is called *net property income from abroad*.

GNP = GDP + net property income from abroad

NET NATIONAL PRODUCT (NNP)

Some of the existing capital equipment in a country will wear out over the year. We call this **depreciation**. Part of the value of output will be needed to *replace* these items. What is left after paying for depreciation is called **net national product**. In some ways NNP is a better measure of the true addition to output in the year, having allowed for replacement of capital equipment that wears out (depreciates) during the year.

NNP = GNP – depreciation

We have already said that there are three possible methods for measuring national income. Here we look at each in a little more detail.

OUTPUT METHOD

We can measure the value of all the incomes received in the economy by measuring the value of all the **output** they are used to produce.

We must be careful not to **double-count**. Suppose a firm sells *components* for £50 to a manufacturer of knitting machines which then uses these components to make a knitting machine selling at £100. If we included the output of *both* firms in national income we would get £150 altogether. But this would be double-counting because £50 worth of components was also included in the £100 price of the knitting machine. We must *subtract* from the knitting machine firm's output of £100 the £50 already paid for components, giving a **value added** of £50 by that firm. We must measure only the *value added* at each stage of production, if we are to avoid double-counting.

National income is the value of output in a particular year. So second-hand sales do not count – the value of the second-hand car etc. was included in national income in the year when it was first produced.

INCOME METHOD

Here we measure the **incomes** received from factor services which helped to produce the output in that year.

Remember to omit **transfer payments**. These are incomes received by people who have *not* contributed to **current production**, e.g. pensions, unemployment benefits, etc. We include only the incomes of people who have contributed to production in the current year. Remember to include the income of salesmen etc. *dealing* in second-hand goods. The *service* they perform takes place in the current year, even though the goods may have been produced in a previous year.

For company income, in the form of profits, you have to consider **stock appreciation**. A company's stocks might increase in value (i.e. **appreciate**) through inflation during the year, boosting profits artificially. We must *subtract* this stock appreciation from the firm's profit figures since it does *not* arise from the firm's contribution to current output.

The income method uses recorded figures, based on Inland Revenue returns. Some income is not declared – this is called the **hidden economy**, so there will always be a difference between the value of output and the value of income declared.

EXPENDITURE METHOD

Here we measure the value of national income by looking at the **expenditure** on the goods and services produced.

Expenditure is measured at the price paid by consumers, which includes taxes (e.g. **VAT**) and subsidies. Taxes *raise* prices above the value of the goods and services when they were produced. Subsidies *reduce* prices below the value of the goods and services when they were produced. When expenditure is measured with taxes and subsidies *included*, we have national income at **market prices**. When expenditure is measured with taxes *subtracted* and subsidies *added*, we have national income at **factor cost**. In other words, income is measured at the 'true' cost of providing the goods and services, and is not distorted by taxes and subsidies as it is when we use market prices.

Some government expenditure goes to pay for pensions, benefits, etc. We have already seen that these transfer payments are not rewarding a contribution to current production. We must therefore subtract the value of the transfer payments from total government spending when we use the expenditure method for calculating national income.

The national income data can be used to judge a country's **standard of living**. Suppose we are looking at the standard of living of a particular country through time. We want to eliminate any rise in national income that was due purely to inflation. In other words, we want *real* national income, not *money* national income. We also need to check the *number of people* the national income has to support. If national income doubled, but so did the population, national income per head would be the same. The standard of living can therefore best be measured by the **real national income per head of population**.

Figure 13.4 shows the considerable increase in the standard of living in the UK over the past two decades or so. It uses real disposable income, i.e. national income after allowing for inflation and for taxes etc. being taken out. It measures what the average person has available to be spent on consumption. We can see that real disposable income per head of population increased significantly in the 1980s.

These are data showing the increase in standard of living *through time*. Question 2 on p. 139 gives you some comparisons of the standard of living *across countries*.

Although such comparisons are interesting, we should be careful how we interpret the data, especially across countries. People in a hot country could have the same standard of living with a lower national income per head than people in a cold country. This is because they will need to spend less on heat and clothing to keep warm than people living in a cold climate.

Can you think of other reasons why comparisons of the standard of living across countries could be misleading? The answer to Question 2 might help you.

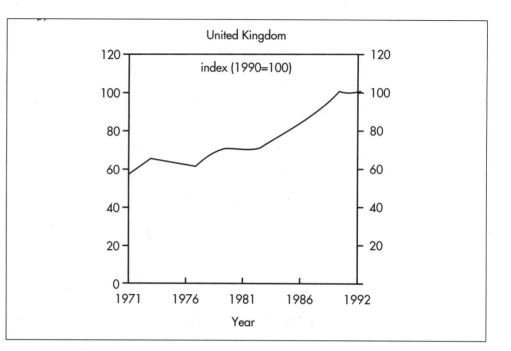

Figure 13.4 Real household disposable income per head

Source: Central Statistical Office

7 ▷ OUTPUT AND EMPLOYMENT

Changes in the value of national income (output) will have an important effect on the level of *employment*. We have already looked at productivity, i.e. output per person. If the total output in the economy is rising, then with present technology we will need more people to produce that output. If employment rises, then *unemployment* should fall. To what extent will, of course, depend upon *type* of unemployment.

UNEMPLOYMENT

● **Demand-deficient unemployment:** This type of unemployment is due to a lack of *overall* demand. So a rise in national output will tend to reduce demand-deficient unemployment.

● **Structural unemployment:** This unemployment is due to a change in the *pattern* of demand. For example, a decline in demand for shipping has led to many shipbuilders being unemployed. A rise in demand *as a whole* may not help to reduce this type of structural unemployment.

● **Regional unemployment:** This is often linked to structural unemployment. Whole industries such as shipbuilding, textiles, coal mining, etc. have grown up in particular **regions**. When these basic industries decline, unemployment in the region in which they are located rises sharply.

● **Frictional unemployment:** People are continually moving into and out of jobs for their own personal reasons. This is an inevitable part of labour mobility.

● **Technological unemployment:** This refers to unemployment caused by changes in technology, e.g. automation, robotics, etc. The new technology will raise the productivity of labour, so that fewer people will be needed to produce a given output. Unless output rises *more than* the increase in productivity, employment will fall, i.e. there will be *technological* unemployment.

A rise in national output will clearly help to reduce some of these types of unemployment more than others.

TYPICAL EXAM QUESTION

1 i) Compare and contrast structural and regional unemployment.
   ii) Why might it take some time for a rise in national output to reduce demand-deficient unemployment?
2 Use the information given in the diagram to compare the standard of living in the UK with that in the other countries mentioned.

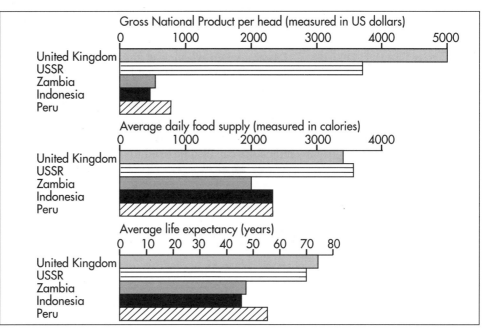

Figure 13.5

TUTOR'S ANSWER TO Q.1 AND Q.2

1. i) Structural unemployment is caused by changes in demand in an economy which bring about a decline in a whole industry and a loss of jobs. Structural unemployment has occurred in the UK since the 1930s with the decline of textiles, coal, steel and shipbuilding. The decline in demand for the output of these industries in the UK came about because of either cheap imports (textiles) and/or better substitutes (coal replaced by gas for energy).

   Regional unemployment occurs when a geographical area of the UK suffers levels of unemployment above the national average. Regional unemployment is often linked to structural unemployment because of the localization of whole industries within particular regions of the UK, e.g. textiles in Lancashire and Yorkshire and shipbuilding in the North-East. These industries originally benefited from external economies of concentration.

   ii) When the output (gross domestic product) of an economy rises, you would expect employment to rise because increased production and spending will require more workers. An increased demand for goods and services should, in theory, increase the demand for labour. However, it is often common for a reduction in unemployment to come about *some time* after output has started rising after a depression. Many firms are able to raise output initially without taking on more workers. This can be done by overtime working or improvements in working practices. Firms are often reluctant to take on workers after only a short period of recovery as it can be quite costly and traumatic for firms to make workers redundant, should the recovery prove to be short-lived. Thus firms may take on new workers only after a sustained rise in demand. There is often a *time-lag* between an increase in an economy's output and resulting falls in unemployment.

2. GNP per head is a useful index of the standard of living. Clearly Gross National Product per head (measured in US dollars) is highest in the UK: almost 50 per cent higher than in the USSR, more than 5 times higher than in Peru, and around 10 times higher than in Zambia.

Again, the difference in true 'quality of life' may not be fully reflected in these figures. Certainly the UK fares best in 'life expectancy', but only just better than the USSR. In the other countries the average life-span is between the late forties and mid fifties and although less than the UK's early seventies, the difference is not as great as the National Income figures might suggest.

Again, when we look at the average daily food supply (in calories), the USSR does better than the UK and the gap between the UK and the other countries is less than 50 per cent, as was the case for income.

A similar narrowing of the difference between countries can be seen in the information for life expectancy between countries.

Clearly GNP per head is an important indicator of standard of living, but other indicators can also be used to obtain a more complete picture.

IDEAS FOR COURSEWORK

Try to find out the level and **type** of unemployment in your town or region. Can you put unemployment into categories which make economic sense? Can you suggest policies which will help to reduce unemployment in your area? Talk to your local Job Centre and Chamber of Commerce.

SOURCES OF INFORMATION

See the list at the end of Chapter 4. See also:

- *Department of Employment Gazette*, HMSO
- *Economic Trends*, Central Statistical Office
- *National Income and Expenditure*, Central Statistical Office
- *UN Statistical Yearbook*, HMSO
- *World Development Report*, World Bank

REVIEW SHEET

1   How is national income per head measured?

_____

_____

2   If over a period of time income per head is constant, does this mean that the standard of living is constant?

_____

_____

3   Which of the following are transfer payments:
   i)   pensions
   ii) winnings from gambling
   iii) the profits of a bookmaker
   iv) a soldier's pay
   v)   donations to charity?

4   What is the difference between an injection and a leakage?

_____

_____

5   Classify the following as injections or leakages:
   i)   taxation
   ii) expenditure on imports
   iii) investment.

6   When is it true that expenditure = income = output?

_____

7   When calculating the value of output produced, why do we not count the gross value of the steel industry's output and the gross value of the car industry's output?

_____

_____

8   When calculating expenditure, why must we deduct indirect taxes and add on subsidies?

_____

_____

9   The diagram shows the circular flow of income and expenditure in an economy. Which of the flows marked A to D represents:
   i)   factor income
   ii) taxes
   iii) private consumption
   iv) government spending?

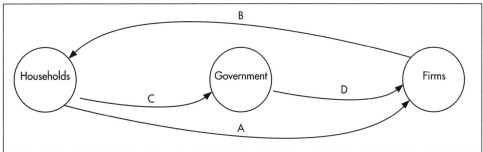

10 Which one of the following is most likely to increase the circular flow of income:
   i)   increased personal savings
   ii) increased import spending
   iii) reduced taxation
   iv) reduced government spending?

11 How is national income per head measured?

_____

_____

12 If over a period of time income per head is constant, does this mean that the standard of living is constant?

_____

_____

13 Which of the following are transfer payments:
  i) pensions
  ii) winnings from gambling
  iii) the profits of a bookmaker
  iv) a soldier's pay
  v) donations to charity?

14 What is the difference between an injection and a leakage?

_____

_____

15 Classify the following as injections or leakages:
  i) taxation
  ii) expenditure on imports
  iii) investment.

16 When is it true that expenditure = income = output?

_____

17 When calculating the value of output produced, why do we not count the gross value of the steel industry's output and the gross value of the car industry's output?

_____

_____

18 When calculating expenditure, why must we deduct indirect taxes and add on subsidies?

_____

_____

INTERNATIONAL TRADE & PAYMENTS

GETTING STARTED

No country is totally self-sufficient in the production of all the goods and services its inhabitants consume. This means that all countries trade internationally. Goods which are produced at home but sold abroad are referred to as **exports**, and goods which are bought from abroad are referred to as **imports**.

The fact that all countries trade internationally does not mean that there are no restrictions on trade. Sometimes countries adopt policies specifically designed to restrict trade. They can do this by taxing imports and therefore raising their price, or by allowing only a certain amount of a good or service to be imported.

At the end of each year most countries prepare a **balance of payments** statement. This is simply a record of earnings from abroad and expenditure made abroad. When a country earns more from abroad than it spends abroad, it has a **balance of payments surplus**. When the opposite is true, and the country spends more abroad than it earns abroad, it has a **balance of payments deficit**.

REASONS FOR INTERNATIONAL TRADE

ABSOLUTE ADVANTAGE

COMPARATIVE ADVANTAGE

BARRIERS TO INTERNATIONAL TRADE

THE TERMS OF TRADE

THE BALANCE OF PAYMENTS

SURPLUSES & DEFICITS

EXCHANGE RATES

ESSENTIAL PRINCIPLES

1 ▷ **REASONS FOR INTERNATIONAL TRADE**

THE NEED FOR IMPORTS

The most obvious reason for international trade is that countries have different climates and different amounts and types of raw materials. For example, Japan has to import most of its oil, and the UK has to import nickel and copper. However, with modern technology it is possible for many countries to produce most, if not all, of the goods they consume. It follows that there must be other reasons to explain the large quantities of goods and services that are traded across international frontiers.

EFFICIENCY OF PRODUCTION

The main reason for international trade is that some countries can produce some goods more cheaply than others. Countries might be able to produce the same goods, but they cannot all produce them with equal efficiency. If countries are more *efficient* in the production of some goods than other countries, then this means that they can produce those goods more *cheaply* than other countries. Because of this, it is often to the advantage of countries to **specialize**, or concentrate on the production of those goods where they have greatest efficiency in comparison with other countries.

When considering international specialization, two situations can be identified. These are **absolute advantage** and **comparative advantage**, and each is discussed below.

2 ▷ **ABSOLUTE ADVANTAGE**

A country is said to have an **absolute advantage** in the production of a good or service when, *using the same amount of resources*, it can produce more of that good or service than another country. This can be illustrated if we take a highly simplified example of two countries, **A** and **B**, each producing only two goods, cars and wheat. Figure 14.1 shows that country **A** has an absolute advantage in the production of cars. Using 10 units of resources it can produce 3 cars, but using the same amount of resources country **B** can produce only 1 car. On the other hand, country **B** has an absolute advantage in the production of wheat. Using 10 units of resources it can produce 15 tonnes of wheat, but using the same amount of resources country **A** can produce only 5 tonnes of wheat.

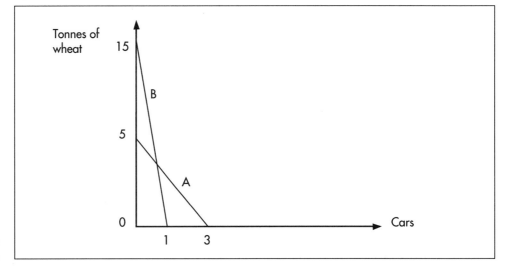

Figure 14.1 Outputs from 10 units of resources

It is easy to see that in this case specialization will lead to an increase in the **combined output** of both countries. For example, suppose each country has only 100 units of resources *in total*, and divides these resources *equally* between the two goods. Then Table 14.1, which is based on the information given in Figure 14.1, shows how much output each country would produce and what the combined total output would be.

	NUMBER OF CARS	TONNES OF WHEAT
Country A	15	25
Country B	5	75
Combined output	20	100

Table 14.1

Suppose that instead of producing both goods, each country specializes in the production of that good in which it has an absolute advantage. If this happened the combined total output of the two countries would increase. This is shown in Table 14.2.

	NUMBER OF CARS	TONNES OF WHEAT
Country A	30	–
Country B	–	150
Combined output	30	150

Table 14.2

The effect of specialization is to increase substantially the combined total output. In this case the combined total output increases by 50 per cent.

It is clear that more output can be produced when countries *specialize* than when they do not. However, this does not mean that both countries will *always* gain from specialization. In this simple example the combined total output of both countries increases, but each country now produces only one good. In order to obtain the other good they must trade with one another. Whether both countries gain from specialization depends on the rate at which goods can be exchanged for one another – in other words, how much of one good must be given up to obtain the other good. This is known as the *terms of trade*.

Countries gain from specialization and trade when this gives them more output than they would have if they did not trade, and instead produced all of their own output. This can happen only when buying from abroad has a **lower opportunity cost** than producing a good domestically. Some figures taken from the example given earlier will make this clear. It is important to remember that each country specializes in the good in which it has an absolute advantage, otherwise it is impossible to increase their combined output.

Look back at Figure 14.1. For country **A**, the opportunity cost of producing 3 cars is 5 tonnes of wheat. This simply means that for every 3 cars country **A** produces, it must *forgo* 5 tonnes of wheat; or for every car it produces, it must forgo $1^2/_3$ tonnes of wheat. Now specialization and trade will be beneficial for country **A** only if for every car it trades it gains *more than* $1^2/_3$ tonnes of wheat.

For country **B**, the opportunity cost of 15 tonnes of wheat is 1 car. This means that in order to produce 15 tonnes of wheat, country **B** must *forgo* 1 car. Specialization and trade will be beneficial for country **B**, therefore, only if, for every 15 tonnes of wheat it produces, it gains *more than* 1 car through trade.

For both countries to gain by specialization and trade the **terms of trade** must lie somewhere between their own domestic opportunity costs of production. In this case the opportunity cost ratio of cars to wheat for each country is $1:1^2/_3$ for country **A** and 1:15 for country **B**. For specialization and trade to benefit both countries, the terms of trade must lie *somewhere between* these two ratios. In other words, the rate at which cars can be traded for wheat must be greater than 1 car: $1^2/_3$ tonnes of wheat but less than 1 car: 15 tonnes of wheat. The terms of trade must be:

$$15 \text{ tonnes of wheat} < \text{car} > 1^2/_3 \text{ tonnes of wheat}$$

It is very important to stress that trade can benefit both countries only if the terms of trade lie somewhere between each country's domestic opportunity cost ratio. If the terms of trade lie *outside* the domestic opportunity cost ratios, one country will benefit from trade but the other will be worse off than if it produced all of its requirements itself. (Question 2 on p. 155 provides you with an opportunity to demonstrate this.)

3 > **COMPARATIVE ADVANTAGE**

In the section above we saw that specialization and trade can benefit countries when each concentrates on the production of that good in which it has an **absolute advantage**, and obtains the other good by trade. However, sometimes a country might have an absolute advantage in the production of *all* the goods it produces. It might seem that in these circumstances it is not possible for specialization and trade to benefit that country *and* the other countries with which it trades. This is *not* the case. Even when one country has an absolute advantage in everything it produces, specialization and trade can still benefit all countries.

To see why this is so let us take another simplified example. Again we will confine ourselves to two countries, A and B, producing two goods, cars and wheat. Figure 14.2 shows that country A has an absolute advantage in the production of both goods. Using 10 units of resources it can produce 4 cars *or* 8 tonnes of wheat. Using the *same amount of resources*, country B can produce only 2 cars *or* 5 tonnes of wheat.

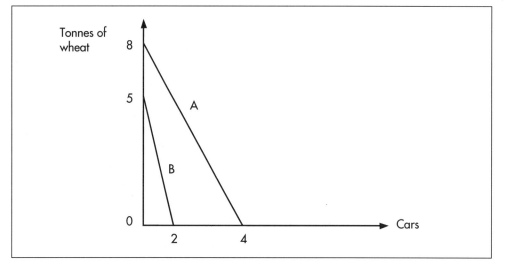

Figure 14.2 Outputs from 10 units of resources

Clearly, country A is more efficient in the production of *both* goods than country B. However, specialization and trade can still benefit both countries if each specializes where it has the greatest **relative efficiency** – in other words, if each country specializes in the production of that good where it has most efficiency compared with the other country. An example, using the information given in Figure 14.2, will make this clear.

For country A the opportunity cost of producing 1 car is 2 tonnes of wheat, because with 10 units of resources it can produce either 4 cars or 8 tonnes of wheat, a ratio of 1:2. For country B the opportunity cost of producing 1 car is $2\frac{1}{2}$ tonnes of wheat, because with 10 units of resources country B can produce 2 cars or 5 tonnes of wheat, a ratio 1:$2\frac{1}{2}$. It is very important to note that the opportunity cost of producing cars and wheat is *different* in each country. This is what gives countries a relative advantage, or **comparative advantage**, in production.

In this example, each time country A produces an extra car it must give up 2 tonnes of wheat, but each time country B produces an extra car it must give up $2\frac{1}{2}$ tonnes of wheat. In other words, country A has a **lower opportunity cost** (alternative forgone) than country B in car production. We say that country A has a **comparative advantage** in the production of cars.

On the other hand, each time country A produces an extra tonne of wheat it must give up 0.5 of a car, but each time country B produces an extra tonne of wheat it must give up only 0.4 of a car. In other words, country B has a **lower opportunity cost** (alternative forgone) in wheat production than country A. We say that country B has a **comparative advantage** in the production of wheat.

> Even countries less efficient in everything can gain from trade

● A country has a comparative advantage in producing that good (or service) for which it has a lower opportunity cost than the other country.

Again we can demonstrate that an increase in the **combined output** of both countries is possible if each specializes in the production of that good in which it has a comparative advantage. We can then show that both countries can gain from trade in the sense that both are able to consume a higher level of output after trade than before trade.

Suppose, at the start, that there is no trade between country A and country B and that each devotes half of its 100 units of resources to the production of each good. Table 14.3 shows this and also the combined output of both countries.

	NUMBER OF CARS	TONNES OF WHEAT
Country A	20	40
Country B	10	25
Combined output	30	65

Table 14.3

Now in order to show that the combined output of both countries can be increased by specialization, it is necessary for each country to concentrate on the production of that good in which it has a comparative advantage. However, if each country concentrates totally on the production of that good in which it has a comparative advantage, the **combined output** of both countries will give *more* cars but *less* wheat. In order to have more of *both* goods it is necessary for country A (the country with the absolute advantage in the production of both goods) to specialize *partly* in cars, in which it has a comparative advantage, and for country B to specialize *fully* in wheat, in which it has a comparative advantage. For simplicity let us assume that country A uses 80 per cent of its resources to produce cars and the remaining 20 per cent to produce wheat. Country B on the other hand, uses all of its resources to produce wheat. Table 14.4 shows how much output each country produces and the combined value of their output.

	NUMBER OF CARS	TONNES OF WHEAT
Country A	32	16
Country B	–	50
Combined output	32	66

Table 14.4

Clearly, even though country A has an **absolute** advantage in both goods, specialization according to **comparative** advantages gives a potential for greater **combined output** in the economy. The extra output can be shared between the countries so that both gain.

Whether they *do* both gain from specialization and trade depends on the **terms of trade**. For both countries to gain from specialization and trade the terms of trade must be somewhere between the domestic opportunity cost ratios. In this case the terms of trade must be somewhere between 1 car : 2 tonnes of wheat and 1 car : 2½ tonnes of wheat:

$$2\tfrac{1}{2} \text{ tonnes of wheat} < \text{car} > 2 \text{ tonnes of wheat}$$

ASSUMPTIONS

In our discussion of absolute advantage and comparative advantage, several assumptions were made. These were ignored earlier to keep the discussion simple. However, for completeness some of the more important assumptions are now considered briefly.

● **Transport costs ignored:** It was assumed that there were no transport costs involved in international trade. In fact, if transport costs are greater than the savings made from buying a good abroad, there is no advantage in international trade.

● **Barriers to trade ignored:** It was assumed throughout our discussion that there was nothing to prevent countries from trading with each other. In reality governments sometimes impose **restrictions** designed to limit trade. These are discussed more fully on pp. 148–9. Here we need only note that if governments limit international trade, this will reduce the benefits of specialization and trade that countries might otherwise gain.

● **Factor immobility ignored:**   In the examples we assumed that resources were highly **mobile**. It was assumed that countries could specialize partially or completely in the production of one good or another, and that there would be no difficulty in transferring resources between goods. In reality this is not the case. We have seen in Chapter 5 that there are many factors which limit the mobility of labour. Similarly, the mobility of the other factors of production, such as capital equipment, might also be limited. If factors of production are *not* highly mobile, then specialization between countries will be more difficult.

❝❝ Whether a particular country gains depends on the terms of trade ❞❞

4 ⟩ BARRIERS TO INTERNATIONAL TRADE

Countries do not always allow free trade to take place. Instead, they impose **barriers** which restrict trade. Such barriers can take many forms. Here we discuss only five.

TARIFFS

A **tariff** is a tax which is payable on, or levied on, an imported good. The effect of this is to raise the price the consumer must pay to buy an imported good. Because price is higher than it otherwise would be, consumption will almost certainly be lower. Tariffs therefore restrict international trade.

QUOTAS

A **quota** is an upper limit on the amount of a particular good that can be imported within a particular period, usually one year. Once the quota, or limit, is reached, no further imports of that good are allowed into the country until the next year (or whatever period the quota runs for).

EXCHANGE CONTROLS

When goods are imported, the person buying them must pay for them in foreign currency. If the Government does not supply the amount of foreign currency that importers require, they will be forced to reduce the amount spent on imports. Limiting the amount of foreign currency available is known as *exchange control*. It is a very effective method of restricting imports although it is not widely used by developed countries.

SUBSIDIES

Another effective way of limiting international trade is to **subsidize** domestic goods. We have seen in Chapter 7 that a subsidy on a product will lower its price. The lower price will encourage consumers to buy domestic output instead of imported substitutes, because the subsidy will make domestic output cheaper.

RED TAPE

This is the newest kind of restriction on trade. It involves the deliberate use of **rules and regulations** to delay or prevent imports, such as imposing safety standards that are excessive. The general idea is to make it difficult for foreign goods to be sold in the domestic economy.

Reasons for imposing barriers to trade

Countries impose barriers to trade for many reasons. When barriers are imposed we say that domestic industry is being *protected* from foreign competition. Barriers to trade are therefore sometimes referred to as **protection**. Some of the more common arguments for protection from imports are considered below.

● **To protect an infant industry:**   A very popular argument for protection concerns a domestic industry in the early stages of its 'life'. This industry may be prevented from growing because it is unable to compete with cheaper imported substitutes. By imposing tariffs, or by using some other restriction, it is possible to shield, or protect, the domestic 'infant industry' from foreign competition. It is hoped that this will allow the industry to grow and gain economies of scale, the aim being that these economies of scale, by lowering the average cost of production, will eventually enable the domestic producer to compete with imports. At this point it will no longer need protection.

● **To reduce a balance of payments deficit:** Another popular argument for imposing barriers to trade is that by reducing imports it is possible to reduce, or even eliminate, a balance of payments deficit. There is no doubt that protection can reduce imports, but it might also lead to a reduction in exports. This would happen if one country erected barriers to trade, and other countries **retaliated** by erecting their own barriers against that country. If this happened, exports and imports would fall and the balance of payments deficit might actually become worse.

● **To encourage a reallocation of resources:** Countries are sometimes faced with the problem of a declining industry. In the UK, for example, the textile and coal industries are declining. The problem is that when an industry declines suddenly, the people who work in that industry become unemployed. This is particularly serious when the industry is highly **localized**. In this case whole areas can be affected. For example, in Cornwall the decline of the tin industry has had a serious effect on local employment. Much of Lancashire has been badly affected by the decline of the cotton industry, and the decline of the steel and shipbuilding industries has increased unemployment sharply in the North-East.

Protection can be used as a way of reducing the impact of the decline in a major industry. For example, where a domestic industry is declining because of foreign competition, quotas could be used to limit the quantity of imports. By gradually increasing the quota limit, the industry could be allowed to decline more gradually. The aim is to avoid the disruption that occurs when an industry declines rapidly.

● **To eliminate 'unfair' competition:** One argument sometimes suggested for protection is that advanced economies, like that of the UK, cannot compete with products from developing countries because **labour costs** in these countries are much lower. It is certainly true that average wages are much lower in developing countries than in the UK, but this does not always mean that **labour costs** are lower in these countries. Also although wages are lower in developing countries, so too is output per head (which we referred to as 'productivity' on p. 34). In advanced economies output per head is much greater, so that although wages are higher, the **labour cost per unit** of output can still be lower.

● **Strategic arguments:** Despite the benefits of specialization and trade, countries might protect certain industries deliberately to avoid becoming dependent on another country for their continued supply. Countries might fear that in times of war or economic blockade the supply of commodities on which they depend, such as food and raw materials, might be cut off.

THE WORLD TRADE ORGANIZATION (WTO)

The WTO was set up in 1948 with the aim of reducing tariffs world-wide. Member countries of the WTO (formerly GATT) meet periodically to hold a round of talks. The latest of these was the Uruguay Round which ended in 1993.

We defined the **terms of trade** (see p. 145) as the rate at which a country's exports can be exchanged for imports. However, in modern economies which export and import many hundreds of goods it is not possible to measure the terms of trade as so much of this good for so much of that good. Instead, the terms of trade are measured as an **index** (see p. 163) or average of the ratio of export prices to import prices. This sounds complicated but is in fact quite easy, as the following equation shows:

$$\text{terms of trade} = \frac{\text{index of export prices} \times 100}{\text{index of import prices}}$$

In the **base year**, that is, the year which is taken as the starting point, all index numbers have a value of 100. The terms of trade must therefore have a value of 100 in the base year. In subsequent years, when export prices and import prices rise, the terms of trade will change. When the value of the terms of trade rises, we say there has been a **favourable** movement in the terms of trade. When the value of the terms of trade falls, we say there has been an **unfavourable** movement in the terms of trade. We can see the terms of trade for the UK over a ten-year period in Table 14.5.

YEAR	TERMS OF TRADE
1985	100.1
1986	96.1
1987	96.4
1988	97.4
1989	99.1
1990	100.0
1991	101.1
1992	102.6

Table 14.5 *Source: Economic Trends*, HMSO

Favourable and unfavourable movements in the terms of trade sometimes cause confusion. A favourable movement always occurs when export prices rise *relative* to import prices. An unfavourable movement always occurs when import prices rise *relative* to export prices. Such price changes are called favourable and unfavourable because of the effect they have on the rate at which exports exchange for imports. For example, if export prices rise while import prices are unchanged, the terms of trade will have moved favourably because a *given amount of exports* will now be worth, or exchange for, a *greater amount of imports*.

Now this seems simple enough. The problem is that the *effect* of any price changes might not be favourable. For example, if a rise in export prices results in less being sold, while a reduction in import prices results in more being sold, then although the terms of trade will have moved favourably, the effect on the balance of payments may actually be unfavourable.

6 ▶ THE BALANCE OF PAYMENTS

The **balance of payments** is a record of a country's earnings from, and expenditures with, the rest of the world over some given period of time, usually a year. Using the example given in Table 14.6 we can see the way in which the different items that make up the balance of payments are classified.

THE CURRENT ACCOUNT

This part of the balance of payments accounts deals with goods and services. Each item is detailed separately.

● **Visible trade:** This consists of exports and imports of **goods** only. No services are included in this account. The difference between the value of exports and imports of goods is called the **visible balance** or the **balance of trade**. Table 14.6 shows that for the UK in 1993 the visible balance was –£13 423m.

● **Invisible trade:** This consists mainly of the export and import of **services**. Some examples of invisible exports are tourists from overseas visiting the UK, British ships transporting foreign goods to different parts of the world, the use of the UK banking industry by foreigners and so on. Table 14.6 shows that in 1993 the invisible balance, that is, the difference between invisible exports and invisible imports, was £2753m for the UK.

When the total **visible balance** is added to the total **invisible balance** the resulting figure is the **current balance**. The current balance for the UK in 1993 was –£10 670m (a deficit).

INVESTMENT AND OTHER CAPITAL FLOWS (TRANSACTIONS ACCOUNT)

Sometimes transactions between one country and the rest of the world result in payments being made that have nothing to do with the purchase of sale or goods and services, for example when a UK citizen buys shares in a Japanese company, or an American company builds a factory in the UK. Clearly, these financial flows also affect the balance of payments, though they are neither visible nor invisible trade. This section of the balance of payments accounts also includes official transactions undertaken by the Government to ensure that the overall balance of payments is zero.

This may mean drawing from or adding to the Government's foreign exchange reserves at the Bank of England or borrowing or lending abroad (see below).

	£m
Visible exports	120 907
Visible imports	134 330
Visible balance	–13 423
Invisible balance	2 753
Current balance	–10 670
Net transactions in assets and liabilities	8 900
Balancing item	1 770
	0

Table 14.6   *Source:* HMSO

Such transactions as these are grouped together in the **investment and other capital flows** section of the balance of payments account. The **net** figure, that is, the difference between inflows and outflows, for investment and other capital flows for the UK for 1993 was +£8900m.

THE BALANCING ITEM

The Bank of England keeps a record of total inflows and total outflows of currency, but it has no way of knowing where these funds came from or what they have been spent on. In fact, the expenditure and earnings figures for each entry in the balance of payments are **estimates**. The difference between these estimates and the Bank of England's record is known as the **balancing item**. It represents the total of all **errors and omissions** from the estimated figures. In 1993 the value of the balancing item was +£1770m.

7 ▷ SURPLUSES AND DEFICITS

Now, it is a fact that the balance of payments must always balance, and yet we often read of a balance of payments deficit or a balance of payments surplus. The reason for this apparent confusion is simple. The *overall* balance of payments account is *brought into balance*. There are two ways in which this can be done: either by **borrowing or lending** abroad (borrowing if there is a deficit, lending if there is a surplus), or by changes in the **reserves**. The reserves consist mainly of foreign currencies that can be used to settle debts with foreign countries, and gold, which is acceptable in settlement of a debt everywhere in the world.

When there is a balance of payments deficit, a country must settle this deficit. The country must either borrow abroad, or use its reserves to settle the deficit, or a combination of both. This borrowing or reduction in the reserves is what makes the balance of payments balance. In total, the borrowing plus any reduction in the reserves must exactly equal the deficit.

When there is a balance of payments surplus, the opposite situation exists. A country can either lend part or all of the surplus abroad, or it can add the surplus to the reserves, or a combination of both. Again the overall balance of payments is brought into balance at zero.

However, while the balance of payments must always balance overall, this does *not* mean that the balance of payments can never be a problem. A deficit (and in some cases a surplus) on any one of the accounts which make up the balance of payments account can create difficulties for a country.

THE IMPORTANCE OF THE CURRENT ACCOUNT

We have seen earlier that the current account consists of visible trade and invisible trade. When there is a surplus on visible trade we say that the balance of trade is **in the black**. When the balance of trade is **in the red**, this means that there is a deficit on visible trade.

The current account is particularly important because it shows the extent to which a nation is able to pay for its imports of goods and services by its exports of goods and services. One reason why this is important is that the production of goods and services adds to a nation's **standard of living**. The more goods and services a nation produces, the more goods and services it can consume and therefore the higher its

▶▶ Visible + invisible = current account ◀◀

material standard of living. However, this does not mean that a nation's standard of living can always be increased by producing every good and service it consumes. We have already seen the benefits of specialization and trade.

It is true that when a country has a current account deficit it is able to *consume* an amount greater than it currently *produces*. This can raise the standard of living of the deficit country in the short term. However, in the long term all imports must be paid for by exports and therefore the standard of living cannot be increased permanently by running a current account deficit.

A country can adopt a range of policies to deal with a balance of payments deficit. It can seek to cut consumer spending *generally*, using **fiscal** or **monetary** policy. Some of the cut in consumer spending will help reduce the demand for imports. Alternatively the Government can use **protection** (see p. 148). Another possibility is to lower the **exchange rate**. This makes exports cheaper and imports dearer. We now take a closer look at exchange rates.

Countries require foreign exchange to pay for their imports or to finance investment overseas. Exchange rates are the rate at which one country's currency can be exchanged for another country's currency.

In the UK the most frequently quoted exchange rate is the sterling–dollar exchange rate. Changes in this exchange rate are frequently reported in the news and, if you check, you will see that some newspapers report daily on the rate of exchange that was *quoted* the previous day.

Institutions such as banks or other public companies obtain foreign exchange through the **foreign exchange market** which, in the UK, is located in London.

FLOATING EXCHANGE RATES

When exchange rates are determined by the free play of market forces they are described as **floating** or **flexible** exchange rates. In this context the free play of market forces simply means that the exchange rate for a country's currency is determined by the amount *supplied* to the foreign exchange market and the amount *demanded* on the foreign exchange market. In order to understand what determines exchange rates we need to know what determines the supply of currency to the foreign exchange market and what determines the demand for currency on the foreign exchange market. For simplicity we consider the exchange rate for sterling against the dollar. Between October 1990 and September 1992 sterling joined the **exchange rate mechanism (ERM)** which fixed the exchange rate of the pound against other European Union currencies. Since leaving the ERM the pound has floated against other currencies.

DEMAND FOR STERLING

Demand for any country's currency on the foreign exchange market is determined by demand for that country's exports of goods and services and by changes in foreign investment in that country. This is because when foreigners buy another country's exports of goods or services they must pay for these in the currency of the exporting country. The same is true if foreigners invest in that country. It is this which gives rise to demand for foreign currency on the foreign exchange market.

This might be clearer if we take sterling as our currency. The demand for sterling on the foreign exchange market is determined by the amount of goods and services foreigners wish to buy from the UK, and by the amount foreigners wish to invest in the UK. For example, a foreign firm wishing to buy goods or services from the UK must pay for them in sterling.

The demand for a country's currency on the foreign exchange market, like the demand for any other good, is influenced by its price. When the price of a country's currency *rises*, the demand for that currency is likely to **fall**. The reason for this is simple. Take the case of a car costing £10 000 in the UK. With an exchange rate of £1 = $2, this car would cost $20 000 in the USA if it were exported. In other words, at a rate of exchange of £1 = $2, a citizen in the USA would have to give up $20 000 in order to obtain the £10 000 necessary to purchase the car from the UK.

However, if the rate of exchange increased to £1 = $2.5, the same car costing £10 000 in the UK would now cost $25 000 if it were exported to the USA. In other words, at the higher rate of exchange it is necessary for the US citizen to give up $25 000 in order to obtain £10 000. Thus an increase in the rate of exchange increases the cost of exports of goods and services from the UK (as well as the cost of overseas investment in the UK). The higher price in the USA would reduce the amount of exports from the UK demanded in the USA. (It would also reduce USA investment in the UK.) Because of this we normally assume that less sterling would be needed at a higher exchange rate, and therefore less sterling would be demanded on the foreign exchange market. So as the sterling exchange rate rises, the quantity of sterling demanded falls.

SUPPLY OF STERLING

The supply of sterling on the foreign exchange market is determined by UK demand for imports of goods and services, and by UK investment in foreign countries. The reason is simple. In order to buy from abroad or to invest abroad UK citizens must obtain foreign currency. They do this by exchanging sterling for foreign currency on the foreign exchange market. Each time UK citizens buy foreign currency from the foreign exchange market, they supply sterling to it.

Again, the supply of sterling to the foreign exchange market is influenced by its price. Like the supply of other goods, a rise in price will result in an increase in the quantity supplied. If we consider the case of sterling again it is easy to see why this is so.

At an exchange rate of £1 = $2 a book costing $40 in the USA will cost £20 if it is imported into the UK. However, if the rate of exchange increases to £1 = $2.5 the same book costing $40 in the USA will now cost only £16 in the UK. In other words, an increase in the rate of exchange will reduce the price of any good or service imported (or the cost of investment abroad). This is likely to increase the amount of imports (as well as investment abroad). In order to pay for these we assume that more dollars will be demanded on the foreign exchange market and consequently more sterling will be supplied to the foreign exchange market. Thus as the sterling exchange rate rises, the quantity of sterling supplied increases.

THE EQUILIBRIUM RATE OF EXCHANGE

In a free market the rate of exchange is determined by market forces, that is, supply and demand. We have seen that demand for a country's currency increases as its price falls and supply of a country's currency increases as its price rises. The equilibrium price of a country's currency in a free market is therefore that price, or exchange rate, at which the supply of currency and the demand for currency are equal.

In Figure 14.3, SS represents the supply of sterling to the foreign exchange market, and DD represents the demand for sterling on the foreign exchange market.

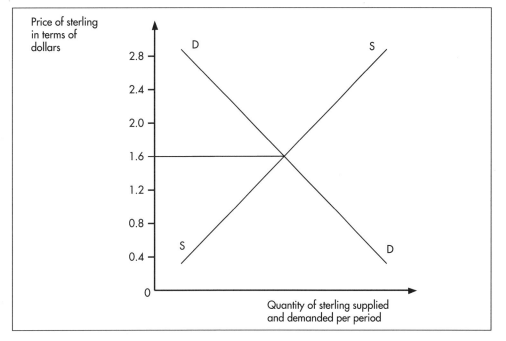

Figure 14.3

The quantity of sterling supplied and demanded is measured with respect to the **price of sterling in terms of dollars**, that is, the quantity of dollars that can be exchanged for (or bought with) £1. In this case the equilibrium exchange rate, that is the exchange rate at which supply and demand are equal, is £1 = $1.60. At any other rate of exchange there will be either a surplus of sterling on the foreign exchange market or a shortage of sterling. Only when the rate of exchange is £1 = $1.60 is there neither a shortage nor a surplus of sterling.

APPRECIATION AND DEPRECIATION

It is clear that in a free market, exchange rates can change only if there is a change in the supply of a country's currency and/or a change in the demand for that currency. For example, if all other things remain equal, an increase in the demand for a country's currency will cause an upward movement in that country's exchange rate.

> Remember a fall in the exchange rate makes exports cheaper and imports dearer

When there is an upward movement in a country's currency we say that the exchange rate has **appreciated**. For example, if supply and demand for sterling are initially given by SS and DD in Figure 14.4, the equilibrium exchange rate will be £1 = $1.60. If demand for sterling now increases to D′D′, the equilibrium exchange rate will rise to £1 = $1.80. In this case we would say that sterling has appreciated on the foreign exchange market, or that there has been an appreciation of sterling on the foreign exchange market.

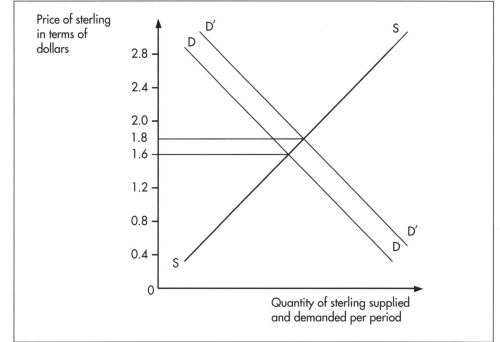

Figure 14.4

When the value of a country's currency falls on the foreign exchange market we say that its currency has **depreciated**. For example, in Figure 14.4 if supply and demand for sterling are initially given by SS and D′D′ respectively the equilibrium exchange rate will initially be £1 = $1.80. If demand now falls to DD, the exchange rate for sterling will fall to £1 = $1.60. In this case we say that sterling has depreciated on the foreign exchange market, or that there has been a depreciation of sterling on the foreign exchange market.

TYPICAL EXAM QUESTIONS

1

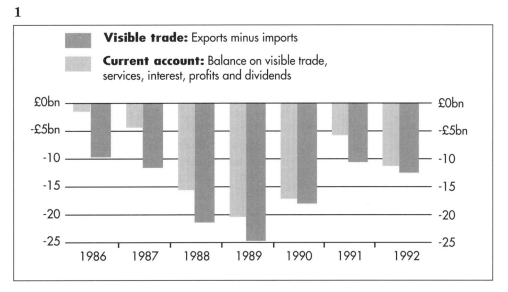

Study the above information of the UK's balance of payments.
i) What is the current account deficit in 1991?
ii) Why, over the period shown, is the invisible balance always in surplus?

WJEC, 1994

2   i) Describe *two* main features of the single market as exists in the European Union (EU).
   ii) Explain the economic reasons why the UK buys
      a) wines from France, b) cars from Germany.
   iii) Discuss the view that membership of the EU has produced serious problems for consumers in the UK.

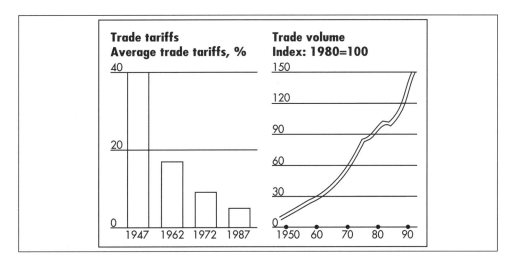

3   i) Why do most economists believe that there are advantages to be gained from the removal of tariffs and the promotion of free trade in the world economy?   [8]
   ii) Despite the advantages of free trade why do some countries impose tariffs on imported goods?   [8]
   iii) The UK's exchange rate has fallen since it left the EU's exchange rate mechanism (ERM) in September 1992. How might this affect the UK economy?   [8]

WJEC, 1994

OUTLINE ANSWERS TO Q.1 AND Q.2

1 i) – £6bn
   ii) The invisible balance must have been in surplus because the current account was not as heavily in deficit as the visible balance. The current account = visible balance + invisible balance.

2 i) Elimination of barriers to trade between member countries. Free movement of labour and capital. Erection of a common tariff against non-member countries.
   ii) Both parts of this question are about the benefits of trade. One benefit is that consumers have greater choice when trade takes place. Another benefit is that trade allows a more efficient use of resources. We have seen that if countries specialize according to comparative advantages, then *all* countries can gain from trade. Go into some detail on this point.
   iii) There are several points that should be discussed in this section. They are summarized below.

   A common criticism of EU membership is that it has led to higher food prices because of the Common Agricultural Policy. This sets minimum guaranteed prices for agricultural goods, which are sometimes higher than they would be in a free market, the result being the familiar surpluses of 'wine lakes', 'butter mountains', etc.

   Another criticism is that consumer choice has been reduced because of the Common External Tariff which increases the price of imports from outside the EU. Higher taxation because of contributions to the EU budget might also have reduced consumers' disposable income.

   However, there are arguments *in favour* of membership which should be briefly considered:

   Removing tariff barriers between member countries increases the scope for international specialization and trade. This can lead to a more efficient allocation of resources and to a greater consumer choice.

   A larger market might enable firms to expand production and so gain economies of scale. This might lead to lower costs and therefore lower prices.

   Increased competition might lead to better products and lower prices.

TUTOR'S ANSWER TO Q.3

i) The use of tariffs is part of a policy of protection which is designed to reduce the number of imports entering a country. Tariffs raise the price of imports making them less attractive to home consumers. The reduction in imports should improve the country's balance of payments.

By removing tariffs and promoting free trade economies should benefit from the following. First, countries will specialize in the production of goods for which they have a comparative advantage. They will import other goods from countries which have a comparative advantage in their production. Second, free trade gives consumers more choice in a competitive market in which the quality of goods will probably improve. Third, as a result of specialization, output will rise for those goods being produced, enabling the benefits of economies of scale to be gained. It can be seen from the data given in the question that as the average level of tariffs has fallen over the years the volume of world trade has increased. This seems to support the view that free trade promotes employment and output in the world economy.

ii) A country may impose tariffs for the following reasons. By reducing the number of imports, domestic consumers are more likely to buy home-produced goods. This will preserve employment in the affected industries. In recent years, cheaper imports caused many people in the UK textile industry to lose their jobs. Sometimes a developing country may impose tariffs on imports from developed countries, partly because it could worsen their balance of payments and also because developing economies may wish to establish their own industries rather than rely on imports. Some countries impose tariffs in order to reduce imports and so correct balance of payments deficits, or as a retaliation against other countries which have themselves imposed import controls or engaged in 'unfair' trade practices. Some countries have to impose tariffs as a condition of membership of a customs union such as the European Union (EU).

iii) The fall in the UK's exchange rate led to lower export prices and higher import prices. This should lead to an improvement in the UK's balance of payments because demand for exports will rise and demand for imports will fall. The increased demand for exports should also lead to a rise in output and employment in the economy. Fewer imports should lead to a further benefit to home industries. However, a fall in the exchange rate will raise import prices, possibly leading to higher inflation. More expensive imported raw materials could trigger 'cost-push' inflation in the economy.

IDEAS FOR COURSEWORK

It is possible to investigate how a country's trade and trading partners have changed over the years. Data could be presented in a variety of ways and it might be possible to attempt some sort of explanation for the changing pattern of trade.

Information in newspapers such as *The Independent, Financial Times* and *The Times* can be used to monitor changes in the exchange rate for several currencies against sterling. By looking at how the **balance of trade** has changed for the UK with those countries it might be possible to suggest reasons why the value of sterling has changed.

Examine the UK's trade balance in recent years and compare it with other members of the European Union.

SOURCES OF INFORMATION

- *Annual Abstract of Statistics*, Central Statistical Office
- *Economic Trends*, Central Statistical Office
- *Monthly Digest of Statistics*, Central Statistical Office
- *UK Balance of Payments* (Pink Book), Central Statistical Office
- Newspapers, e.g. *Financial Times, The Times, Guardian, Daily Telegraph, The Independent*

MONEY & FINANCIAL INSTITUTIONS

GETTING STARTED

It is difficult to define money in a precise way. Economists simply say that '**money is as money does**'. In other words, anything which performs the **functions** of money, is money. In the course of history this has led to many different things acting as money including stones, shells, cattle and metal. The functions which money performs are discussed in the Tutor's answer to Question 1 at the end of this chapter.

In the modern world there are two things which function as money: notes and coin, which are sometimes referred to as **currency**, and **bank deposits**. It is easy to see that currency functions as money, but care must be taken when considering bank deposits. In particular it is important to realize that cheques are not money. They are simply the means of *transferring* a bank deposit from one person to another in payment for something. A cheque drawn on a bank account which contains insufficient funds to honour it might well be dishonoured (or 'bounced') by the bank. In these circumstances the cheque is worthless!

A term used in this chapter is **liquidity**. This is a term economists often use when considering financial assets. The more easily an asset can be turned into money the greater its liquidity. Another term used is **securities**. There are different types of securities but the ones we are concerned with in this chapter are simply **IOUs**. The Government is the main issuer of securities but commercial banks and local authorities also issue securities. These IOUs have to be repaid when they **mature**, i.e. reach the date printed on the security.

In this chapter, and elsewhere, you will come across the term **monetary policy**. Remember that this refers to changes in the *supply* of money and/or changes in the *price* of money. By 'price' of money we mean the rate of interest.

ESSENTIAL PRINCIPLES

Notes and coin are a far less important part of the money supply than bank deposits. Over 90 per cent of the money supply in the UK consists of bank deposits.

One important way in which bank deposits are created is when a customer opens an account and makes a deposit. In cases like this, or when existing customers add to their deposits, a bank acquires assets. On the other hand, when bank deposits are used to make purchases, a bank's assets fall. Now on any particular day a bank's assets might rise or they might fall, but *over time* assets have a tendency to rise. Even on days when assets fall they rarely fall significantly and any reduction in assets is quickly made up. This is very important because it means that only a fraction of the deposits lodged with a bank will be withdrawn on any particular day. The remainder can be lent to customers who wish to borrow. It is this process of lending which leads to the **creation of credit** by the banking system, or, as it is sometimes called, **the multiple expansion of bank deposits**.

THE CREATION OF CREDIT

When a bank grants a customer a loan it creates a bank deposit in that customer's name. This will be used to make purchases, almost certainly by writing a cheque against the bank deposit. This will be paid into somebody else's bank account and will appear as an increase in another bank's assets. This increase in the other bank's assets will be used to make a further loan. After being used to make purchases this will be re-deposited with yet another bank and will make possible still further lending. In this way, by expanding their loans, banks can **create credit**.

However, in the real world banks cannot create credit without limit. We have already seen that on any particular day a bank's assets might fall. In particular, banks must be prepared to meet demands for cash by their customers. This means they must keep part of their assets in the form of cash, or in assets that can quickly be turned into cash. Suppose that all banks in the economy maintain a ratio of 10 per cent between the amount of cash they hold and their total assets, and that they plan to maintain the same cash ratio in the future. In this case banks will lend 90 per cent of any increase in their assets.

To understand what this means let us consider a bank which receives an increase in assets in the form of a deposit of £100. The bank will keep £10 to maintain its cash ratio and lend out £90. When this is spent, it will be re-deposited with another bank (or perhaps even the same bank). Whichever bank receives the deposit of £90 will experience an increase in assets of £90. In order to maintain its cash ratio of 10 per cent it will lend £81, that is, 90 per cent of £90. This £81 will be re-deposited with another bank and again 90 per cent, or £72.9, will be lent.

You can see that each time money is lent and re-deposited it leads to another loan, but of a smaller amount. Because the amount the bank lends at each stage falls, the process of credit creation cannot go on indefinitely. In fact, credit can be created only as long as the ratio of cash to total deposits is greater than 10 per cent. This means that the banking system can create credit until the entire amount of the original £100 deposit represents 10 per cent of the total increase in deposits – in other words, when lending has increased by £900 which, including the original £100 cash deposit, means that total deposits have increased by £1000.

Now if we are given the cash ratio that banks intend to maintain, we can work out the **credit multiplier**. This is simply the number that an original increase in deposits must be multiplied by in order to obtain the final increase in bank deposits. The credit multiplier is given by the formula:

$$\text{credit multiplier} \quad = \quad \frac{1}{\text{cash ratio}}$$

In the example above, the cash ratio is 10 per cent and therefore the credit multiplier is $1 \div 0.1 = 10$. If we multiply the original increase in deposits of £100 by 10 we obtain the final increase in total deposits, which is £1000.

2 ❯ THE LONDON MONEY MARKET

The **London Money Market** is a market in short-term liquid assets. The main assets traded in this market are bills (securities which usually have a maturity of up to six months), although other securities with up to a year to maturity might be traded.

The securities traded on the London Money Market are basically IOUs which can be bought and sold; but who would want to buy an IOU? The answer is mainly institutions, such as commercial banks, which buy bills for less than their maturity value. For example, a commercial bank might buy for £950 000 a bill which matures in twelve months' time with a maturity value of £1m. If the bank holds this bill to maturity it collects £1m, and therefore earns a return of £50 000 for holding the bill.

The return to an institution for holding a bill is usually expressed as a **rate of discount**. This is easily calculated. In the example above the bank buys a bill for £950 000. It is therefore making a loan to the **drawee**, or **debtor**, of £950 000. In this case the rate of discount is:

$$\frac{£50\,000}{£950\,000} \times 100 = 5.26\%$$

Two of the most important bills which are traded in the London Money Market are Treasury bills and commercial bills of exchange.
● **Treasury bills:** These are bills issued by the Government with 91 days to maturity. They are issued weekly and are the means by which the Government finances its short-term borrowing.
● **Commercial bills of exchange:** These are bills issued by buyers of goods, usually with three to six months to maturity. Sellers of goods can sell or discount these bills of exchange in the London Money Market and obtain ready cash.

3 ❯ COMMERCIAL BANKS

The main functions of a **commercial bank** are to accept deposits and to make loans. They are often called profit-maximizing institutions because they exist to make a profit for their shareholders. They do this mainly by paying interest to attract deposits and charging a higher rate of interest on their loans. They participate in the London Money Market because they are prepared to borrow and lend (often by discounting securities) in the short term.

The most important commercial banks are known as **clearing banks** because they are members of the **London Clearing House**. This is simply a meeting place where the clearing banks settle their indebtedness to each other. Every day cheques are drawn on a deposit in one bank and paid into a different bank. Naturally, a great many of these will cancel each other out. Rather than adding them all together and insisting on payment, the banks simply swap bundles of cheques of specific sums drawn on each other's accounts and settle the difference. For example, if at the beginning of clearing Lloyds has cheques drawn against deposits in Barclays of £50m, and Barclays has cheques drawn against deposits in Lloyds of £55m, then at the end of clearing Lloyds will owe Barclays £5m.

This debt will be settled by Lloyds drawing a cheque on itself in favour of Barclays. The deposit against which this cheque is drawn is held at the Bank of England for this purpose. These deposits are called **operational deposits** and in this case the operational deposits of Lloyds will go down by £5m and this £5m will be transferred to Barclays' account at the Bank of England. Barclays' operational deposits will therefore rise by £5m.

All clearing banks (as well as many other institutions) must hold operational deposits at the Bank of England equal to at least $\frac{1}{2}$ per cent of their **eligible liabilities**. The main part of the commercial banks' eligible liabilities is their loans to customers. We shall see (below) that operational deposits play an important part in implementing the Government's **monetary policy**.

4 ❯ MERCHANT BANKS

Merchant banks were originally set up to finance trade and they still provide loans for this purpose. However, over the years they have acquired additional functions. One function they perform which is important in the London Money Market is *accepting* bills of exchange. This simply means the merchant bank guarantees payment on the bill if the drawee is unable to pay when the bill matures. This is important, because once a bill is accepted it is virtually risk-free and is therefore easy to sell in the money market.

DISCOUNT HOUSES

The **London Discount Market Association** consists of twelve **discount houses** which, as their name suggests, specialize in discounting securities. In practice they often discount newly issued securities and then sell these to the commercial banks as they approach maturity. (The commercial banks require such securities because they are highly liquid and can easily be converted into cash to meet a sudden increase in demand for cash by the public.)

Another important function of the discount houses is to provide the commercial banks with highly liquid assets. They do this by borrowing funds from the commercial banks which are repayable on demand. Such loans to the discount market are referred to as **call money** because the commercial banks can call for their immediate repayment.

The discount houses have a special relationship with the Bank of England. On the one hand the London Discount Market Association agrees collectively to buy up all of the Treasury bills issued weekly by the Government. They therefore guarantee to meet the Government's short-term borrowing requirements. On the other hand, if they are ever short of funds, the Bank of England will always lend to the discount houses. This is referred to as **lender of last resort**, because the discount houses will try to obtain funds elsewhere before borrowing from the Bank of England.

Again, we shall see on below that the discount houses are important in implementing the Government's monetary policy.

THE BANK OF ENGLAND

The Bank of England is the central bank of the UK. It has many functions, and these are listed briefly below.

- It is banker to the banks. We have seen that commercial banks and licensed deposit takers are obliged to maintain deposits at the Bank of England. These deposits are used to settle debts between the banks.
- It is the Government's bank and handles the Government's revenue and expenditure. Receipts from taxation are paid into the Government's account at the Bank of England and payments are made to various Government departments to meet their expenditures.
- It has responsibility for managing the **national debt**. The national debt is simply the value of securities issued by the Government but not yet redeemed. The Bank of England therefore arranges the issue of new securities, the repayment of maturing securities and the payment of interest to the holders of Government securities.
- It is the sole issuer of notes in England and Wales.
- It is the **lender of last resort** and, as explained earlier, will lend to the banking system.
- It acts in the foreign exchange market for the Government so as to influence the value of sterling on the international markets.
- It is responsible for implementing the Government's monetary policy.

THE MONEY SUPPLY

We have seen that the money supply of the UK consists mainly of bank deposits. In fact there are several definitions of the money supply. It is certainly no easy matter to define the money supply, and the different definitions exist because different assets have different degrees of liquidity. Some assets, such as cash, are much more liquid than others, such as **time deposits**. If we are concerned with the level of immediate spending potential in the economy, then we will consider only the most liquid assets. However, if we are concerned with potential spending over a period of time, such as a week, we will need to include some assets which are less liquid than others. Which definition of the money supply is appropriate therefore depends on the level of liquidity we are considering.

Some of the more important measures of the money supply in the UK are considered below. These measures of the money supply are sometimes referred to as the **monetary aggregates**.

● **M0:** This is sometimes referred to as the **monetary base** or **narrow money**. It consists of notes and coin in circulation with the public plus banks' **till money** (the amount of cash banks have on their premises) and banks' operational deposits at the Bank of England.

● **M4:** This is sometimes referred to as **broad money**. M4 includes M0 plus deposits in banks and building societies (see Table 15.1 and Figure 15.1)

	M0 NARROW MONEY	M4 BROAD MONEY
1987	15 665	304 096
1988	16 868	357 737
1989	17 825	425 481
1990	18 299	477 580
1991	18 854	504 402
1992	19 380	520 084
1993	20 529	546 571

Table 15.1

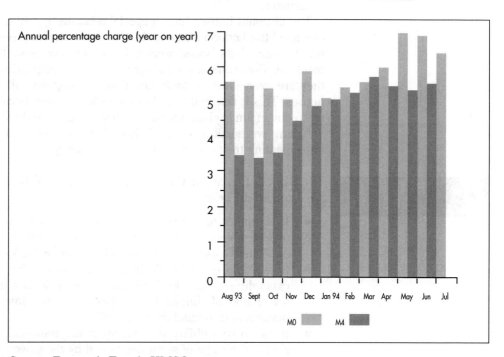

Figure 15.1 Percentage growth in M0 and M4, 1993 to 1994

Source: Economic Trends, HMSO

8 ▷ MONEY SUPPLY AND PRICE

One of the oldest known relationships in economics is that between changes in the money supply and changes in the price level. There is no doubt among economists that, *if all other things remain equal*, an increase in the money supply will cause an increase in the price level. When economists refer to a rise in the price level they simply mean that, on average, prices have increased. An increase in average prices is usually referred to as inflation. Thus, if all other things remain equal, changes in the money supply lead to changes in the rate of inflation.

The belief that changes in the money supply *cause* changes in the rate of inflation is associated particularly with those economists who are referred to as *monetarists*. Their views are expressed in the **quantity theory of money** which predicts that an increase in the money supply will lead to a roughly proportional increase in the price level. In other words, if the money supply grows by 5 per cent, the rate of inflation will be roughly 5 per cent.

Figure 15.2 shows the relationship between changes in the money supply and changes in the rate of inflation. There is no doubt that the rate of inflation and changes in the money supply are linked. However, there is no agreement among economists that a change in the money supply *always* causes a proportional change, or any other kind of change, in the price level. Some economists argue that a change in the price level can occur *independently* of a change in the money supply, and that only *after prices have increased* is there an increase in the money supply.

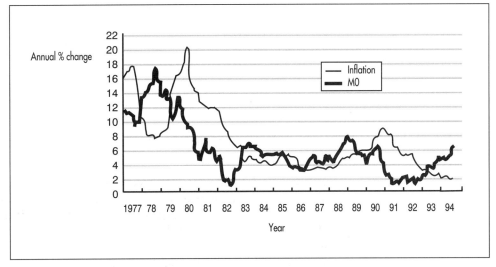

Figure 15.2 Money supply, M0 and inflation

Source: Bank of England, CSO

The reason for disagreement among economists on this issue is clear from Figure 15.2. At times it seems that a *large* increase in money supply in a year is linked to a *large* rise in prices, but at other times only a *small* rise in prices occurs. There is no simple answer to this and the debate among economists will continue for many years to come.

MEASURING CHANGES IN THE VALUE OF MONEY

When prices rise, the value of money falls. This must be so because when prices rise, a given amount of money will buy fewer goods and services. For example, if all prices in the economy double, a given amount of money will buy only half as much after prices have increased.

> A *rise* in the price level is a *fall* in the value of money

But how do we *measure* changes in the price level? After all, we never have a situation where all prices in the economy double. In fact, we rarely have a situation when all prices in the economy move in the same direction! Even during periods when the rate of inflation is rising, the prices of some goods will be falling. For example, during the summer months the prices of many fruits and vegetables fall.

In practice economists use a technique known as **index numbers** to measure changes in the price level. This simply measures changes in the average price of a collection, or **basket**, of goods. The average price is expressed as a percentage and this enables us to measure the percentage change in prices over some period of time.

However, it would be very misleading if we took a simple average of price changes, because changes in the prices of some goods and services are far more important to most people than changes in the prices of other goods and services. Changes in the prices of those goods which are bought frequently, such as foodstuffs, are far more important to most people than changes in the price of household consumer durables, such as refrigerators, which are bought infrequently.

Because of this, each item in the basket of goods is **weighted** according to its importance to the 'average consumer'. In the first year the index is started, that is, the **base year**, the price of each item in the index is given the value 100. In subsequent years changes in the price of an item are measured as percentage changes in the price that existed in the base year. To work out a weighted index number for each item we simply multiply the index number by the weight. The weighted index number of each item is then added across all the items and the result is divided by the sum of the weights to give an index of prices.

This sounds complicated but in fact is quite easy, as the example below illustrates. For simplicity we consider a basket of only three goods, A, B and C. We assume the weights of these goods are 4, 1 and 5 respectively. Year 1 is the base year.

Good	Weight	Year 1 Price	Index	Weighted Index	Year 2 Price	Weighted Index	Index
A	4	£2.00	100	400	£2.50	125	500
B	1	£5.00	100	100	£4.00	80	80
C	5	£1.00	100	500	£1.50	150	750
	10			1000			1330

Price index in year 1 = 1000/10 = 100   Price index in year 2 = 1330/10 = 133

Between year 1 and year 2 the weighted index of prices has increased by 33 per cent. This is the technique used to measure changes in the rate of inflation. In the UK the main index used for this purpose is the **retail price index (RPI)** (see Figure 15.3). (Question 2 on p. 166 provides you with an opportunity to calculate an index number for yourself.)

Quite apart from the calculation, there are a number of problems with using index numbers. These problems are also discussed in the 'Tutor's answer to Q. 2' on pp. 168–9. They are very important and you should pay careful attention to them. Because of these problems, index numbers should be interpreted with a certain amount of caution.

Figure 15.3 Inflation: a 20-year view

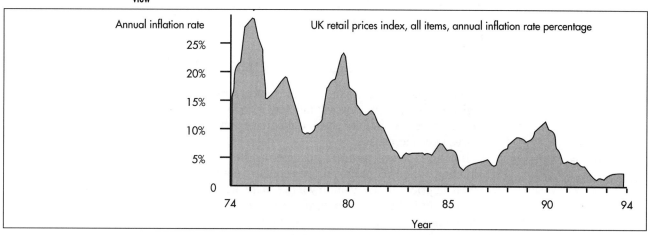

Source: Department of Employment

9 ▷ THE CAUSES OF INFLATION

Economists identify two types of inflation: **cost** (or **cost-push) inflation** and **demand** (or **demand-pull) inflation**. These types of inflation have different causes.

COST INFLATION

As its name suggests, **cost inflation** is caused by rising costs. In other words, prices rise because costs of production rise. We have seen in Chapter 7 how an increase in costs shifts the individual firm's supply curve upwards and leads to an increase in price. For the economy as a whole, when there is a *general* increase in costs there will be a *general* increase in prices.

Cost-push and demand-pull are terms often used

There are many reasons why costs might rise, but the two that have attracted most attention in the UK are rising imported raw materials costs and rising labour costs. The UK imports vast amounts of raw materials and when sterling depreciates on the foreign exchange market the cost of these imported raw materials rises. These higher costs lead to higher final prices for the goods that use these raw materials in their production.

Rising labour costs are caused by wage increases which are greater than productivity increases. These also will push up costs of production. This is especially important in industries which are labour-intensive. For example, if labour costs in a particular industry account for 70 per cent of total costs, an increase in wages of 10 per cent (assuming all other things remain equal) will lead to an increase in total costs of $10 \times 0.7 = 7$ per cent. If, on the other hand, labour costs account for only 15 per cent of total costs, the same increase in wages of 10 per cent (again assuming all other things remain equal) will lead to an increase in total costs of only $10 \times 0.15 = 1.5$ per cent.

It is often argued that cost inflation is particularly likely when there is full employment in the economy. In these circumstances there will be shortages of labour generally but, even more important, acute shortages in certain types of skilled labour. Because of this, organized trade unions are in a strong bargaining position and can bid up wages above increases in productivity.

This explanation of how inflation is caused no longer commands the attention it once did. This is partly because of developments in economic theory, especially the growing influence of the monetarists, whose views on inflation are discussed below. However, another reason is that in more recent years there have been higher levels of unemployment in the UK economy than used to be the case.

DEMAND INFLATION

As its name suggests, **demand inflation** is caused by rising demand. We have seen in Chapter 7 how an increase in demand for a single product leads to an increase in the price of that product. Now if there is a *general* increase in demand for all products in the economy, prices in *general* will tend to rise.

Traditionally, economists have argued that demand inflation is much more likely when there is full employment in the economy. The reason for this is that when resources are fully employed, it is difficult or even impossible to increase production. In other words, supply is inelastic. In these circumstances a general increase in demand will lead to a general increase in prices.

There are several factors that might cause an increase in demand. One possible cause is a depreciation of the exchange rate. This will increase the domestic price of imports and reduce the foreign price of exports. If, as a consequence, domestic residents buy fewer imports and turn to domestic substitutes, while foreigners buy more exports because of their lower price, demand in the domestic economy will rise. If the economy is already at full employment, it will be impossible to increase output and prices will be pulled upwards.

Another possible cause is a reduction in taxation. If taxes on incomes, that is, direct taxes, are reduced, there will be an increase in **disposable income**. As disposable income rises, the demand for most goods and services will rise. A reduction in indirect taxes, that is, taxes on goods and services such as VAT, will mean that a given amount of income will now buy a greater volume of goods and services. Here again there will be an increase in demand for most goods and services.

THE MONETARIST VIEW OF INFLATION

Monetarism is a term used to describe the views of those economists who believe that the only cause of inflation is an increase in the money supply. Their argument is simple. When the money supply increases, the extra money must be held by someone. It will be held by people receiving increased wages, by firms receiving increased profits, by individuals receiving increased pensions and so on. Now, we know that when people receive more money they will increase their spending. Because of this, an increase in the money supply will lead to an increase in spending on most goods and services. In other words, there will be an increase in demand for most goods and services.

The monetarists also believe that in the *long run* the economy will operate at full employment. This means that it will be impossible to increase supply other than by increases in productivity. Remember that when productivity increases, resources are used more efficiently and it is therefore possible to *increase output* by using the *same resources*. However, the monetarists believe that productivity grows only slowly over time, so that when resources are fully employed, output cannot be increased. Quite simply, more resources are required to increase output and these are not available when there is full employment. Because output cannot be increased, the monetarists argue that an increase in the money supply will always lead to an increase in prices in the long run.

Now, a great deal of this aspect of monetarist analysis would be accepted by a number of economists, many of whom would not claim to be monetarist. A major difference between monetarists and other economists is that monetarists claim that an increase in the money supply is the *only* cause of inflation. They argue that if costs in one industry rise, for example because of a rise in wages, and this leads to higher prices in that industry, then unless the money supply increases so that people can pay these higher prices, there will be *no* long-term rise in prices. This is because the quantity demanded of the higher-priced products will fall, together with a fall in demand for other products. This will happen because if the money supply is fixed, people's incomes will be fixed and therefore the *total level of spending* in the economy will be fixed. Greater spending on one product must mean lower spending on another. As demand for other products falls, the prices of these will also fall. Therefore, the **average price level** will be unchanged. In other words, there will be no inflation.

10 **CONSEQUENCES OF INFLATION**

Inflation is usually taken to mean a fall in the value of money. Therefore, to a certain extent, the effects of inflation depend on how rapidly the value of money falls. With this in mind we can identify some of the general consequences of inflation.

● **People on fixed incomes suffer:**   Pensioners and others on incomes that do *not* keep pace with inflation will find the real purchasing power of their incomes falling. Many pensions and benefits now rise *automatically* with inflation to prevent this happening.

● **Balance of payment problems:**   If prices of goods and services in the UK rise *faster* than those of our trading partners, then UK exports will become less competitive in prices. On the other hand, imports from abroad will become more attractive than the now more expensive home goods. So exports may fall in value, and imports rise in value, so that the **current account** of the balance of payments deteriorates.

● **Savings may be discouraged:**   With inflation, the future purchasing power of money saved may be reduced. The rate of interest savers receive is often *lower than* the rate of inflation. This may discourage saving, so that there is less money available for investment in the economy.

● **Debtors gain:**   People who *owe* money may benefit from inflation. The *real* value of the amount they will have to repay in the future will be falling.

TYPICAL EXAM QUESTIONS

1 Increased use of bank accounts means less need for cash.

i)   a) What is meant by the term 'money'?   [2]
     b) Describe and distinguish the main forms of money in the UK.   [6]
ii) Describe and explain the functions of money.   [8]
iii) What factors may affect the amount of money saved and borrowed in the UK economy?   [8]

WJEC, 1994

2 You are given the following information about the expenditure of a typical household in the same week of two different years.

Good	Year 1 Price	Year 1 Quantity bought	Year 2 Price	Year 2 Quantity bought
A	£1.00	3	£1.50	3
B	£2.40	5	£2.70	5
C	£4.00	2	£3.00	2
D	£1.60	3	£2.00	3
E	£2.20	1	£1.76	1

i)   Calculate an index of prices for this household.
ii) What are the problems with using an index such as this to estimate the rate of inflation?
iii) Why is it necessary to change periodically the weights of index numbers?

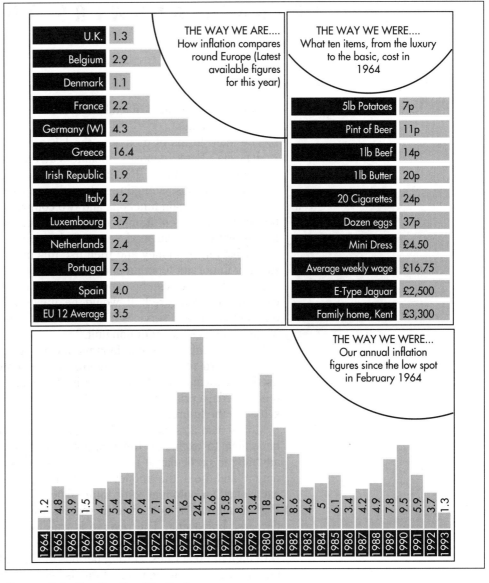

Source: Solo Syndication Limited

3 i) Which European Union (EU) countries have an inflation rate below the EU average? [2]

ii) In which year was the UK inflation rate a) lowest, b) highest? [2]

iii) a) What was the average weekly wage in 1964? [1]

   b) Why did people live quite well on this wage in 1964 but would not be able to survive on it in 1994? [2]

iv) The UK has experienced inflation every year since 1964. Explain *two* causes of inflation. [4]

v) Using the information on inflation rates in EU countries explain why Greece and Portugal may have balance of payments deficits with other EU members. [4]

vi) Explain the meaning of the phrase *'the inflation rate is falling but prices are still rising'*. [4]

WJEC, 1994

TUTOR'S ANSWERS TO Q.1 AND Q.2

1 i) a) Money, as a medium of exchange, is anything which is accepted as a means of settling a debt.

b) The main forms of money in the UK are notes and coin (cash) and bank deposits. Bank deposits include current and deposit accounts at the commercial banks. Building society accounts and National Savings accounts are also sometimes classed as money.

ii) Money has two main functions and two comparatively minor functions. One of the main functions of money is that it is a medium of exchange. This simply means that goods and services are exchanged for money. A person can sell his or her labour for money and then use this money to buy goods and services. Another important function of money is that it provides a measure of value. All goods and services can be expressed in money values and their relative values can then be compared. It would be impossible to compare the values of different goods and services if they were not expressed in some common unit. Money provides that common unit.

In performing these functions money also performs other functions. It acts as a standard of deferred payments. This simply means that money can be used as a means of settling debts in the future as well as in the present. In other words, a price can be agreed for something now, but the account can be settled in the future.

Money also acts as a store of value. Suppliers of goods and services might be willing to exchange their output, but might not wish to exchange it for anything in particular at present. Because of money, individuals can sell their output and hold the money obtained as a store of value which can be exchanged for output at some future date.

iii) Higher interest rates tend to increase saving, making it more attractive, and decrease borrowing. The reverse is true for low interest rates. This may be distorted by inflation, because high inflation can make saving unattractive even with high interest rates. During periods of high inflation, savings will lose their purchasing power if the interest rate is below the inflation rate.

During periods of depression in an economy, people may be less inclined to borrow and instead build up their savings, fearful of their job security. If taxation on savings falls this may attract more savers. This was the result of the creation of Tax Exempt Special Savings Accounts (TESSAs) a few years ago. As incomes and living standards rise in an economy people may save a bigger proportion of their incomes, and also feel confident enough to borrow more, for instance by taking out higher mortages for house purchases.

2 i) In this case the weight is given by the quantity bought. Thus we have:

Weighted index in year 1 = 1400/14 = 100

Weighted index in year 2 = 1617.5/14 = 115.5

ii) There are many reasons why the RPI might not reflect the rate of inflation that any individual has experienced. Pensioners and single parent families have a different index for this reason. There are also likely to be regional differences, such as between London and some rural areas, and differences in the nature of the retail outlets from which goods are bought by different individuals. Easy access to a supermarket will tend to lower the price of certain items. Taking an average bundle of goods will inevitably produce a result which is not strictly accurate for any particular individual or family. Nevertheless, we must remember that the RPI is computed in the same way each month and therefore it is likely to measure the trend of inflation for any particular group very accurately.

iii) It is periodically necessary to change the weights of the different goods in the RPI to take account of changes in consumer tastes and income. Over time, some goods become less important to households. Other goods not available at the time the index was first constructed will also change the pattern of consumer spending. Additionally, shopping habits will change. The trend towards supermarkets has changed the pattern of consumer spending and it has been necessary to change the weights accordingly.

| Good | Year 1 | | | | Year 2 | | | |
	Price	Quantity bought	Index no	Weighted index no	Price	Quantity bought	Index no	Weighted index no
A	£1.00	3	100	300	£1.50	3	150	450
B	£2.40	5	100	500	£2.70	5	112.5	562.5
C	£4.00	2	100	200	£3.00	2	75	150
D	£1.60	3	100	300	£2.00	3	125	375
E	£2.20	1	100	100	£1.76	1	80	80

STUDENT'S ANSWER TO Q.3 WITH EXAMINER COMMENTS

(i) UK (1.3), Belgium (2.9), Denmark (1.1), France (2.2), Irish Rep. (1.9), Netherlands (2.4).

(ii) (a) 1964

(b) 1975

(iii) (a) £16.75

(b) Inflation rates were very low in 1964. From 1964 inflation will mean the purchasing power of the money in 1964 is not the same as in 1994 as the money will have decreasing in value.

(iv) 1. Demand pull inflation – If demand exceeds supply then this will push the price up. E.G. if the amount of blazers for a shop supplied were 300 and the demand for them was 600 this would push the price up.

2. Cost push inflation – If the cost of production increases for a product then this will also push the price up. E.G. if raw materials increased in price.

(v) Greece and portugal have high inflation rates, meaning their purchasing power if less than that of another country with low inflation rates. When Greece + portugal buy imports they may find it is more expensive and when exporting many countries are not going to buy at their high prices which they have to charge to cover their costs. As such things as raw materials are more expensive, this is why their products are high in price.

(vi) Prices are rising still but not as much.

66 Imports from other countries will appear cheaper! 99

66 It is possible for prices to be rising at a decreasing rate, i.e inflation may be 10% in year 1 and 5% in year 2 99

IDEAS FOR COURSEWORK

List a range of items in your home, some of which are clearly money, some 'near' to being money, and some of which have little to do with money. For each item, consider the *features* which help/hinder its use as a unit of money.

From local branches of a major bank, find out about the services it offers. Compare these with those offered by a local building society. How similar/different are they? You could use this as a basis for talking about changes in the UK financial system, i.e. how the commercial banks and the building societies have begun to compete more directly with one another in recent years.

You could construct a questionnaire asking people about the prices and quantities of different goods and services they buy in a typical week. Are the *proportions* of income spent on items such as food, drink, tobacco, heat, etc. similar to the 'weights' assumed for people in general in the retail price index? You could do this for a specific group of people, e.g. pensioners, and see if there is any difference. This could be a useful basis for considering the use of a price index in measuring changes in people's cost of living.

SOURCES OF INFORMATION

- *Family Expenditure Survey*, HMSO
- *Annual Abstract of Statistics*, Central Statistical Office
- *Economic Trends*, Central Statistical Office
- *Social Trends*, Central Statistical Office

R E V I E W   S H E E T

1   What are the missing words in the following sentence? When one country can produce more of a good than another country when they both use the same amount of resources, it is said to have an _____ _____ in the production of that good.

2   Using the same amount of resources, two countries, A and B, can produce the following outputs:

	Number of cars		Tonnes of wheat
Country A	10	or	18
Country B	8	or	16

   i)   In the production of which good(s) does country A have an absolute advantage?

   _____

   _____

   ii) In the production of which good does country A have a comparative advantage?

   _____

   _____

   iii) In the production of which good does country B have a comparative advantage?

   _____

   _____

   iv) Will both countries gain from trade if the terms of trade are

        a) 1 car = 1.9 tonnes of wheat

   _____

   _____

        b) 1 car = 1.7 tonnes of wheat

   _____

   _____

        c) 1 car = 1.5 tonnes of wheat?

   _____

   _____

   Explain your answer in each case.

   _____

   _____

3   In which of the following circumstances will a country's terms of trade **improve**? Explain your answer in each case.

   i)   Export prices rise and import prices fall.

   _____

   _____

   ii) Export prices rise by *more* than import prices rise.

   _____

   _____

   iii) Export prices fall by *more* than import prices fall.

   _____

   _____

4 You are given the following information on the prices of a country's exports and imports in different years. Complete the following by obtaining the terms of trade for each year.

Year	Index of export prices	Index of import prices	Terms of trade index
1	100	100	—
2	105	108	—
3	110	111	—
4	116	113	—
5	118	117	—

In which years did the terms of trade move
i) favourably
ii) unfavourably?

5 The following is a list in random order of various items in the balance of payments of a country:

	£m
Investment and other capital flows overseas	–250
Exports	95
Invisible imports	–45
Change in reserves	–20
Imports	?
Balancing item	10
Investment and other capital flows from abroad	225
Invisible exports	130

i) What is the value of this country's imports of goods?

_____

ii) What is the value of the balance of trade for this country?

_____

iii) What is the value of the current balance for this country?

_____

iv) Does this country have a surplus or deficit in its balance of payments?

_____

v) What is the size of the balance of payments surplus or deficit?

_____

6 What happens to import prices and export prices when the foreign exchange rate of a country's currency
i) appreciates

_____
_____

ii) depreciates?

_____
_____

7 Name some items included in the invisible account of the UK's balance of payments.

_____
_____

8 Distinguish a 'quota' from a 'tariff'.

_____
_____

9 What is included in the balancing item on the UK's balance of payments?

_____
_____

10 What is the major objective of the WTO/GATT?

_____

_____

11 Over the centuries a wide variety of assets have functioned as money. What qualities must an asset possess to function as money? Can you find some assets in your own home that could
(i) function as money

_____

_____

(ii) never function as money?

_____

_____

12 What is meant by the term 'liquidity' and what is the most liquid asset of all?

_____

_____

13 What is the relationship between the liquidity of an asset and its profitability?

_____

_____

14 List the following assets in ascending order of liquidity, that is, most liquid first: a postal order, a five-pound note, shares in ICI, a Treasury bill.

_____

_____

15 If all banks in an economy maintain a ratio of 12½ per cent cash to total deposits, what is the value of the money supply multiplier?

_____

_____

16 What do
(i) accepting houses accept

_____

_____

(ii) clearing banks clear

_____

_____

(iii) discount houses discount?

_____

_____

17 If a Treasury bill with a maturity value of £250 000 is discounted for £200 000, what is the discount rate?

18 This question is based on the following list of assets:
banks' till money
Treasury bills
cash in circulation with the public
private sector sterling sight deposits
operational deposits at the Bank of England
private sector sterling time bank deposits
private sector holdings of sterling bank certificates of deposit.

i) Which one of these is included in all definitions of the money supply except M0?

_____

_____

ii) Which of these assets is included in M0 but in no other definition of the money supply?

_____

_____

iii) Which of these assets is not included in M0 or M4?

_____
_____
_____

19 Why is the 'basket of goods' used to calculate the RPI weighted?

_____
_____
_____

20 Using the following information, calculate how an index of prices changed between years 1 and 2.

Good	Weight	Year 1 Price	Year 2 Price
A	25	£1.50	£2.25
B	15	£2.00	£1.75
C	40	£5.00	£6.00
D	20	£1.00	£1.10

_____
_____
_____
_____
_____

PUBLIC REVENUE, EXPENDITURE & POLICY

GETTING STARTED

Public revenue and expenditure involve the public sector, that is, central government, local authorities and public corporations. In this chapter we look at how the public sector raises revenue and spends funds.

The major source of government revenue is taxation. Of course, if there were no expenditure there would be no need to raise revenue. This does not, however, mean that there would be no taxation. As we shall see, the Government might wish to levy taxes for particular purposes rather than simply to raise revenue.

There are also a number of reasons why the Government might wish to spend money.
● **Provision of goods and services:** The state provides certain public goods and certain merit goods (see pp. 19–20).
● **Redistribution of income:** There are many ways in which the state redistributes income through its expenditure. In particular it provides **supplementary benefits** to low-income families, together with many other allowances.
● **Industrial policy:** The Government provides grants to influence the location of firms and to finance research and development. It also provides funds to encourage training for school-leavers and the unemployed.
● **Control of the economy:** Central government has certain economic aims, and to achieve these it is involved in expenditure. For instance, it might wish to inject money into the economy in times of slump (remember the circular flow analysis). The use of government spending (injection) and taxation (leakage) to influence the level of national income is called **fiscal policy**.

THE GOVERNMENT'S EXPENDITURE PLANS

THE BUDGET

THE PSBR

THE NATIONAL DEBT

DIRECT TAXATION

INDIRECT TAXATION

DIRECT VERSUS INDIRECT TAXES

LOCAL AUTHORITY FINANCE

PUBLIC POLICY

ESSENTIAL PRINCIPLES

Each autumn the Chancellor of the Exchequer (usually referred to simply as the Chancellor) presents **The Budgets** to Parliament. On this occasion the Chancellor reviews the performance of the economy as a whole, and outlines his or her **expenditure** and **taxation** plans for the coming financial year. This runs from 1 April to 31 March. The expenditure and taxation plans for the financial year 1995–96 are set out in Figure 16.1. We shall return to this figure later when discussing **revenue**.

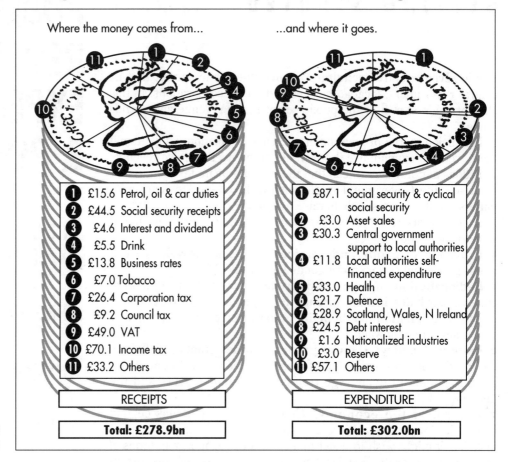

Figure 16.1 Balancing the books
1995-96 (£bn)

Source: Financial Times, November 1994

The Budget is the occasion when the Chancellor outlines his or her plans for raising the revenue with which to finance the expenditure plans. The main source of revenue is, of course, taxation. There are two types of taxation: **direct** and **indirect**. Usually, government expenditure (G) exceeds government revenue (T) and we call this a budget deficit. From figure 16.1 you can see that the Government will have a budget deficit in 1995–96. Unusually, in the late 1980s, the Government had a budget surplus, when government expenditure was less than taxation revenue. Although a budget deficit is the , the present Government plans to balance the budget (G = T) by 1998–99.

IMPORTANCE OF BUDGET DEFICITS AND SURPLUSES

The size of the budget deficit or surplus is very important. In terms of our discussion of the circular flow of income in Chapter 13, we can see that one effect of a **budget deficit** (G>T) is to increase **net injections** into the circular flow of income. If all other things were to remain equal, this would lead to an increase in national income. On the other hand, a **budget surplus** (G<T) would lead to **net withdrawals** from the circular flow and, other things remaining equal, a tendency for national income to fall.

However, it is the effect of the budget on the **money supply** which has been the focus of attention in recent years. We have already seen that an increase in the money supply is important because of its effect on inflation. But what is the connection between the budget and the money supply? If the Government has a budget deficit, that is, expenditure is greater than revenue, then it must *borrow* that part of its expenditure not covered by revenue. It is the amount the Government borrows, and more importantly from whom it borrows, that affects the money supply.

Remember that when the Government borrows it issues securities. If these are bought by banks and other financial institutions, as some of them inevitably will be, there will be an increase in *bank deposits* and therefore an increase in the money supply. When banks or other financial institutions buy government securities, they pay for these by running down their operational deposits at the Bank of England. These deposits are not included in most definitions of the money supply and therefore the money supply is not affected by this. However, the Government now has additional bank deposits which it will use to finance its expenditures. When the Government spends this money it will eventually flow back into the banking system. When this happens the banks will experience an increase in deposits and they will therefore increase their lending. It is this which causes an increase in the money supply.

Of course, with the present budget surplus the opposite can now occur. That is, the money supply can be reduced below the level it would otherwise be, due to less need for government borrowing.

3 ▷ THE PSBR

The **PSBR**, or the **public-sector borrowing requirement**, is the amount the whole of the public sector needs to borrow to finance its expenditure plans in the coming financial year. It therefore consists of borrowing by central government, by local authorities and by public corporations. The planned PSBR for 1995–96 is £23.1 bn. Of course, with a budget surplus, the PSBR is negative in a particular year. This means that the Government can use that year's surplus to pay back some of the borrowing made in previous years (see Figure 16.2).

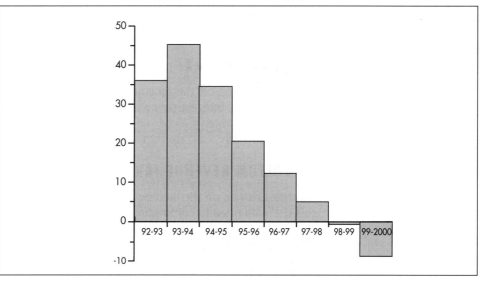

Figure 16.2 Public sector borrowing requirement (£bn)

Source: Economics Today (Courtesy of Anforme Ltd.).

4 ▷ THE NATIONAL DEBT

The **national debt** is the total amount of borrowing undertaken by central government which has not yet been repaid. In other words, it is the sum of all outstanding central government debt. At one time the size of the national debt gave great cause for concern, because it was thought that the bigger the debt, the greater the problem of repayment. In addition, the bigger the debt, the greater the burden of interest payments to holders of the national debt. It was thought that as the size of the national debt increased, higher taxes would have to be levied for both of these reasons.

This idea no longer gives such cause for concern. It is now realized that for the most part, the national debt is a debt which the nation owes to itself. When the national debt increases, the Government borrows mainly from citizens of the UK. When interest is paid to holders of the debt, or the debt is repaid, those who receive the money are mainly residents of the UK. Therefore, when government securities are held by domestic residents, the *community as a whole* is neither better off nor worse off.

However, about 10 per cent of the national debt is held by overseas residents. That part of the national debt held overseas is called the **external debt**. The size of this part of the national debt still gives cause for concern. When government securities are sold abroad and interest is paid on these, people overseas receive sterling. This flow of money out of the country makes the balance of payments deteriorate.

Despite these considerations the important question is what central government *does* with the money it has borrowed. When the funds are invested in capital this will enable the nation to increase the amount of output it can produce. This in turn will make it easier to pay off previous debts or to pay the interest on them.

As can be seen from Figure 16.1, **income tax** and **national insurance** contributions (social security receipts) account for almost £115bn of government revenue. These are called **direct** taxes and are collected by the Department of Inland Revenue. They are called *direct* taxes because the person who pays the tax cannot pass on the burden to somebody else. The following are the most important direct taxes collected in the UK.

INCOME TAX

This tax is collected on all incomes received by private individuals after certain allowances are made. As can be seen from Figure 16.1, income tax is the most important of all taxes in terms of the amount raised. In 1995–96 over £70 bn was raised through income tax.

Not all income is taxed. Everyone with an income has a **non-taxable allowance** which is determined by many factors, such as whether a person is married or not. This allowance is deducted from **gross** income to leave **taxable** income. It is this amount on which tax is levied.

Income tax is a **progressive** tax. This means that as income rises the *proportion* of income paid in taxation rises. In the UK, the lowest rate of income tax is 20 per cent and the highest is 40 per cent.

CORPORATION TAX

This tax is levied on the income of companies after deductions have been made for operating costs, interest payments and so on. It is a **proportional** tax which is levied at the constant rate of 33 per cent (25 per cent for 'small' companies). In the tax year 1995–96, £26.4bN was raised through corporation tax (see Figure 16.1).

PETROLEUM REVENUE TAX

This tax is levied on the income from exploiting North Sea oil and gas. Companies pay this tax *in addition* to corporation tax.

INHERITANCE TAX

This tax is levied on the value of wealth transferred from one person to another either at death or during a lifetime. The rate of tax is 40 per cent.

CAPITAL GAINS TAX

This tax is levied on the increase in value of certain assets when they are sold compared with their value when they were bought. For example, any increase in the value of shares at the time of sale is subject to capital gains tax. In the UK this is a **progressive** tax.

Indirect taxes are collected by the Customs and Excise Department. These taxes fall mainly on expenditures, that is, they are paid when money is spent on goods and services. They are known as **indirect** taxes because it is possible for the person who pays the tax to pass the burden of the tax on to someone else.

VALUE ADDED TAX (VAT)

This is the most important indirect tax levied in the UK in terms of revenue raised. As Figure 16.1 shows, in 1995–96, £49.0 bn was raised in revenue from VAT. In the UK, VAT is a **proportional** tax and is levied at the rate of 17½ per cent, although some goods such as fuel are taxed at 8 per cent. As its name suggests VAT is a tax levied on the *value added* at each stage of production. A simple example is set out in Table 16.1. We assume here that VAT is levied at each stage at 10 per cent.

Notice that 10 per cent of the value added at each stage is paid to the Customs and Excise Department and that the retailer's selling price is the price which the consumer pays. In this example it is clear that the entire burden of VAT is passed on to the consumer.

In practice, the burden of VAT might not be passed on in full to the final consumer. Figure 16.3 shows that in the case of normal supply and demand curves, part of the tax is borne by the producer and part is borne by the consumer. In other words, the price has *not* risen by the full amount of the tax. Can you see that the *more elastic* (flatter) the demand curve, the *smaller* the proportion of tax borne by the consumer. In other words the *smaller* the price rise.

In practice, VAT is not levied on all goods and services. In some cases output is *exempt*. This means that for the stage of production where the exemption is granted, no VAT is levied on the value added at that stage. However, VAT is levied on all other stages where an exemption has not been granted. Other products, such as medicines, exports, books and children's clothing, are **zero rated**. This means that no VAT is levied at all.

SUPPLIER	BUYING PRICE £	VALUE ADDED £	SELLING PRICE £	PAYMENT TO CUSTOMS AND EXCISE £
Primary producer	–	50	50	5
Manufacturer	50	100	150	10
Wholesaler	150	40	190	4
Retailer	190	60	250	6
Total				25

Table 16.1

Figure 16.3

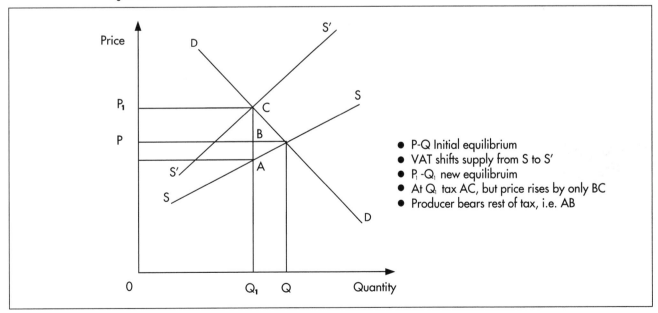

- P-Q Initial equilibrium
- VAT shifts supply from S to S'
- P₁-Q₁ new equilibruim
- At Q₁ tax AC, but price rises by only BC
- Producer bears rest of tax, i.e. AB

7 ▷ DIRECT VERSUS INDIRECT TAXES

The present Government has frequently announced its intention to reduce the burden of direct taxation, and in particular the burden of income tax. There are several reasons for this but the most important is that it is thought that an increase in direct taxes affects **incentives** to a far greater extent than an equivalent increase in indirect taxes. Indeed, this was a major reason behind the Government cutting income tax rates in the 1980s.

Various kinds of incentive are thought to be reduced by relatively high rates of direct taxation.

INCENTIVE TO WORK

It is thought that relatively high rates of income tax reduce the incentive for many unemployed people to accept offers of employment. After payment of income tax, national insurance contributions and the additional cost (bus fares etc.) of going to work, many people are not better off financially in work than out of work. It is also possible that relatively high rates of income tax reduce the incentive for workers to move to different parts of the country to accept employment.

Economists refer to this as the **unemployment trap**. By reducing income tax it is thought that many people will be encouraged to accept work. The reduction of income tax is therefore an important part of the present Government's policy to reduce unemployment.

INCENTIVE TO INCREASE PRODUCTIVITY

It has been argued that workers may make less attempt to increase productivity because the after-tax earnings from doing so do not merit the increased effort. If this is true, higher taxation is responsible for reducing the growth of living standards. We have seen that a nation's standard of living depends on the amount produced per head. Anything which discourages production therefore hampers the growth of living standards. It is therefore argued that lower rates of income tax will encourage production and improve living standards.

INCENTIVE TO INVEST

It has been suggested that relatively high rates of tax on company profits, by reducing the amount available for distribution as dividends, might discourage individuals from investing in companies by buying their shares. Again, if true, this will restrict productivity. Investment in new plant and machinery is one of the most important sources of higher productivity, but this will depend on the company being able to raise finance. One of the cheapest ways of doing this is by issuing new shares to the public.

INCENTIVE TO DECLARE INCOME

One effect of relatively high rates of income tax is to encourage the growth of the *black* or *hidden economy*. This is simply those activities which generate taxable incomes, but which are untaxed because they are not declared to the authorities. If lower rates of taxation persuade individuals to declare these transactions on their tax returns, this will partly offset any financial loss from lower rates of taxation.

Questions 1, 3 and 4, and their respective answers give more detail on taxes, and the direct versus indirect issue.

Local authorities obtain income in a variety of ways.

GRANTS

Central government provides certain grants. Some are allocated for particular purposes, such as financing the police service. However, by far the largest grant is the **revenue support grant**, which the local authorities can spend as they see fit.

RENTS AND CHARGES

The most important item here is rents from council housing. However, other sources of income include charges for entry into certain municipal undertakings, such as swimming pools.

COUNCIL TAX

The **council tax** is set by local councils to help pay for local services. There is one bill per dwelling, and it is based on the relative value of each property to others in the local area. The value of each home has been assessed by the Valuation Office Agency (part of the Inland Revenue). Each home has been placed on a **valuation list** in one of eight council tax *valuation bands*.

In the example below, a district council's basic charge is based on the assumption that two people live in a house valued between £68 000 and £88 000. The band a house is placed in will determine what percentage of that basic charge each household is expected to pay.

Occupants of a house in Band C – valued between £52 000 and £68 000 – would pay 89 per cent of that basic charge, while a house in Band H – valued in excess of £320 000 – would pay double the basic charge (see Table 16.2). As the basic charge is based on two people living in a house, if more than two people liable to pay the tax live in a house, it will be up to the person to whom the bill is sent to arrange payment.

Table 16.2

BAND	VALUE	RELATIVE PAYMENT %
A	up to £40 000	67
B	up to £52 000	78
C	up to £68 000	89
D	up to £88 000	100
E	up to £120 000	122
F	up to £160 000	144
G	up to £320 000	167
H	over £320 000	200

If, in the above example, the council's basic charge is £553 then the house in Band D will pay this amount. A house in Band A will pay 67 per cent of this figure, i.e. £369, and a house in band H will pay 200 per cent of £553 which is £1106. The basic charge is fixed once local councils have received from central government their **standard spending assessments**, from which are assessed their **revenue support grants (RSGs)**. Once councils have received their RSGs, they can assess the basic council tax for their authority. A separate system of local taxation on business properties is levied through **business rates**.

9 ▷ PUBLIC POLICY

In various parts of this book we have looked at a whole range of **policy objectives**, and ways in which governments try to meet these objectives. It will be helpful here to review the main points and to take some a little further.

TARGETS

The main objectives of the Government are often called **targets**. We can list some obvious ones.

- low inflation (stable prices)
- high employment (low unemployment)
- high growth (increase in national income)
- balance of payments equilibrium

Of course, we could add others, such as a balance of opportunities between regions, between different sexes, ethnic groups, etc.

The problem of having such targets is that the various objectives may **conflict**. If we have high economic growth, with rising incomes, then we know that expenditure will rise. This extra demand will tend to raise output, and with it employment. However, the extra spending may also pull up prices (inflation) and cause imports to rise (balance of payments problems). So in meeting two objectives, high growth and higher employment, we may create problems for two others, low inflation and equilibrium in the balance of payments. Governments may therefore have to **weigh** the various objectives against each other. Are we willing to have a little more employment at the expense of a little more inflation?

INSTRUMENTS

In achieving the various objectives, the Government has a variety of policy measures or **instruments** it can use. We have already discussed many of these in earlier chapters. It can use the Budget (Chapter 16), monetary policy (Chapter 15 and below), exchange rate policy (Chapter 14), regional policy (Chapter 12), industrial policy (Chapter 11) and so on.

By way of illustration we will take one of the policy instruments already discussed, and take it a little further. Here we choose the highly topical instrument of monetary policy.

MONETARY POLICY

We have seen in Chapter 15 that there is a close relationship between changes in the money supply and changes in the price level. It is argued that this relationship is *causal* – in other words, that an increase in the money supply *causes* an increase in the rate of inflation and that there can be *no inflation without an increase in the money supply*.

Control of the rate of inflation is one of the major aims of the present Government and, since it is believed that inflation is caused by increases in the money supply, control of the money supply is an important part of the Government's economic policy. Because of this the Government sets target rates of growth for the money supply.

In its attempts to control the money supply, the Government works through the **monetary authorities**. This term is used to describe the **Bank of England** and the **Treasury**. Each of these performs different functions. Basically, the Treasury has responsibility for *coordinating* the Government's economic policy and the Bank of England, acting on instructions from the Treasury, *implements* the Government's monetary policy.

The target rates of growth for the money supply are set to achieve the Government's particular target for inflation. Having established its target rate of growth for the money supply, the Government attempts to ensure that this target is met. In order to do this the Government uses the **instruments** of monetary policy.

The instruments of monetary policy

We have seen that definitions of the money supply include notes and coin in circulation with the public. However, this is a relatively unimportant part of the money supply, and the monetary authorities make no attempt to control the amount of notes and coin in circulation. Instead, the efforts of the monetary authorities are directed towards controlling the *rate of growth of bank deposits*. If the rate of growth of bank deposits can be controlled, the rate of growth of the money supply can be controlled.

The instruments of monetary policy refer to the techniques available to the monetary authorities in their efforts to control the rate of growth of bank deposits. Since 1980 the authorities have used three basic techniques for controlling the money supply: fiscal policy, sales of debt to non-banks, and interest-rate policy. Each of these is considered in turn.

● **Fiscal policy:** We have seen on pp. 176–7 that borrowing by the public sector, and more importantly the way such borrowing is financed, can lead to changes in the money supply. The main component of borrowing by the public sector is undoubtedly the budget deficit of central government. The size of the budget deficit is determined by the Government's fiscal policy, that is, the difference between government spending and government revenue which comes mainly from taxation. The Government's fiscal policy therefore has an important influence on the money supply.

The present Government has been concerned to reduce the level of direct taxation. This, coupled with its aim of reducing government borrowing, explains why it has sought to control its own expenditure. In other words, fiscal policy has been geared towards achieving the Government's monetary policy.

● **Debt management:** The Bank of England has responsibility for carrying out the Government's monetary policy. In particular it is responsible for selling securities to finance the Government's borrowing, for paying interest on such securities, for repaying holders of securities when they mature and for buying securities when the Government has surplus funds, so as to avoid the Government paying unnecessary interest. The buying and selling of securities by the Bank of England is known as **open-market operations**.

When carrying out open-market sales of securities, the Bank of England aims to sell at the lowest rate of interest that will persuade people to buy whatever amount of securities it wishes to sell. However, because of the importance given to the effect on the money supply of changes in government borrowing, that is, sales of government debt, the Bank of England aims to sell securities to *non-bank institutions* and *private individuals* wherever this can be done. It will try to do this at a rate of interest that is below, or equal to, the rate of interest that would be necessary to persuade *banks* to buy securities. When this is not possible, a conflict exists. The Bank of England must then choose between offering a higher rate of interest to encourage the **non-bank sector** to buy securities, and the increase in the money supply which increased sales of debt to the **banking sector** would involve.

● **Interest-rate policy:** A different approach to controlling bank lending is to raise the rate of interest. In other words, by raising the price of loans, the monetary authorities aim to reduce the *demand* for loans.

In the UK, the Bank of England is in a powerful position to influence the rate of interest. We have seen that the Bank of England is **lender of last resort**. This means that when there is an increase in demand for cash by the public and the commercial banks call in their call loans from the discount market, the discount market will be unable to obtain funds from within the monetary sector and will be forced to request assistance from the Bank of England.

As lender of last resort, the Bank of England will always lend to the discount market. It will do so by **rediscounting eligible bills** from the discount market. Eligible bills are simply Treasury bills, local authority bills or bills accepted by commercial banks or merchant banks. When these are rediscounted, the Bank of England simply buys them from the discount market. However, because the discount market has no alternative but to sell securities to the Bank of England to relieve its shortage of cash, the Bank of England can buy, or discount bills, at whatever price it wishes.

We have seen that there is a relationship between the price paid for securities and the rate at which they are discounted. By lowering the price at which it is prepared to rediscount a bill, the Bank of England can *increase* its discount rate. This will result in an immediate increase in the rate of discount offered by the discount houses. If the discount houses did not increase their own rate of discount they would lose money if they were forced to borrow again from the Bank of England.

As the rate of discount offered by the discount market increases, all *short-term* rates of interest in the money market will rise. In particular, the commercial banks will raise their rates of interest on loans to customers, including call loans to the discount market. In this way the authorities can bring about an increase in interest rates.

However, even when the discount market is not short of funds, the authorities can *bring about* such a shortage. If the authorities sell securities, these will be paid for by a reduction in bank deposits. As cheques are cleared, operational deposits at the Bank of England will fall and banks will call in loans to the discount market to restore their operational deposits to the required level.

This example of a *particular* policy instrument, monetary policy, should give you an idea of how difficult real-world policy-making is. Even if the Government sets out with a clear idea of what it wants in terms of growth in money supply, it can be blown off course by problems with the budget deficit, with interest rates and so on.

In the real world, policy-making is about being flexible, and constantly adjusting both the policy instruments and the policy objectives in the light of events.

TYPICAL EXAM QUESTIONS

1 i) What is a 'progressive' tax?   [2]

   ii) To what extent may each of the following taxes be described as 'progressive':
   a) personal income tax
   b) value added tax
   c) council tax?   [9]

   iii) Discuss the view that everyone should receive exactly the same income.   [9]

2 i) Explain the difference between central government expenditure and central government revenue.[2]

   ii) a) Identify the major sources of central government income.   [3]
   b) Indicate the major items of control government expenditure.   [3]

   iii) How does central government taxation and expenditure policy
   a) affect/influence the distribution of personal income in the UK   [4]
   b) reduce inequalities in the living standards of various sections of the UK population?   [4]

   iv) Suggest ways in which spending on education could be on a) capital goods, b) consumer goods.

   NICCEA 1988 specimen

3 i) Give *two* reasons why governments levy taxes.   [4]

   ii) Explain the *main* difference between income tax and value added tax.   [6]

   iii) Assess the economic effects of a cut in income tax on
   a) the availability of jobs
   b) public expenditure
   c) the rate of inflation.   [6]

   WJEC specimen

4 Study the two extracts below which refer to government revenue and expenditure, and then answer the questions which follow.

'The Economy is in Recession', says Chancellor

'Output in the UK has now fallen for the second quarter in succession. This is having serious effects on our tax revenues and our expenditure. The budget deficit is likely to be larger than expected.'

This was the bad news from the Treasury yesterday.

Public Money 1991–92
(pence in every £1)

Where it comes from		Where it goes to	
Income tax	24.5	Social security	29.5
National insurance contributions	15.5	Education and Science	13.5
Value added tax	15.0	Defence	10.0
Local authority rates	9.0	Law & order	5.5
Excise duties	9.5	Transport	4.0
Corporation tax	8.0	Other services	17.5
Capital taxes	1.0	Debt interest	7.5
Interest, dividends	2.5	Other	0.5.
Petroleum revenue tax and oil royalties	0.2		
Borrowing	6.0		
Other	9.0		
Total	**100.0***		**100.00***

*Figures do not sum due to rounding

(Source: *The Budget in Brief*, H.M. Treasury, March 1992.)

   i) List a) *two* taxes paid by individual people, b) *two* different taxes paid by companies.   [2]

   ii) a) What is meant by the term 'budget deficit'?   [1]

b) How do the figures show that there was a budget deficit in 1991–92? [1]

iii) Suggest *two* ways in which a government can reduce a budget deficit. [2]

iv) Explain the meaning of the headline, 'The Economy is in Recession'. [2]

v) During a recession a government may receive less revenue from income tax and value added tax. It may also spend more on social security and education. Explain why these changes in revenue and expenditure may occur. [8]

ULEAC, 1994

OUTLINE ANSWERS Q.1 AND Q.3

1 i) Strictly, a progressive tax is one where the marginal rate of taxation exceeds the average rate of taxation. This simply means that as taxable income rises, the amount, paid in tax rises *more than proportionately*.

ii) a) This is a progressive tax. Higher taxable **bands** ensure that as taxable income rises, tax paid rises more than proportionately. Clearly, the non-taxable allowances which are the same for all income groups make personal income tax progressive. These points should be discussed with examples.

b) This is a proportional tax because it is levied at a constant percentage rate. However, it acts *regressively* because the poorer members of society pay a higher proportion of their earnings in VAT than the wealthier members of society. However, this regressive effect is partly offset because some goods are **zero rated** while others are **exempt** altogether. You must explain these points fully.

c) The amount paid in council tax is not related to current income and penalizes those who have used their past income to buy better property. It is thus possible to argue that the tax is, on the whole, regressive. However, it can be argued that as their income rises people buy larger houses and as a result pay more in council tax. Certain discounts have been built into the council tax system for people on low incomes and people living alone, thus mitigating some of its more regressive effects.

iii) Many factors could be discussed here. However, you must take great care simply to discuss advantages and disadvantages. One advantage is that it might reduce the problem of poverty. Another is that it might make the choice of career easier and reduce the number of people leaving their present job in the hope of finding a better paid one.

The disadvantages include a reduced incentive to take on certain unpleasant jobs or those that require extensive training. There is less incentive to increase effort at work or to accept greater responsibility. It would probably encourage greater emigration and consequent loss of skills. All of these have serious implications for the economy which should be discussed.

3 i) Governments levy taxes partly to finance their expenditures. In answering this part of the question it would be helpful to outline *briefly* some major reasons for government expenditure, such as the provision of public goods. A second reason governments levy taxes is to influence the distribution of income. This is best illustrated by the progressive nature of income tax. (A third reason might be to influence the allocation of resources. Some demerit goods, such as cigarettes, might be taxed to discourage consumption.)

ii) Income tax is a direct tax, whereas VAT is an indirect tax. You must explain precisely what this means in terms of the government department which collects the tax and the person on whom the burden falls. You might also point out that income tax is progressive whereas VAT is proportional.

iii) a) If a cut in income tax leads to greater spending on domestic output, firms will increase production and more jobs will be created. However, if government expenditure is unchanged it is possible that a cut in income tax will lead to inflation (see (c) below). If inflation is increased, the availability of jobs might be adversely affected.
   b) There is no clear relationship here but it is unlikely that if income tax receipts fall, public expenditure will be increased (indeed it is likely to fall). In answering this part of the question it would help to outline *briefly* the reasons for public expenditure to show the absence of a clear link.
   c) In answering this part of the question you should outline the relationship between government expenditure and the money supply and the relationship between changes in the money supply and the rate of inflation.

TUTOR'S ANSWER TO Q.4

i)   a) Income tax and value added tax.
     b) Corporation tax and petroleum revenue tax.
ii) a) A budget deficit occurs when a government's expenditure is greater than its revenue which comes mainly from taxation.
     b) There was a budget deficit because the Government had to borrow to meet all its expenditure requirements.
iii) A government can reduce a budget deficit by either raising more revenue from taxation or cutting its expenditure. For example the Government could raise the basic rate of income tax or cut defence spending.
iv) Recession occurs in an economy when output (gross domestic product) is falling leading to a rise in unemployment.
v)   Revenue from income tax will fall because with more people unemployed fewer people will be paying the tax. Also, as income growth is slower during a recession even those in work will not be subject to major increases in tax payments. The increase in unemployment and slower growth in incomes will mean less spending in the economy and thus VAT revenues will be lower.

Spending by the Government on social security will rise because more people will be claiming the job seekers' allowance and income support because of rising unemployment. Education spending will rise because more people may stay in full-time education after 16 or go back to college so that they have a better chance of finding work. Education is a better alternative than being unemployed.

STUDENT'S ANSWER TO Q.2 WITH EXAMINER COMMENTS

66 Good, and to the point 99

66 Some strange points here, especially PSBR! 99

2 i) Central government expenditure refers to the expenditure by governments on such things as defence and other public goods and merit goods. It also includes expenditure on transfer payments made out of tax revenue. Central government revenue refers to the income generated through the various measures of taxation, e.g. direct and indirect tax.

Check Figure 16.1

ii) a) Major sources of income are through taxation, PSBR, interest, dividend and profits from investments either at home or abroad.

b) defence, education, health, transfer payments.

Better

iii) a) Progressive – takes higher proportion as income rises although now there has been a tax cut. Thus higher wage earners would be distributing their taxes to the unemployed etc. in the form of transfer payments. Thus if progressive taxation is taking place, the marginal rate of tax is greater than average rate of tax, which means it should distribute income more evenly. If the government contrives to spend on transfer payments, some will fall in the unemployment trap. They would rather remain unemployed and hence government would have to support them with benefits which can only be done by increasing taxation which in the end would result in the fall in the level of personal income.

Good definition

Good point

A bit unclear, though I can see your point

b) Lower net income. Also some will fall in employment and poverty trap. If however tax is cut as it is, this will lead to less revenue and support distribution of benefits. Thus tax lowers standards of living as many would be living in poverty due to no incomes, no jobs etc.

Rather confused!

iv) Capital – desks, buildings, computer, i.e. investment, teachers, apparatus. Consumer – food, stationery (ie books, pens) TV sets.

Some good examples

IDEAS FOR COURSEWORK

Find out from your local council as much as you can about the council tax in your area. How is the council tax for your own home calculated? Do you think that the council tax is progressive or regressive?

SOURCES OF INFORMATION

See the list at the end of Chapter 15.

THE DISTRIBUTION OF INCOME & WEALTH

DEFINING INCOME

MEASURING INEQUALITY

FACTORS AFFECTING INCOME DISTRIBUTION

WEALTH

GETTING STARTED

We have seen how real national income per head gives a useful guide to the standard of living in a country. However, this tells us something only about the *average* person in the country. There may in reality be a big gap between those who are well off and those who are poor, so that the 'average' figure is misleading. In other words, we need to know something about the **distribution of income**.

We will also look at wealth in this chapter and consider how this is distributed in the UK.

ESSENTIAL PRINCIPLES

1 ▷ DEFINING INCOME

Before we look at how equal or unequal incomes are, we must have a clear definition of the term. **Income** is defined in theory as the amount a person could have spent, without running down the value of his or her assets. On this definition we should include capital gains as income, e.g., the extra you get from selling a house, car, painting, etc., over what you originally paid for it. However, because it is so difficult to get satisfactory data on capital gains, these are in practice *not* included in income. Again, many people could, in theory, rent out part of their house and get extra money. They could then spend that money without reducing their assets. So, strictly, we should put some value on the owner-occupied house and count that as income. But again it would be so difficult to do this in practice that we ignore this potential source of income.

The definition *actually used* for income is based on what is declared on tax returns to the Inland Revenue.

2 ▷ MEASURING INEQUALITY

If there was perfect equality in the UK, 50 per cent of all the people would get 50 per cent of the income, and so on. In other words, if we plotted **cumulative percentage people** against **cumulative percentage income**, as in Figure 17.1, we would get the diagonal line A of 'perfect equality'. In practice, the *actual* curve after tax looks something like line B, the bottom 20 per cent of people getting only 6.9 per cent of all income, and the bottom 50 per cent of people getting only 24.9 per cent of income.

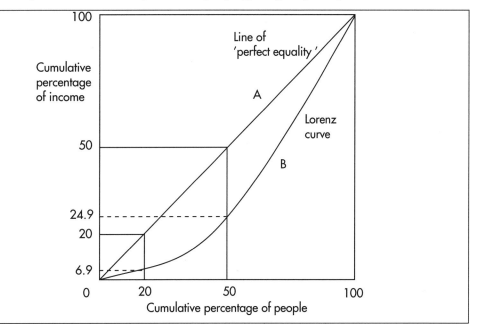

Figure 17.1 The Lorenz curve

If we plot the various points for the UK on the diagram and connect them together, we get a curve. This is called the **Lorenz curve**. The closer this curve is to the diagonal, the closer we are to 'perfect equality'. The further this curve is away from the diagonal, the further away we are from 'perfect equality'. Figure 17.2 gives recent data on income distribution in the UK.

It can be seen that in 1992 over 25 per cent of the population lived in households which earned less than half the national average income compared with less than 10 per cent in 1979. In addition, it can be seen that the richest ten per cent of the population enjoyed an increase in income of over 60 per cent between 1979 and 1992. For the poorest ten per cent, incomes fell by 15 per cent over the same period.

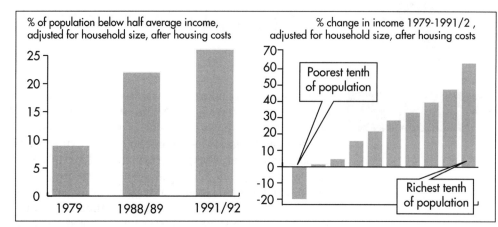

Figure 17.2

Source: Commission on Social Justice/IPPR

TAX REVENUE

We have looked at tax revenue in Chapter 16. A progressive tax system will take a bigger proportion of high incomes in tax than of low incomes. So raising taxes on high-income groups and reducing taxes on low-income groups will help to make income more equal.

PUBLIC EXPENDITURE

Again in Chapter 16 we looked at the various aspects of public expenditure. Increasing benefits and supplements to the lower paid and taking them away from the higher paid will make income more equal.

OCCUPATIONAL FACTORS

Different occupations receive different incomes, as we saw in Table 10.1. If the gap between the earnings of these different occupations were to narrow, then incomes would become more equal.

Of course, there is nothing in the operation of markets to suggest that the gap between the earnings of different occupations *will* narrow. If there is extra demand for a certain type of worker, then in a free market the wage rate will rise for that occupation, and vice versa. As the economy changes, so there will always be some occupations where demand is increasing, and others facing a declining demand.

It is not only the market that determines wages. Some occupations are more highly unionized than others, and a powerful union may be able to secure a higher wage. Equally, some occupations have well-organized employer groups and little unionization, which can help to keep wages low.

4   WEALTH

Income is not the same as wealth. We have seen that income is a **flow of money**. But wealth is a **stock of assets**, usually built up over a long period, through savings or inheritance.

The most obvious forms of wealth are land, housing, stocks and shares and other financial assets. Households also own durable goods, such as cars, electrical goods, carpets, furnishings, etc., which are also a type of asset. Even pension rights can be thought of as an asset, and therefore wealth.

It is difficult to obtain satisfactory information on wealth in the UK. Britain has no wealth tax and so no regular wealth valuations are made. Attempts have been made, however, to estimate wealth using sample surveys and figures provided by the Inland Revenue and via Inheritance Tax.

PERCENTAGE OF WEALTH OWNED BY	1976	1981	1986	1991
Most wealthy 1%	21	18	18	18
Most wealthy 5%	38	36	36	37
Most wealthy 10%	50	50	50	50

Table 17.1

Source: Social Trends, 1994

Table 17.1 gives a picture of the wealth distribution in the UK over a period of time. We can see that the distribution is again unequal. In 1991, the most wealthy 1 per cent of the population owned 18 per cent of the wealth, and the most wealthy 10 per cent owned 50 per cent of the wealth.

However, wealth distribution has become more equal over time. A major reason has been the impact of death duties and capital gains tax in reducing the real value of inherited wealth. Whereas the most wealthy 1 per cent had 21 per cent of all wealth in 1976 that figure had fallen to 18 per cent by 1991.

Table 17.2 gives a more detailed breakdown of the ownership of wealth in the UK. We can see that houses (dwellings) accounted for almost 33 per cent of wealth in 1992. Building society shares and National Savings each provided around 8–10 per cent of net wealth, and stocks and shares 9 per cent.

	NET WEALTH (UK) %		
	1981	1991	1992
Dwellings (net of mortgage debt)	36	37	33
Other fixed assets	10	6	5
Non-marketable tenancy rights	12	8	8
Shares and deposits with building societies	8	8	8
National Savings, notes and coin and bank deposits	10	10	10
Stocks, shares and unit trusts	8	8	9
Life assurance and pension funds	16	27	31
Other financial assets net of liabilities	0	–4	–4
Total (= 100%) (£ billion)	740	2270	2300

Table 17.2

Source: Social Trends, 1994

IDEAS FOR COURSEWORK

You could compare the income distribution of the UK over the last fifteen years, and try to suggest why any changes you observe have taken place (similarly with wealth). What are the economic/social consequences of inequality? What policies might reduce inequality?

SOURCES OF INFORMATION

See the list at the end of Chapter 15. See also:

- *New Earnings Survey*, HMSO
- *World Development Report*, World Bank
- *UN Statistical Yearbook*, HMSO
- *Social Trends*, Central Statistical Office.

REVIEW SHEET

1   What is meant by the **incidence** of a tax?

_____

2   In what circumstances will the incidence of an indirect tax fall on
i)   the consumer of a product

_____

ii) the supplier of a product?

_____

3   This question is based on the diagram below which shows the proportion of
income paid in tax as income rises.
Which line shows
i)   a progressive tax
ii) a proportional tax
iii) a regressive tax?

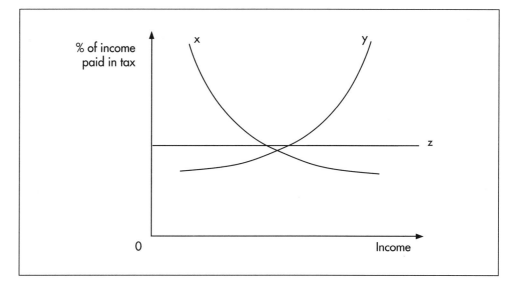

4   Central government borrowing is equal to the difference between what?

_____

5   What is the difference between the PSBR and the national debt?

_____

_____

6   Which individuals and institutions hold the national debt and in what forms is it
held?

_____

_____

7   In which ways might a budget deficit affect national income?

_____

_____

8   Give two examples of expenditures which are not subject to VAT.

_____

_____

9   Is it possible to levy VAT so that it acts progressively?

_____

_____

10 What is the 'unemployment trap'?

_____

_____

11 Distinguish between a **stock** and a **flow**.

_____

_____

12 Classify the following as a stock or a flow:
   i)   wages

_____

   ii) savings out of current income

_____

   iii) the total value of savings

_____

   iv) rent from the ownership of property.

_____

13 How would the distribution of _wealth_ be affected by the introduction of a steeply progressive income tax?

_____

_____

14 What are the major factors that affect the distribution of income?

_____

_____

15 If the distribution of income became more equal, would the distribution of wealth become more equal?

_____

_____

16 Distinguish _wealth_ from _income_.

_____

_____

17 Now does Inheritance Tax help to create a more even distribution of wealth in the UK?

_____

_____

18 How can wealth generate income?

_____

_____

19 What is a Lorenz curve?

_____

_____

20 How would you calculate the value of the wealth of the average family?

_____

_____

INDEX